GOD
WITH US

GOD
WITH US

365 DEVOTIONS
ON THE PERSON AND WORK
OF CHRIST

JUSTIN S. HOLCOMB

BETHANYHOUSE
a division of Baker Publishing Group
Minneapolis, Minnesota

© 2021 by Justin Holcomb

Published by Bethany House Publishers
11400 Hampshire Avenue South
Bloomington, Minnesota 55438
www.bethanyhouse.com

Bethany House Publishers is a division of
Baker Publishing Group, Grand Rapids, Michigan

Printed in the United States of America

ISBN 978-0-7642-3440-8 (cloth)
ISBN 978-1-4934-2820-5 (ebook)

Library of Congress Cataloging-in-Publication Control Number: 2021019026

Scripture quotations are from The Holy Bible, English Standard Version® (ESV®), copyright © 2001 by Crossway, a publishing ministry of Good News Publishers. Used by permission. All rights reserved. ESV Text Edition: 2016

Language has been updated for today's reader.

Excerpt from *Reformed Dogmatics* volume 3 by Herman Bavinck, copyright © 2006. Used by permission of Baker Academic, a division of Baker Publishing Group.

Excerpt from *Reformed Dogmatics* volume 4 by Herman Bavinck, copyright © 2008. Used by permission of Baker Academic, a division of Baker Publishing Group.

Author is represented by Wolgemuth and Associates.

Cover design by Studio Gearbox

21 22 23 24 25 26 27   7 6 5 4 3 2 1

Dedicated to my daughters,
Sophia and Zoe.
My deepest hope is that you
will continue to enjoy and explore
the abundance, capacity, and immensity
of Christ's love for you.

ACKNOWLEDGMENTS

I am grateful for the research assistance from Kathy Larson, Ellen Ceely, and Steve Rustin. I would like to thank Zach Williams and the Reverend Dr. Dave Johnson for their wise input and Andy McGuire and Hannah Ahlfield at Bethany House for their support of this project.

INTRODUCTION

The goal of this devotional is to expand upon a simple yet elegant line from George Herbert that captures two essential features of the Christian teaching about Jesus Christ: "In Christ two natures met to be thy cure."*

The first is the person of Jesus Christ, who is fully God and fully man. At the Father's bidding and by the power of the Holy Spirit, the Son assumed human nature at the incarnation: "The Word became flesh and dwelt among us" (John 1:14). The divine nature and human nature "met" in the one person of Jesus Christ.

The second is the work of Christ. The Lord took on the form of a servant to be our "cure." By subjecting himself to the frailties and temptations of our condition and yet remaining without sin, He condemned sin in the flesh, undoing the consequences of sin. In His incarnation, obedience, death, resurrection, ascension, and future return, Jesus Christ accomplished redemption.

Let us ponder the astonishing truth that, as the Nicene Creed eloquently states, the Son of God "for us and for our salvation came down from heaven and became incarnate by the Holy Spirit and of the Virgin Mary, and was made man." The Nicene Creed, the cornerstone of orthodox Christian belief, attaches saving significance not only to Christ's death and resurrection but also to His incarnation and birth.

*George Herbert, from *The Temple* (1633). For more on the two essential features of the Christian teaching about Christ, see Scott R. Swain, "In Christ two natures met to be thy cure," *Modern Reformation* 24:6 (2015), 20–23.

This book celebrates that Jesus Christ is God with us and God for us. It explores the abundance, capacity, and immensity of Christ's tender and powerful love for you. It explores His sovereign rule as Lord and King. We will see that the person and work of Christ have very personal implications for you. Those same implications are also comprehensive for all creation. The Lord delights in showing mercy to you, and He is making all things new.

The selected texts in this devotional display the wonder of the person of Christ, the fullness of His marvelous works, and the tenderness of the very heart of God incarnate. These excerpts from classic Christian writers, theologians, and pastors have been gently edited to enhance their readability.

Matthew 1:23: "They shall call his name Immanuel" (which means, God with us).

It was of supreme importance that He who was to be our Mediator should be both true God and true man. If the necessity be inquired into, it was not what is commonly termed simple or absolute but flowed from the divine decree on which the salvation of humanity depended. What was best for us our most merciful Father determined. Our iniquities, like a cloud intervening between Him and us, having utterly alienated us from the kingdom of heaven, none but a person reaching to Him could be the medium of restoring peace. But who could reach to Him? Could any of the sons of Adam? All of them shuddered at the sight of God. Could any of the angels? They had need of a superior, by connection with whom they might adhere to God entirely and inseparably. What then? The case was certainly desperate if the Godhead himself did not descend to us, it being impossible for us to ascend to Him. Thus, the Son of God took it upon himself to become our Emmanuel, *i.e.*, God with us; and in such a way, that by mutual union, His divinity and our nature might be combined; otherwise, neither was the proximity near enough, nor the affinity strong enough, to give us hope that God would dwell with us; so great was the divide between our lost state and the spotless purity of God.

Had humans remained free from all corruption, they were of too humble a condition to approach God without a Mediator. What, then, of humanity's true state, when by fatal flaw they were condemned to death and hell, defiled by sin, made loathsome through the curse, in complete and utter despair? It is not without cause, therefore, that Paul, when he sets forth Christ as the Mediator, distinctly declares Him to be man. "For there is one God," he says, "and there is one mediator between God and men, the man Christ Jesus" (1 Timothy 2:5). He might have called Him God, or called Him man; but because the Spirit, speaking through him, knew our infirmity, he provides for it by the most appropriate remedy: setting the Son of God familiarly before us as one of us.

—JOHN CALVIN, *Institutes of the Christian Religion*, vol. 2, trans. Henry Beveridge (Edinburgh: The Calvin Translation Society, 1845), 2–3 (*Institutes*, 2.12.1).

Matthew 9:36: When he saw the crowds, he had compassion for them, because they were harassed and helpless, like sheep without a shepherd.

Compassion is no doubt the emotion we would naturally expect to find most frequently attributed to Jesus, whose whole life was a mission of mercy, and whose ministry was so marked by deeds of generosity that it was summed up in the memory of His followers as a going through the land "doing good" (Acts 10:38). In fact, this is the emotion that is most frequently attributed to Him. The term *compassion* first appears in common use in this sense in the Synoptic Gospels.

The divine mercy has been defined as that essential perfection in God "whereby He pities and relieves the miseries of His creatures." It includes two parts: an internal movement of pity and an external act of kindness or generosity. It is the internal movement of pity that is emphasized when our Lord is said to be "moved with compassion," as the term is sometimes excellently rendered in the English versions. In the appeals made to His mercy, a more external word is used; but it is this more internal word that is employed to express our Lord's response to these appeals: the petitioners sought Him to take pity on them; His heart responded with a profound feeling of pity for them.

His compassion fulfilled itself in outward acts; but what is emphasized by the term used to express our Lord's response is the profound internal movement of His emotional nature. This emotional nature was aroused in our Lord as well by the sight of individual distress as by the spectacle of humanity's universal misery. The sight of their desperate plight awakens our Lord's pity and moves Him to provide the remedy.

—B. B. WARFIELD, "On the Emotional Life of Our Lord," in *Biblical and Theological Studies* (New York: Charles Scribner's Sons, 1912) 40–42.

Mark 2:17: "Those who are well have no need of a physician, but those who are sick. I came not to call the righteous, but sinners."

Just as the use of common remedies is the way to physical health, so Jesus took up sinners to heal their souls and restore them. And just as doctors, when they bind up wounds, do it carefully, and neatly, so as not to cause further discomfort, so Jesus by His assumption of humanity adapted to our wounds, our suffering, our helplessness. And just as one who ministers to a bodily injury in some cases applies the contrary, such as cold to hot, moist to dry, and does not fit the same bandage or treatment to all cases, in the same way the wisdom of God in healing humanity has applied himself to his cure, being himself both healer and medicine. Seeing, then, that humanity fell through pride, Jesus restores them through humility. We were ensnared by the "wisdom" of the serpent; we are set free by the "foolishness" of God. Moreover, just as the former was called wisdom, when it was the folly of those who did not trust God, so the latter is called foolishness, when it is true wisdom in those who overcome the devil.

We used our immortality so badly as to incur the penalty of death; Christ used His mortality so well as to restore us to life. The disease was brought in through a woman's disobedience; the remedy came through a woman's submission to God's will. To the same class of opposites, it belongs that our sins are cured by His sinless sacrifice. On the other hand, the following are, as it were, applications made to match the wounds to which they are applied: He was born of a woman to deliver us who fell through a woman; He came as a man to save us who are human; as a mortal to save us who are mortals; and by death to save us who were spiritually dead.

—AUGUSTINE OF HIPPO, *On Christian Doctrine*, in *St. Augustin's City of God and Christian Doctrine*, A Select Library of the Nicene and Post-Nicene Fathers of the Christian Church, 1st ser., vol. 2, ed. Philip Schaff, trans. J. F. Shaw (Buffalo, NY: Christian Literature Company, 1887), 526 (Augustine, *On Christian Doctrine*, 1.14).

> **1 John 2:1–6:** My little children, I am writing these things to you so that you may not sin. But if anyone does sin, we have an advocate with the Father, Jesus Christ the righteous. He is the propitiation for our sins, and not for ours only but also for the sins of the whole world. And by this we know that we have come to know him, if we keep his commandments. Whoever says "I know him" but does not keep his commandments is a liar, and the truth is not in him, but whoever keeps his word, in him truly the love of God is perfected. By this we may know that we are in him: whoever says he abides in him ought to walk in the same way in which he walked.

Jesus is the only high priest of all, and the only king of every creature, and the Father's only supreme prophet of prophets.

—EUSEBIUS, *Ecclesiastical History*, trans. S. E. Parker (London: Samuel Bagster and Sons, 1847), 43 (*Ecclesiastical History*, 1.3).

The three miserable consequences introduced by sin—ignorance, guilt, and bondage to sin—required Christ to fulfill three roles for us. Ignorance is healed by Christ the Prophet; guilt by Christ the Priest; the tyranny and bondage to sin by Christ the King. Prophetic light scatters the darkness of error; the merit of the Priest takes away guilt and procures a reconciliation for us; the power of the King removes the bondage of sin and death. The Prophet shows God to us; the Priest leads us to God; and the King joins us together and glorifies us with God. The Prophet enlightens the mind by the Spirit of illumination; the Priest by the Spirit of consolation tranquilizes the heart and conscience; the King by the Spirit of sanctification subdues rebellious desires and emotions.

—FRANCIS TURRETIN, *Institutes of Elenctic Theology*, vol. 2, trans. George Musgrave Giger (Phillipsburg: Presbyterian and Reformed Publishing, 1994), 393.

John 6:35: "I am the bread of life; whoever comes to me shall not hunger, and whoever believes in me shall never thirst."

It is not in our nature to be holy, to submit to Christ, to give up our own will and pleasure, selfish love, earthly hope, and a heart after this world and its carnal ways. But the call goes out: Come to Christ! See what He offers, find new life and hope in Him. He is the nearest, surest way to be relieved of all your earthly burdens. I can vouch for the fact that you shall be dearly welcomed by Him; He waits to impart to you joy as you have never known on this earth. I daresay, neither angels' pens nor angels' tongues can convey all that He can and will be to you if you submit yourself to His keeping. Having been a prisoner myself to sin and selfishness, I cannot describe the depth of His compassion, His sweetness, His longing to commune with us. Oh, for a soul wide enough and deep enough to contain His love! It is wider and deeper than we could ever comprehend. And yet it is available to us. Oh, wonder of wonders! If my soul could but rest within the fragrance of His love, could but grasp its fullness! I long for the day when I shall know Him as He longs to be known to us!

And oh, what awaits those who truly believe and trust in Him for the salvation of their souls: that fair orchard of the new paradise; to see, and smell, and touch, and kiss that fair field flower, that evergreen Tree of Life! Even His mere shadow would be enough; the sight of Him would be heaven itself! We have neglected what is right beside us, wasted our lives upon some loathsome object, and Christ waits for us to come. Woe, woe unto us! The world is full of madmen, seeking a fool's paradise, even some good and desirable things, but without and apart from Christ, nothing in this world can satisfy our deepest needs and longings. Will you not set Christ, the well of life, before you and drink your fill?

—SAMUEL RUTHERFORD, *The Letters of Samuel Rutherford*, ed. Andrew Alexander Bonar (Edinburgh and London: Oliphant, Anderson and Ferrier, 1891), 172–173.

Acts 2:32–35: This Jesus God raised up, and of that we all are witnesses. Being therefore exalted at the right hand of God, and having received from the Father the promise of the Holy Spirit, he has poured out this that you yourselves are seeing and hearing. For David did not ascend into the heavens, but he himself says,

> "The Lord said to my Lord, 'Sit at my right hand, until I make your enemies your footstool.'"

In Christ, we have our own flesh in heaven.
—THE HEIDELBERG CATECHISM, Q. and A. 49.

Let us, therefore, never be ashamed of the cross of Christ. Though others may hide it, let us openly write it, even upon our forehead, that the devils may behold the royal sign and flee away. Make then this sign of the cross, whether eating or drinking, sitting or lying down, rising, walking or, in a word, in everything we do. For He who was crucified is in heaven above. If after being crucified and buried He had remained in the tomb, we should have had cause to be ashamed of the cross; but, in fact, He who was crucified has risen from the dead, having gone down into hell and come up again, He ascended into heaven, His Father addressing Him, and saying, "Sit at my right hand, until I make your enemies your footstool."
—CYRIL OF JERUSALEM, "The Catechetical Lectures of S. Cyril, Archbishop of Jerusalem," in *S. Cyril of Jerusalem, S. Gregory Nazianzen*, A Select Library of the Nicene and Post-Nicene Fathers of the Christian Church, 2nd ser., vol. 7, ed. Philip Schaff and Henry Wace, trans. Edwin Hamilton Gifford (Buffalo, NY: Christian Literature Co., 1894), 135.

DAY

7

> **Luke 2:6–7:** The time came for her to give birth. And she gave birth to her firstborn son and wrapped him in swaddling cloths and laid him in a manger, because there was no place for them in the inn.

The Word of the Father, by whom all time was created, was made flesh and was born at the right time for us. He, without whose divine permission no day completes its course, wished to have one day [set aside] for His human birth. In the bosom of His Father, He existed before all the cycles of ages; born of an earthly mother, He entered upon the course of the years on this day. The Maker of humans became Man that He, Ruler of the stars, might be nourished at His mother's breast; that He, the Bread of Life, might be hungry; that He, the Eternal Fountain, might thirst; that He, the Light of the World, might sleep; that He, the Way, might be wearied by the journey; that He, the Truth, might be accused by false witnesses; that He, the Judge of the living and the dead, might be brought to trial by a mortal judge; that He, true Justice, might be condemned by the unjust; that He, the innocent, might be scourged with whips; that He, the King of kings, might be crowned with thorns; that He, our foundation, might be suspended upon a cross; that Strength might know weakness; that the Healer might be wounded; that the Giver of Life might die.

To endure these and like indignities for us, to free us, unworthy creatures, He who existed as the Son of God before all ages, without a beginning, humbled himself to become the Son of Man. He who submitted to such great evil for our sake had done no evil, and although we, who were the recipients of so much grace at His hand, had done nothing to merit these benefits. Begotten by the Father, He was not made by the Father; He was made human through a human mother, whom He himself had made, so that He might exist here for a while, for our sakes.

—AUGUSTINE OF HIPPO, *Sermons on the Liturgical Seasons*, ed. Hermigild Dressler, trans. Mary Sarah Muldowney, vol. 38, *The Fathers of the Church* (Washington, DC: The Catholic University of America Press, 1959), 28–29.

> **John 1:1–3:** In the beginning was the Word, and the Word was with God, and the Word was God. He was in the beginning with God. All things were made through him, and without him was not any thing made that was made.

For as no one has known the Father, but the Son, so no one, on the other hand, can know the Son fully, but the Father alone, by whom He was begotten. For who but the Father has thoroughly understood that Light which existed before the world was—that intellectual and substantial wisdom, and living Word, which in the beginning was with the Father, before all creation and any production, visible or invisible? He was the first and only offspring of God, the prince and leader of the spiritual and immortal host of heaven, the angel of the mighty council, the agent to execute the Father's secret will, the maker of all things with the Father, the second cause of the universe next to the Father, the true and only Son of the Father, and the Lord and God and King of all created things. He has received rule and dominion with divinity itself, and power and honor from the Father.

All this is evident from those more obscure passages in reference to His divinity: "In the beginning was the Word, and the Word was with God, and the Word was God" (John 1:1). "All things were made through him, and without him was not any thing made that was made" (John 1:3). This, too, we are taught by Moses, when, under the influence of the divine Spirit, he describes the creation and arrangement of all things. He also informs us that the Creator and Maker of the universe yielded to Christ, and to none but to His divine and first begotten Word, the formation of all subordinate things, and communed with Him respecting the creation of humans: "Let us make man in our image, after our likeness" (Genesis 1:26). This expression is confirmed by another of the prophets, who, speaking of God in the Psalms, declares, "Let them praise the name of the LORD! For he commanded and they were created" (Psalm 148:5).

—EUSEBIUS, *Ecclesiastical History*, trans. S. E. Parker (London: Samuel Bagster & Sons, 1847), 35–36 (*Ecclesiastical History*, 1.2).

> **Luke 22:39–45:** And he came out and went, as was his custom, to the Mount of Olives, and the disciples followed him. And when he came to the place, he said to them, "Pray that you may not enter into temptation." And he withdrew from them about a stone's throw, and knelt down and prayed, saying, "Father, if you are willing, remove this cup from me. Nevertheless, not my will, but yours, be done." And there appeared to him an angel from heaven, strengthening him. And being in agony he prayed more earnestly; and his sweat became like great drops of blood falling down to the ground. And when he rose from prayer, he came to the disciples and found them sleeping.

Jesus would not have been less good had He not taken my feelings on himself. Therefore, He grieved on my account, when He had cause for grief on His own; and having put aside the bliss of His eternal divinity, He labored under the heaviness of my infirmity. Yes, He took my sorrow on himself that He might bestow His bliss, and He came down to walk in our steps to the point of death so that He might call us to walk in His steps to life. Therefore, I speak with confidence of His sorrow because I proclaim the cross; for it was not the appearance of incarnation that He assumed but the reality. He had also to take on grief, that He might vanquish our sorrow. Isaiah speaks of a man in suffering and affliction and knowing how to bear the infirmities of others.

For how could we imitate You, Lord Jesus, if we did not follow You as a man, if we had not seen Your wounds and believed You dead? How could the disciples have believed that You were going to die, had they not discerned the sorrow of one about to die? Up to this point, they slept and knew nothing of grief, while You grieved for them: for so we read that You bore our sins and grieved for us. Therefore, Lord, it is not Your wounds but ours that You grieved for, not Your death but our infirmity; and we deemed that the grief was Yours when you were grieving not for yourself but for us.

—AMBROSE, *Exposition of the Gospel of Luke*, in Ambrose of Milan, *Exposition of the Holy Gospel According to St. Luke with Fragments on the Prophecy of Isaiah*, trans. T. Tomkinson (Etna, CA: Center for Traditionalist Orthodox Studies, 1998), 406–407.

> **John 5:30:** "I can do nothing on my own. As I hear, I judge, and my judgment is just, because I seek not my own will but the will of him who sent me."

What Christ did, what obedience He rendered unto the law of God in the discharge of His office ("Behold, I have come to do your will, O God, as it is written of me in the scroll of the book" Hebrews 10:7), was of His own free choice, and was resolved on His own. It is our duty likewise to willingly, freely, and cheerfully obey all that He commands. Obedience is a matter of the will. And there is no obedience outside our willingness to choose God's way. But even before our acts of the will, we are required to be obedient. From the very constitution of our nature we are necessarily subject unto the law of God. All that is left unto us is a voluntary compliance with unavoidable commands; with Christ it was not so. An act of His own will and choice preceded all obligation as to obedience. He obeyed because He chose to, rather than because He had to. He said, "I have come to do your will, O God," before He was obliged to do that will. By His own choice, and that in an act of infinite humility and love, as we have seen, He was "made of a woman," and thereby "made under the law." In His divine person He was Lord of the law—above it—no more subject to its commands or its curse. Neither was He not only under the law's curse because He was innocent but also because He was in every way above the law itself, and all its power.

This was the original glory of His obedience. This wisdom, the grace, the love, the humility He chose animated His every act, every duty He fulfilled, rendering it good in the sight of God, and useful to us. So, when He went to John to be baptized, John knew Jesus didn't need baptism and told Him so; but Jesus replied, "Let it be so now, for thus it is fitting for us to fulfill all righteousness" (Matthew 3:15). In other words, to say, "This I have undertaken willingly, of my own accord, without any need of it for myself, and therefore I will go through with it." For Him, who was Lord of all universally, submitted himself to universal obedience, carrying along with it the evidence of glorious grace.

—JOHN OWEN, *The Works of John Owen*, vol. 1, ed. William H. Goold (Edinburgh: T&T Clark, 1862), 339.

> **Galatians 3:24:** So then, the law was our guardian until Christ came, in order that we might be justified by faith.

The uniqueness of the religion of Israel does not consist exclusively or primarily in its ethical monotheism. The substance of the revelation that came to Israel, and the core of the religion that corresponds with it in Israel, consists in something else. In order to find this, we must go back to the prophets and psalmists, to Jesus and the apostles, and they all teach us unanimously and clearly that the content of the divine revelation does not consist primarily in the unity of God, in the moral law, in circumcision, in the Sabbath, in short, in the law, but appears primarily and principally in the promise, in the covenant of grace, and in the Gospel.

Not the law, but the Gospel, is in both the Old and New Testaments, the core of the divine revelation, the essence of religion, the whole of the Holy Scriptures. Every other view fails to do justice to special revelation, limits its difference from general revelation, degrades the Old Testament, rends apart the two economies of the same covenant of grace, and gradually changes the gospel of the New Covenant into a law, and makes Christ into a second Moses. The law is therefore temporary, transitory, a means in the service of the promise, but the promise is eternal; it had its beginning in paradise, was preserved and developed by revelation in the days of the Old Covenant, received its fulfillment in Christ, and is now extended to the whole human race and all peoples. God places himself in a special relationship to a particular person and people (Israel). This relationship is not grounded in nature; it is not a matter of course; it does not exist by virtue of creation; it is not instituted on the part of humanity, by their conscience or reason, by their feeling of dependence or need. Rather, it is a historical product; the initiative came from God; He so reveals himself, by the act of revelation, to receive a particular person and people into communion with himself.

—HERMAN BAVINCK, *The Philosophy of Revelation* (New York: Longman, Green, and Co., 1909), 191–192.

Hebrews 2:17–18: Therefore he had to be made like his brothers in every respect, so that he might become a merciful and faithful high priest in the service of God, to make propitiation for the sins of the people. For because he himself has suffered when tempted, he is able to help those who are being tempted.

Christ was made subject to human experiences and feelings, that He might be a merciful and faithful high priest. For it is a rare thing for those who are always happy and content to empathize with the sorrows of others. The Son of God had no need of experience that He might know the emotions of mercy. But we could not be persuaded that He is merciful and ready to help us had He not become acquainted by experience with our miseries. But this, as so many other gifts and benefits, has been given as a favor to us.

Therefore, whenever any evil comes upon us, let us remember that nothing happens to us but what the Son of God has himself experienced the same in order that He might empathize with us; nor let us doubt that He is present with us just as though He suffered with us. An acquaintance with our sorrows and difficulties so inclines Christ to compassion that He is continually asking God to help us.

—JOHN CALVIN, *Commentaries on the Epistle of Paul the Apostle to the Hebrews*, trans. John Owen (Edinburgh: The Calvin Translation Society, 1853), 74–76.

> **1 Corinthians 13:7–8:** Love bears all things, believes all things, hopes all things, endures all things. Love never ends. As for prophecies, they will pass away; as for tongues, they will cease; as for knowledge, it will pass away.

There is much in our Lord's pantry that will satisfy His children, and much wine in His cellar that will quench all their thirst. Hunger for Him until He fills you. He is pleased with the requests of hungry souls. If He delays, do not despair, but fall at His feet. Every day we may see some new attribute in Christ. His love has neither measure nor limit. How blessed are we to enjoy this invaluable treasure, the love of Christ; to allow ourselves to be mastered and subdued by His love, so that Christ is our all, and all other pursuits are as nothing. Oh, that we might be ready for the times when our Lord's trials and triumphs call for us! There are infinite depths to His love that the saint will never be able to fully uncover. I urge you to seek a closer and growing communion with Christ. There are depths of His character that we have not yet seen. There are new discoveries yet to be found. Dig deep, take pains to know Him, and set aside as much time each day for Him as you can; He will be won with your efforts.

Live on Christ's love alone. He seeks to make your heart His throne. It is our loss to divide our limited love. Give it all to Christ. Lay your cares and your burdens upon God; make Him your beloved. Your goal in this life is to make sure you spend eternity with Christ. Your love, if it could be more than all the love of angels, would be only Christ's due. Look up to Him and show Him your love. Love and live! My counsel is that you come, and leave all else, that you let Christ have your whole heart. Let those who love this present world have it; Christ is the more worthy and noble portion; blessed are those who choose Him.

—SAMUEL RUTHERFORD, *The Letters of Samuel Rutherford*, ed. Andrew Alexander Bonar (Edinburgh and London: Oliphant, Anderson and Ferrier, 1891), 492, 323, 383, 284, 215, 279, 380, 375, 347, 495–496.

> **Ephesians 3:14–19:** For this reason I bow my knees before the Father, from whom every family in heaven and on earth is named, that according to the riches of his glory he may grant you to be strengthened with power through his Spirit in your inner being, so that Christ may dwell in your hearts through faith—that you, being rooted and grounded in love, may have strength to comprehend with all the saints what is the breadth and length and height and depth, and to know the love of Christ that surpasses knowledge, that you may be filled with all the fullness of God.

Coming sinner: I have a word for you: Be of good comfort. He will not cast you out. Of all men, you are blessed of the Lord; the Father has sent His Son to be a sacrifice for you, and Jesus Christ, your Lord, has gone to prepare a place for you. What more shall I say to you? You come to a full Christ!

He is full of truth, full of grace and truth.

He is full of wisdom. He is made unto us God's wisdom, wisdom to manage the affairs of His Church in general, and the affairs of every sinner in particular.

He is a storehouse full of all the graces of the Spirit.

He is full of compassion: You shall feel it and find it when you come to Him for life. He can bear with your weaknesses. He pities your ignorance. He is touched with the feeling of your infirmities. He will mercifully forgive your transgressions. He will heal your backsliding and love you freely.

Coming sinner: Jesus, to whom you are coming, is lowly in heart. He does not despise you: not your outward wretchedness, nor your inward weakness, nor because you are poor, or base, or even a fool. He has chosen the foolish, the base, and despised things of this world, to confound the wise and mighty.

—JOHN BUNYAN, *Come, and Welcome to Jesus Christ* (Carlisle, PA: Banner of Truth, 1681/2011), 214–218.

> **Galatians 3:13–14:** Christ redeemed us from the curse of the law by be-
> coming a curse for us—for it is written, "Cursed is everyone who is hanged
> on a tree"—so that in Christ Jesus the blessing of Abraham might come to
> the Gentiles, so that we might receive the promised Spirit through faith.

I cannot think little of sin when I look at the cross of Christ. Do I want to know the fullness and completeness of the salvation God has provided for sinners? Where will I see it most vividly? Shall I go to the general declarations of God's mercy in the Bible? Shall I rest in the general truth that God is a God of love? No! I must look at the cross of Christ. I find no other evidence that equals that. I find no balm for my conscience, my troubled heart, like the sight of Jesus dying that cruel death for me on that wretched tree.

There I see the full payment that has been made for my enormous debt. The curse of the law that I have broken has come down on the Most Holy One, who suffered there in my place. The demands of that law are satisfied. Payment has been made for me to the uttermost farthing. It will not be required again. I might sometimes imagine I was too far gone to be for-given. My own heart sometimes whispers that I am too wicked to be saved. But in my better moments, I know this is all my foolish unbelief. I read an answer to my doubts in the blood shed on Calvary. I feel certain, when I look at the cross, that there is a way to heaven for the very vilest of men.

—J. C. RYLE, *Startling Questions* (New York: Robert Carter & Brothers, 1853), 287–288.

In Jesus Christ, God himself has acted in place of the human race. In Him, God not only demands but gives what He demands.

—KARL BARTH, *Church Dogmatics*, vol. 4, part 1 (Edinburgh: T&T Clark), 1956), 280.

> **Romans 5:19-21:** For as by the one man's disobedience the many were made sinners, so by the one man's obedience the many will be made righteous. Now the law came in to increase the trespass, but where sin increased, grace abounded all the more, so that, as sin reigned in death, grace also might reign through righteousness leading to eternal life through Jesus Christ our Lord.

The obedience of Christ has two praiseworthy effects: first, we are freed from the punishment we deserve because of our sin; second, through the cancellation of sin we are given the right to eternal life, and salvation is acquired for us. For as sin has brought upon us two evils—the loss of life and exposure to death—so redemption must provide the two opposite benefits—deliverance from death and a right to life, escape from hell and an entrance into heaven.

—FRANCIS TURRETIN, *Institutes of Elenctic Theology*, vol. 2, trans. George Musgrave Giger (Phillipsburg: Presbyterian and Reformed Publishing, 1994), 447.

To justify, therefore, is nothing else than to acquit from the charge of guilt, as if innocence were proven. Hence, when God justifies us through the intercession of Christ, He does not acquit us on a proof of our own innocence, but by giving us righteousness, so that we are not righteous in ourselves, but we are deemed righteous in Christ.

—JOHN CALVIN, *Institutes of the Christian Religion*, vol. 2, trans. Henry Beveridge (Edinburgh: The Calvin Translation Society, 1845), 304–305 (*Institutes*, 3.11.2).

2 Corinthians 9:15: Thanks be to God for his inexpressible gift!

O God of grace, teach me to know that grace precedes, accompanies, and follows my salvation; that it sustains the redeemed soul, that not one link of its chain can ever be broken.

> From Calvary's cross, wave upon wave of grace reaches me,
> deals with my sin, washes me clean, renews my heart,
> strengthens my will, draws out my love,
> kindles a flame in my soul, rules throughout my inner man,
> consecrates my every thought, word, and work, and
> teaches me Your immeasurable love.
> How great are my privileges in Christ Jesus!
> Without Him I stand far off, a stranger, an outcast,
> in Him I draw near and touch His kingly scepter.
> Without Him I dare not lift my guilty eyes,
> in Him I gaze upon my Father God and Friend.
> Without Him I hide my lips in trembling shame,
> in Him I open my mouth in petition and praise.
> Without Him all is wrath and consuming fire,
> in Him all is love, and the repose of my soul.
> Without Him is gaping hell below me, and eternal anguish,
> in Him its gates are barred to me by His precious blood!
> Without Him darkness spreads its horrors before me,
> in Him an eternity of glory is my boundless horizon.
> Without Him all within me is terror and dismay,
> in Him every accusation is covered with joy and peace.
> Without Him all things external call for my condemnation,
> in Him they minister to my comfort,
> and are to be enjoyed with thanksgiving.
> Praise be to You for grace, and for the unspeakable gift of Jesus.
> —*THE VALLEY OF VISION: A COLLECTION OF PURITAN PRAYERS AND DEVOTIONS*, ed. Arthur Bennett (Edinburgh: The Banner of Truth, 1975), 284–285.

> **Romans 4:18–25:** In hope [Abraham] believed against hope, that he should become the father of many nations, as he had been told, "So shall your offspring be." He did not weaken in faith when he considered his own body, which was as good as dead (since he was about a hundred years old), or when he considered the barrenness of Sarah's womb. No unbelief made him waver concerning the promise of God, but he grew strong in his faith as he gave glory to God, fully convinced that God was able to do what he had promised. That is why his faith was "counted to him as righteousness." But the words "it was counted to him" were not written for his sake alone, but for ours also. It will be counted to us who believe in him who raised from the dead Jesus our Lord, who was delivered up for our trespasses and raised for our justification.

The resurrection is the day of Christ's crowning. He was Son and Messiah already before His incarnation. He was that also in His humiliation. But then His inner being was hidden beneath the form of a servant.

Now, however, God openly cries out and declares Him to be Lord and Christ, Prince and Savior. Now Christ takes up again that glory that He had before with the Father (John 17:5).

After this He takes on another form, another figure, a different form of existence. He who was dead has become alive, and lives in all eternity, and He has the keys of Death and Hades (Revelation 1:18). He is the Prince of life, the source of salvation, and the one appointed by God to be the Judge of the living and the dead.

Furthermore, the resurrection of Christ is a fountain of good for His Church and for the whole world. It is the "Amen" of the Father upon the "Finished" of the Son. Christ "was delivered up for our trespasses and raised for our justification" (Romans 4:25).

—HERMAN BAVINCK, *Our Reasonable Faith, or The Wonderful Works of God*, trans. Henry Zylstra (Grand Rapids, MI: Wm. B. Eerdmans Publishing, 2016), 350–351.

1 John 5:13–15: I write these things to you who believe in the name of the Son of God, that you may know that you have eternal life. And this is the confidence that we have toward him, that if we ask anything according to his will, he hears us. And if we know that he hears us in whatever we ask, we know that we have the requests that we have asked of him.

When we see that the sum of our salvation, every part of it, is ours through Christ alone, we must beware of deriving even the minutest security from any other source. If we seek true salvation from the power of sin and death, we find it by faith and trust in the name of Jesus Christ alone. If we seek the gifts of the Spirit, they are found through His anointing. There is strength in His government, and empathy with the human condition. Through the purity of His conception, the miracle of His nativity, He was made like us in all respects, in order that He might empathize with us. If we seek redemption, we shall find it in His passion, acquittal in His condemnation, remission of the curse in His cross, satisfaction in His sacrifice, purification in His blood.

We have newness of life and immortality through His resurrection; the inheritance of a celestial kingdom by His entrance into heaven; protection, security, and the abundant supply of every blessing in His kingdom; secure anticipation of a righteous judgment committed to Him. In short, since in Him every blessing and good is found, let us draw all we need from Him, and from no other source. Those not satisfied with Him alone entertain various hopes from others, and though they may continue to look chiefly to Him, they deviate from the right path as their thoughts take them in various directions. Such distrust cannot be sustained once the abundance of His presence and care is properly known.

—JOHN CALVIN, *Institutes of the Christian Religion*, vol. 2, trans. Henry Beveridge (Edinburgh: The Calvin Translation Society, 1845), 72–73 (*Institutes*, 2.16.19).

> **Ephesians 2:14–16:** For he himself is our peace, who has made us both one and has broken down in his flesh the dividing wall of hostility by abolishing the law of commandments expressed in ordinances, that he might create in himself one new man in place of the two, so making peace, and might reconcile us both to God in one body through the cross, thereby killing the hostility.

Jesus does not give recipes that show the way to God as other teachers of religion do. He is himself the Way.

> —KARL BARTH, quoted in Bruxy Cavey, *The End of Religion* (Colorado Springs: NavPress, 2007), 257.

Christianity is in a profound sense the end of all religion. Religion is needed where there is a wall of separation between God and humanity. But Christ who is both God and man has broken down the wall between humanity and God. He has inaugurated a new life, not a new religion. It was this freedom of the early Church from religion in the usual, traditional sense of the word that led the pagans to accuse Christians of atheism. Christians had no concern for any sacred geography, temples, or cult that could be recognized as such by the generations fed with the solemnities of the mystery cults. There was no need for temples built of stone; Christ's body, the Church itself, the new people gathered in Him, was the only real temple. The historical reality of Christ was of course the undisputed ground of the early Christian's faith; yet they did not so much remember Him as know He was with them. And in Him was the end of religion, because He himself was the answer to all religion, to all human hunger for God, because in Him the life that was lost by humanity—and which could only be symbolized in religion—was restored to humanity.

> —ALEXANDER SCHMEMANN, *For the Life of the World* (Crestwood, NY: St. Vladimir's Seminary Press, 2004), 19–20.

> **1 John 5:20:** And we know that the Son of God has come and has given us understanding, so that we may know him who is true; and we are in him who is true, in his Son Jesus Christ. He is the true God and eternal life.

There are many other components to the incarnation of Christ that are to be observed to our advantage. One of them is that it has been demonstrated to humanity what place they have in God's creation. Since human nature could so be joined to God that one person could be made of two substances—God and flesh, so that evil spirits, who interpose themselves as mediators to deceive, do not dare to place themselves above humans because they themselves have no flesh, and chiefly because the Son of God deigned to die in the same flesh, lest they, because they seem to be immortal, should succeed in getting themselves worshiped as gods. Further, that the grace of God might be commended to us in the man Christ Jesus, that He should be joined in such unity with the true God, and should become the Son of God, one Person with Him; whence it is said, "The Word became flesh" (John 1:14).

Then, again, the pride of humanity, which is the chief hindrance against their cleaving to God, can be healed through the humility of God. Humanity learns how far they have strayed from God and what it is worth to God to redeem them when they return through the Mediator. For what greater example of obedience could be given to us who had perished through disobedience than God the Son who was obedient to God the Father, even to the death of the cross? And wherein could the reward of obedience itself be better shown than in the flesh of so great a Mediator, who rose again to eternal life? It owed also to the justice and goodness of the Creator that the devil should be conquered by the same rational creature whom he rejoiced to have conquered!

—AUGUSTINE OF HIPPO, "On the Trinity," in *St. Augustin: On the Holy Trinity, Doctrinal Treatises, Moral Treatises*, A Select Library of the Nicene and Post-Nicene Fathers of the Christian Church, 1st ser., vol. 3, ed. Philip Schaff, trans. Arthur West Haddan (Buffalo, NY: Christian Literature Co., 1887), 179–180 (*De Trinitate*, 13.17.22).

> **Matthew 28:5–6:** "Do not be afraid, for I know that you seek Jesus who was crucified. He is not here, for he has risen."

He is not here. This is the only place of which it could be considered good news to say, Christ is not here. "Christ is here" was good news at Bethany, at Jericho, at Nain, at Capernaum, or on the Sea of Galilee; but Christ is not here is the good news from Joseph's tomb.

A present Christ would be considered the joy and security of other places; it is an absent Christ who is announced as the blessing, the comfort here. He is not here is one of the gladdest sounds that ever fell on human ears. Were He still here, who and where would we have been?

And who is it that you are seeking here? The mortal or the immortal? And what place is this in which you expect to find the Son of God? In a grave? Is this the place for immortality? Is it likely that there should be life in a dwelling of death? Why seek the living among the dead? No; not here—not here; not in this place of death can the Prince of Life be found. He was here, indeed; but He is not here now.

These stone walls and this stone gate could not hold him. He *was* in Gethsemane, in Pilate's palace, on the cross; but not now. These He has visited, but in none of them has He remained. He has left them all behind. With Him it is all life, and incorruption, and glory now. He is not here!

If not here, where? That we soon discover when we follow Him to Emmaus and to Galilee. But even though we knew not, does it matter, except for this, that we may learn that His disappearance has not been a forsaking of earth, nor a turning of His back upon the children of men? His disappearance from the tomb is only the carrying out of His great love.

—HORATIUS BONAR, *The Everlasting Righteousness; or, How Shall a Man Be Just with God?* (London: James Nisbet and Co., 1873), 131–132.

Ephesians 6:10–18: Finally, be strong in the Lord and in the strength of his might. Put on the whole armor of God, that you may be able to stand against the schemes of the devil. For we do not wrestle against flesh and blood, but against the rulers, against the authorities, against the cosmic powers over this present darkness, against the spiritual forces of evil in the heavenly places. Therefore take up the whole armor of God, that you may be able to withstand in the evil day, and having done all, to stand firm. Stand therefore, having fastened on the belt of truth, and having put on the breastplate of righteousness, and, as shoes for your feet, having put on the readiness given by the gospel of peace. In all circumstances take up the shield of faith, with which you can extinguish all the flaming darts of the evil one; and take the helmet of salvation, and the sword of the Spirit, which is the word of God, praying at all times in the Spirit, with all prayer and supplication. To that end, keep alert with all perseverance, making supplication for all the saints.

Christ himself is the Christian's *armory*. When he puts on Christ, he is then completely armed from head to foot. Are his loins girt about with truth? Christ is the *truth*.

Has he put on the breastplate of righteousness? Christ is our righteousness. Are his feet shod with the gospel of peace? Christ is our peace.

Does he take the shield of faith and the helmet of salvation? Christ is that shield and our salvation. Does he take the sword of the Spirit, which is the Word of God? Christ is the Word of God.

Thus he puts on the Lord Jesus Christ; by His Spirit fights the fight of faith; and, in spite of men, of devils, and of his own evil heart, lays hold of eternal life. Christ is all in all.

—JOHN BUNYAN, *The Pilgrim's Progress*, in *The Works of John Bunyan* (London: Blackie and Son, Paternoster Row, 1862), 3:110, n. 2.

> **Ephesians 4:13–15:** Until we all attain to the unity of the faith and of the knowledge of the Son of God, to mature manhood, to the measure of the stature of the fullness of Christ, so that we may no longer be children, tossed to and fro by the waves and carried about by every wind of doctrine, by human cunning, by craftiness in deceitful schemes. Rather, speaking the truth in love, we are to grow up in every way into him who is the head, into Christ.

If the Godhead is to be revealed in the created order, it will be revealed most adequately in manhood, since humanity was created in the image of God. It is fitting, then, that our Lord Jesus Christ, the divine Word who became flesh, should in His one person be both altogether God and altogether man—not something between as so many, from Arius (and before Arius) to Jehovah's Witnesses, have supposed. The more, then, we emphasize our Lord's real humanity, the more we do justice to His true nature, for it is in that real humanity—in it, and not merely through it, that we see the Godhead shine.

—F. F. BRUCE, "The Humanity of Jesus Christ," *Journal of the Christian Brethren Research Fellowship* 24 (1973): 5.

The Gospel of our salvation depends upon the genuineness of our Lord's humanity, and so does the value of His life as an example for His people to follow. The power of that example is weakened if we can say, allowing for our own failure, "It was different, or easier, for Him." Only as He presents himself to us as perfect man can we in turn be validly encouraged to grow up, not only individually but corporately, "to the measure of the stature of the fullness of Christ."

—F. F. BRUCE, "The Humanity of Jesus Christ," *Journal of the Christian Brethren Research Fellowship* 24 (1973): 13.

Matthew 16:24–25: Then Jesus told his disciples, "If anyone would come after me, let him deny himself and take up his cross and follow me. For whoever would save his life will lose it, but whoever loses his life for my sake will find it."

The cross is laid on every Christian. The first Christ-suffering that every person must experience is the call to abandon the attachments of this world. It is that dying of the old man which is the result of his encounter with Christ. As we embark upon discipleship, we surrender ourselves to Christ in union with His death—we give our lives over to death. Thus it begins: the cross is not the terrible end to an otherwise God-fearing and happy life, but it meets us at the beginning of our communion with Christ. When Christ calls a person, He bids them come and die. It may be a death like that of the first disciples, who had to leave home and work to follow Him, or it may be a death like Luther's, who had to leave the monastery and go out into the world. But it is the same death every time—death in Jesus Christ, the death of the old man at His call.

—DIETRICH BONHOEFFER, *The Cost of Discipleship* (London: SCM Press, 1948/2001), 44.

Romans 8:1–2, 9–11: There is therefore now no condemnation for those who are in Christ Jesus. For the law of the Spirit of life has set you free in Christ Jesus from the law of sin and death. . . . You, however, are not in the flesh but in the Spirit, if in fact the Spirit of God dwells in you. Anyone who does not have the Spirit of Christ does not belong to him. But if Christ is in you, although the body is dead because of sin, the Spirit is life because of righteousness. If the Spirit of him who raised Jesus from the dead dwells in you, he who raised Christ Jesus from the dead will also give life to your mortal bodies through his Spirit who dwells in you.

We expect salvation from Him—not because He stands afar off from us, but because by ingrafting us into His body, He not only makes us partakers of all His benefits but also of himself. If you look to yourself, damnation is certain, but since Christ has been presented to you with all His benefits, so that all that is His is made yours, you become a member of Him and hence one with Him. His righteousness covers your sins—His salvation extinguishes your condemnation; He interposes His worthiness, and so prevents your unworthiness from coming before God. It will never do to separate Christ from us, nor us from Him; but we must with conscious effort keep a firm hold on that alliance by which He has joined us to himself. This the apostle teaches: "The body is dead because of sin, the Spirit is life because of righteousness." Our enemy, speaking through those who would deny our Lord's work, might say, "Christ indeed has life in himself, but you, as you are sinners, remain liable to death and condemnation." The truth is that the condemnation that we in ourselves deserve is annihilated by the salvation Christ offers, and to confirm this the apostle further employs the argument that Christ is not external to us, but dwells in us; and not only unites us to himself by an undivided bond of fellowship, but by a wondrous communion brings us daily into closer connection, until He becomes altogether one with us. I cannot deny that faith occasionally suffers certain interruptions when by some distraction or weakness is made to falter and succumb to temptation. Yet even still, true faith ceases not its earnest quest for God.

—JOHN CALVIN, *Institutes of the Christian Religion*, vol. 2, trans. Henry Beveridge
(Edinburgh: The Calvin Translation Society, 1845), 124–125 (*Institutes*, 3.2.24).

> **Luke 22:44:** And being in agony he prayed more earnestly; and his sweat became like great drops of blood falling down to the ground.

The Son of God became man to enable men to become the sons of God.

—C. S. LEWIS, *Mere Christianity* (New York: HarperCollins, 2001), 178.

God could, had He pleased, have been incarnate in a man of iron nerves, the stoic sort who lets no sigh escape him. Of His great humility, He chose to be incarnate in a man of delicate sensibilities, who wept at the grave of Lazarus and sweat blood in Gethsemane. Otherwise, we should have missed the great lesson that it is by His will alone that a man is good or bad, and that feelings are not, in themselves, of any importance. We should also have missed the all-important help of knowing that He has faced all that the weakest of us face, has shared not only the strength of our nature but every weakness of it, except sin. If He had been incarnate in a man of immense natural courage, that would have been for many of us almost the same as His not being incarnate at all.

—C. S. LEWIS, *Letters of C. S. Lewis* (Boston: Houghton Mifflin Harcourt, 1993), 383.

The central miracle asserted by Christians is the incarnation. They say that God became man. Every other miracle prepares for this, or exhibits this, or results from this. Just as every natural event is the manifestation of nature's total character, so every miracle manifests at a particular place and moment the character and significance of the incarnation. There is no question in Christianity of arbitrary interferences simply scattered about. It relates not a series of disconnected raids on nature, but the various steps of a strategically coherent invasion—one that intends complete conquest and occupation. The fitness, and therefore credibility, of a particular miracle depends on its relation to the grand miracle of the incarnation; all discussion of it in isolation from it is futile.

—C. S. LEWIS, *Miracles: The Complete C. S. Lewis Signature Classics* (New York: HarperCollins Publishers Inc., 2002), 270.

> **Romans 3:23–25:** For all have sinned and fall short of the glory of God, and are justified by his grace as a gift, through the redemption that is in Christ Jesus, whom God put forward as a propitiation by his blood, to be received by faith. This was to show God's righteousness, because in his divine forbearance he had passed over former sins.

If the Father did not spare His own Son but delivered Him up to the agony and shame of Calvary, how could He possibly fail to bring to fruition the end contemplated in such a sacrifice.

The greatest gift of the Father was not temporal things, though He has given us much to enjoy. It was not simply our calling, or even our justification and glorification. It was not even the security we have in Him. These are favors dispensed in the fulfilment of God's gracious design.

But the unspeakable and incomparable gift is the giving up of His own Son. So great is that gift, so marvelous its implications, so far-reaching its consequences that all gifts of lesser proportion will surely be given to us.

Christ is given to us; the Father's giving Him up is also to be construed as a gift. Since He is the supreme demonstration of the Father's love, every other grace will follow the gift of Christ.

—JOHN MURRAY, *The Epistle to the Romans*, The New International Commentary on the Old and New Testament, vol. 1 (Grand Rapids, MI; Cambridge, U.K.: Wm. B. Eerdmans Publishing, 1968), 326.

> **Isaiah 40:11:** He will tend his flock like a shepherd. He will gather the lambs in his arms.

Our Good Shepherd has in His flock people with a variety of experiences; some are strong in the Lord, and others are weak in faith, but He is impartial in His care for all His sheep, and the weakest lamb is as dear to Him as the most advanced of the flock.

Lambs tend to stray from the flock, are prone to wander, and apt to grow weary, but from all the danger of these tendencies, the Shepherd protects them with His strong arm. He finds newborn souls, like young lambs, ready to perish; He nourishes them till they become vibrant. He finds weak ones ready to faint and die; He consoles them and renews their strength.

All the little ones He gathers, for it is not the will of our heavenly Father that one of them should perish. What a quick, discerning eye He must have to see them all! What a tender heart to care for them all! What a far-reaching arm to gather them all!

In His lifetime on earth He was a compassionate gatherer of the weaker sort, and now that He dwells in heaven, His loving heart yearns toward the meek and contrite, the timid and frail, the fearful and fainting here below.

How gently did He gather me to himself, to His truth, to His blood, to His love, to His Church! With what effectual grace did He compel me to come to himself! Since my conversion, how frequently has He restored me from my wanderings, and once again folded me within the circle of His everlasting arms!

Best of all, He does it all himself personally, not delegating the task of love, but humbling himself to rescue and preserve His most unworthy servant. How shall I love Him enough or serve Him sufficiently? I want to make His name known unto the ends of the earth, but what can my feeble efforts accomplish for Him?

Great Shepherd, add to Your mercies this one: a heart to love You more truly as I ought.

—CHARLES H. SPURGEON, "October 17—Evening," in *Morning and Evening* (Geanies House, Fearn, Scotland: Christian Focus, 1994), 609.

Psalm 34:18: The LORD is near to the brokenhearted and saves the crushed in spirit.

Only the humble believe Him and rejoice that God is so free and so marvelous that He does wonders where people despair, that He takes what is small and lowly and makes it marvelous. And that is the wonder of all wonders that God loves the lowly. God is not ashamed of the lowliness of human beings. God marches right in. He chooses people as His instruments and performs His wonders where one would least expect them. God is near to the least of men; He loves the lost, the neglected, the unseemly, the excluded, the weak, and the broken.

—DIETRICH BONHOEFFER, *God Is in the Manger: Reflections on Advent and Christmas*, trans. O. C. Dean Jr. (Louisville, KY: Westminster John Knox Press, 2010), 22.

And in the incarnation the whole human race recovers the dignity of the image of God. Henceforth, any attack even on the least of men is an attack on Christ, who took the form of man, and in His own Person restored the image of God in all that bears a human form. Through fellowship and communion with the incarnate Lord, we recover our true humanity, and at the same time we are delivered from self-centeredness, which is a consequence of sin, and we retrieve our solidarity with the whole human race. By being partakers of Christ incarnate, we are partakers in the whole humanity that He bore. We now know that we have been taken up and borne in the humanity of Jesus, and therefore that new nature we now enjoy means that we too must bear the sins and sorrows of others. The incarnate Lord makes His followers the brothers and sisters of all humankind.

—DIETRICH BONHOEFFER, *The Cost of Discipleship*, trans. R.H. Fuller and Irmgard Booth (London: SCM Press, 2015), 231.

Hebrews 10:8–10: When he said above, "You have neither desired nor taken pleasure in sacrifices and offerings and burnt offerings and sin offerings" (these are offered according to the law), then he added, "Behold, I have come to do your will." He does away with the first in order to establish the second. And by that will we have been sanctified through the offering of the body of Jesus Christ once for all.

As all people are, in the sight of God, lost sinners, we hold that Christ is our only righteousness, since, by His obedience, He has wiped away our transgressions; by His sacrifice, He has appeased the divine anger; by His blood, He has washed away our sins; by His cross, He has borne our curse; and by His death, He has paid all our debt.

We maintain that in this way man is reconciled in Christ to God the Father by no merit of his own, no value of his works, but by mercy alone. When we embrace Christ by faith, we come into communion with Him.

—JOHN CALVIN, "Calvin's Reply to Sadoleto," in *A Reformation Debate*, ed. John Olin (Grand Rapids, MI: Baker, 1966/1539), 66–67.

How, then, are we justified by faith? By faith we apprehend the righteousness of Christ, which alone reconciles us to God. Christ justifies no man without also sanctifying him. These blessings are conjoined by a perpetual and inseparable tie. Those whom He enlightens by His wisdom He redeems; whom He redeems He justifies; whom He justifies He sanctifies.

Though we may distinguish them, they are both inseparably comprehended in Christ. Would you obtain justification in Christ? You must first possess Christ. But you cannot possess Him without being made a partaker of His sanctification, for Christ cannot be divided. Since the Lord, therefore, does not grant us the enjoyment of these blessings without giving us himself, he gives both at once, but never the one without the other. So, it is true that we are justified not *without* works, and yet not *through* works, since in our participation of Christ, by which we are justified, we are also sanctified.

—JOHN CALVIN, *Institutes of the Christian Religion*, vol. 2, trans. Henry Beveridge (Edinburgh: The Calvin Translation Society, 1845), 386 (*Institutes*, 3.16.1).

DAY
32

> **1 Corinthians 3:16–17, 21–23:** Do you not know that you are God's temple and that God's Spirit dwells in you? If anyone destroys God's temple, God will destroy him. For God's temple is holy, and you are that temple. . . . So let no one boast in men. For all things are yours, whether Paul or Apollos or Cephas or the world or life or death or the present or the future—all are yours, and you are Christ's, and Christ is God's.

Q. What is your only comfort in life and in death?

A. That I am not my own, but belong—body and soul, in life and in death—to my faithful Savior, Jesus Christ. He has fully paid for all my sins with His precious blood and has set me free from the tyranny of the devil. He also watches over me in such a way that not a hair can fall from my head without the will of my Father in heaven; in fact, all things must work together for my salvation. Because I belong to Him, Christ, by His Holy Spirit, assures me of eternal life and makes me wholeheartedly willing and ready from now on to live for Him.

Q. Why is He called "Christ," meaning "anointed"?

A. Because He has been ordained by God the Father and has been anointed with the Holy Spirit to be our chief prophet and teacher, who fully reveals to us the secret counsel and will of God concerning our deliverance; our only high priest who has delivered us by the one sacrifice of His body, and who continually pleads our cause with the Father; and our eternal king who governs us by His Word and Spirit, and who guards us and keeps us in the freedom He has won for us.

—THE HEIDELBERG CATECHISM, Q. and A. 1 and 31.

Luke 1:41–45: And when Elizabeth heard the greeting of Mary, the baby leaped in her womb. And Elizabeth was filled with the Holy Spirit, and she exclaimed with a loud cry, "Blessed are you among women, and blessed is the fruit of your womb! And why is this granted to me that the mother of my Lord should come to me? For behold, when the sound of your greeting came to my ears, the baby in my womb leaped for joy. And blessed is she who believed that there would be a fulfillment of what was spoken to her from the Lord."

The nativity mystery "conceived from the Holy Spirit and born from the Virgin Mary" means that God became human, truly human, out of His own grace. The miracle of the existence of Jesus, His "climbing down of God" is the Holy Spirit and the Virgin Mary. Here is a human being, the Virgin Mary, and as He comes from God, Jesus comes also from this human being. Born of the Virgin Mary means a human origin for God. Jesus Christ is not only truly God; He is also truly human, like every one of us. He is human without limitation. He is not only *similar* to us but He is also like us.

—KARL BARTH, *Dogmatik im Grundriss* (1947), 125, 127.

Mary's Son first had to be the Child of the Father in order then to become man and be capable of taking upon His shoulders the burden of a guilty world.

—HANS URS VON BALTHASAR, *Unless You Become Like This Child*, trans. Erasmo Leiva-Merikakis (San Francisco: Ignatius Press, 1991), 74.

For me, it is the virgin birth, the incarnation, and the resurrection that are the true laws of the flesh and the physical. Death, decay, and destruction are the suspension of these laws. I am always astonished at the emphasis the Church puts on the body. It is not the soul, it says, that will rise, but the body, glorified.

—FLANNERY O'CONNOR, *The Habit of Being: Letters of Flannery O'Connor* (New York: Farrar, Straus & Giroux, Inc., 1979), 100.

Luke 2:22, 25–35: And when the time came for their purification accord-ing to the Law of Moses, they brought him up to Jerusalem to present him to the Lord. . . . Now there was a man in Jerusalem, whose name was Simeon, and this man was righteous and devout, waiting for the consola-tion of Israel, and the Holy Spirit was upon him. And it had been revealed to him by the Holy Spirit that he would not see death before he had seen the Lord's Christ. And he came in the Spirit into the temple, and when the parents brought in the child Jesus, to do for him according to the custom of the Law, he took him up in his arms and blessed God and said,

> "Lord, now you are letting your servant depart in peace, according to your word; for my eyes have seen your salvation that you have prepared in the presence of all peoples, a light for revelation to the Gentiles, and for glory to your people Israel."

And his father and his mother marveled at what was said about him. And Simeon blessed them and said to Mary his mother, "Behold, this child is appointed for the fall and rising of many in Israel, and for a sign that is opposed (and a sword will pierce through your own soul also), so that thoughts from many hearts may be revealed."

The Lord's generation received testimony not only from angels and prophets, from shepherds and parents, but also from the aged and the righteous. Every age and both sexes, as well as the miraculous occurrences, build up faith: a virgin bears Him, a barren woman gives birth, a dumb man speaks, Elizabeth prophesies, the magi adore, the one enclosed in the womb leaps for joy, the widow confesses Him, and the righteous awaits Him. And the righteous man, Simeon, did well, as he sought the favor not for himself but for the people, desiring for himself release from the toils of his frail body, but waiting to see the fulfillment of the promise. For he knew, blessed were the eyes that saw.

—AMBROSE OF MILAN, *Expositions on the Gospel of Luke*, ed. Carl Schenkl
(Leipzig, 1902), in Corpus Scriptorum Ecclesiasticorum Latinorum (Vienna, 1866–),
32.4, 73–74.

> **Hebrews 2:17–18:** Therefore he had to be made like his brothers in every respect, so that he might become a merciful and faithful high priest in the service of God, to make propitiation for the sins of the people. For because he himself has suffered when tempted, he is able to help those who are being tempted.

The Son of God assumed human nature, and in it He endured all that belongs to the human condition. This is hope for humankind beyond our imagining. Could our pride be cured if the humility of God's Son does not cure it? Could our greed be cured if the poverty of God's Son does not cure it? Or our anger if the patience of God's Son does not cure it? Or our bitterness and selfishness if the love of God's Son does not cure it?

And what could cure our fear of death, if not the resurrection of the body of Christ our Lord? Let us raise our hopes and recognize our redeemed nature; let us observe how high a place it has in the works of God.

Do not despise yourselves, dear ones; the Son of God assumed manhood. God's Son was born of a woman. But do not set your hearts on the satisfactions of the body, for in the Son of God "there is no male and female" (Galatians 3:28). Do not fear insults, crosses, or death itself: for if they did man harm, the humanity that God's Son assumed would not have endured them.

—AUGUSTINE OF HIPPO, *On the Christian Struggle* 12, in *The Later Christian Fathers*, ed. and trans. Henry Bettenson (Oxford University Press, 1973), 218–219.

> **Romans 5:12–14:** Therefore, just as sin came into the world through one man, and death through sin, and so death spread to all men because all sinned—for sin indeed was in the world before the law was given, but sin is not counted where there is no law. Yet death reigned from Adam to Moses, even over those whose sinning was not like the transgression of Adam, who was a type of the one who was to come.

For it was fitting that just as death entered the human race through man's disobedience, so should life be restored by man's obedience. And that just as the sin that was the cause of our damnation had its beginning from a woman, so the author of our justice and salvation should be born from a woman. And that while the devil conquered man through persuading him to taste from the tree, he should be conquered by man through the passion He endured on the tree.

—ANSELM OF CANTERBURY, *Cur Deus Homo* (Oxford and London: John Henry and James Parker, 1865), 6.

This kind of death was especially suitable in order to atone for the sin of our first parent, which was the plucking of the fruit from the forbidden tree against God's command. And so to atone for that sin, it was fitting that Christ should suffer by being nailed to a tree, as if restoring what Adam had stolen. Augustine says in a sermon on Christ's sacrifice: "Adam despised the command, plucking the apple from the tree: but all that Adam lost, Christ found upon the cross."

—THOMAS AQUINAS, *"Summa Theologica" of St. Thomas Aquinas*, trans. Reginaldus de Piperno (London: R. & T. Washbourne, 1922), Book III, Question 46, Article 4.

Philippians 2:6–8: Who, though he was in the form of God, did not count equality with God a thing to be grasped, but emptied himself, by taking the form of a servant, being born in the likeness of men. And being found in human form, he humbled himself by becoming obedient to the point of death, even death on a cross.

Christ was God, is God, and will forever remain God. He was not the Father, or the Spirit, but the Son, the Only Begotten, beloved Son of the Father who became man in the fullness of time. And when He became man and as man went about on earth, even when He agonized in Gethsemane and hung on the cross, He remained God's own Son in whom the Father was well pleased.

But it is a mistake to take this to mean, as some do, that Christ, in His incarnation, in His state of humiliation, completely or partly divested himself of His divinity, and thereupon in the state of exaltation gradually assumed those attributes again. For how could this be, since God cannot deny himself, and as the immutable One in himself far transcends all becoming and change? Even when He became what He was not, He remained what He was, the Only Begotten of the Father. Further, the apostle says that in this sense Christ made himself of no reputation: being in the form of God, He assumed the form of a man and a servant.

One can express it humanly and simply in this way: Before His incarnation, Christ was equal with the Father, not alone in essence and attributes, but He had also the form of God. He looked like God, He was the brightness of His glory, and the expressed image of His person. Had anyone been able to see Him, he would immediately have recognized God.

But this changed at His incarnation. Then He took on the form of a human being, the form of a servant. Whoever looked at Him then could no longer recognize Him as the Only Begotten Son of the Father, except by the eye of faith.

He had laid aside His divine form. He hid His divine nature behind the form of a servant. On earth He was and looked like one of us.

—HERMAN BAVINCK, *Our Reasonable Faith, or The Wonderful Works of God,* trans. Henry Zylstra (Grand Rapids, MI: Wm. B. Eerdmans Publishing, 2016), 305–306.

> **Matthew 9:10–13:** And as Jesus reclined at table in the house, behold, many tax collectors and sinners came and were reclining with Jesus and his disciples. And when the Pharisees saw this, they said to his disciples, "Why does your teacher eat with tax collectors and sinners?" But when he heard it, he said, "Those who are well have no need of a physician, but those who are sick. Go and learn what this means: 'I desire mercy, and not sacrifice.' For I came not to call the righteous, but sinners."

There is not the meanest, the weakest, the poorest believer on the earth, but that Christ prizes him more than all the world.

—JOHN OWEN, *Communion with God* (Fearn, Scotland: Christian Heritage, 2012), 218.

One of the purposes of the incarnation was that Christ should not lead a solitary life but should associate with men. Now, it is most fitting that he who associates with others should conform to their manner of living. According to the words of the apostle (1 Corinthians 9:22): "I have become all things to all people, that by all means I might save some." And, therefore, it was appropriate that Christ should conform to others even in the matter of eating and drinking.

—THOMAS AQUINAS, *"Summa Theologica" of St. Thomas Aquinas*, trans. Reginaldus de Piperno (London: R. & T. Washbourne, 1922), Book 3, Question 40, Article 2.

> **Revelation 3:15–19:** "I know your works: you are neither cold nor hot. Would that you were either cold or hot! So, because you are lukewarm, and neither hot nor cold, I will spit you out of my mouth. For you say, I am rich, I have prospered, and I need nothing, not realizing that you are wretched, pitiable, poor, blind, and naked. I counsel you to buy from me gold refined by fire, so that you may be rich, and white garments so that you may clothe yourself and the shame of your nakedness may not be seen, and salve to anoint your eyes, so that you may see. Those whom I love, I reprove and discipline, so be zealous and repent."

Sinners, are you poor? Christ has gold to enrich you.

Are you naked? Christ has royal robes; He has white raiment to clothe you.

Are you blind? Christ has eye-salve to enlighten you.

Are you hungry? Christ will be manna to feed you.

Are you thirsty? He will be a well of living water to refresh you.

Are you wounded? He has a balm under His wings to heal you.

Are you sick? He is a physician to cure you.

Are you prisoners? He has laid down a ransom for you.

Ah, sinners! Tell me, tell me, is there anything in Christ to keep you from believing? No.

Is there not everything in Christ that may encourage you to believe in Him? Yes.

Then believe in Him, and "though your sins are like scarlet, they shall be as white as snow; though they are red like crimson, they shall become like wool" (Isaiah 1:18).

Then your iniquities shall be forgotten as well as forgiven; they shall be remembered no more. God will cast them behind His back; He will throw them into the bottom of the sea.

—THOMAS BROOKS, "Precious Remedies," in *The Works of Thomas Brooks*, vol. 1, ed. Alexander Balloch Grosart (Carlisle, PA: Banner of Truth, 1666/2001), 143–144.

Philippians 3:4–11: Though I myself have reason for confidence in the flesh also. If anyone else thinks he has reason for confidence in the flesh, I have more: circumcised on the eighth day, of the people of Israel, of the tribe of Benjamin, a Hebrew of Hebrews; as to the law, a Pharisee; as to zeal, a persecutor of the church; as to righteousness under the law, blameless. But whatever gain I had, I counted as loss for the sake of Christ. Indeed, I count everything as loss because of the surpassing worth of knowing Christ Jesus my Lord. For his sake I have suffered the loss of all things and count them as rubbish, in order that I may gain Christ and be found in him, not having a righteousness of my own that comes from the law, but that which comes through faith in Christ, the righteousness from God that depends on faith—that I may know him and the power of his resurrection, and may share his sufferings, becoming like him in his death, that by any means possible I may attain the resurrection from the dead.

Every little thing would hurt my conscience. But one day, as I was passing in the field, suddenly I had this thought: "Your righteousness is in heaven." With the eyes of faith, I saw Jesus sitting at God's right hand. And I suddenly realized—*there* is my righteousness. Wherever I was, or whatever I was doing, God could not say to me, "Where is your righteousness?" for it was right before Him. I saw that my frame of mind could not make my righteousness better nor could it make it worse. My righteousness was in Jesus Christ himself, forever!

Now indeed my chains fell off. I felt delivered from my slavery to guilt and fear. I went home rejoicing for the love and grace of God. Now I could look from myself to Him. Christ is my treasure, my righteousness. Christ is my wisdom, my holiness, and my salvation.

—JOHN BUNYAN, *Grace Abounding to the Chief of Sinners*, 228–232.

1 Corinthians 15:55–58: "O death, where is your victory? O death, where is your sting?" The sting of death is sin, and the power of sin is the law. But thanks be to God, who gives us the victory through our Lord Jesus Christ. Therefore, my beloved brothers, be steadfast, immovable, always abounding in the work of the Lord, knowing that in the Lord your labor is not in vain.

Without the Gospel, everything is useless and vain; without the Gospel we cannot be Christians; without the Gospel riches are as poverty, wisdom is folly; strength is weakness, and the justice of man is under the condemnation of God. But through the knowledge and acceptance of the gospel, we are made children of God, brothers of Jesus Christ, fellow believers with the saints, citizens of the kingdom of heaven, heirs of God with Jesus Christ. It is the power of God unto salvation for all those who believe.

Every good and perfect gift is found in Jesus Christ alone. He was sold to buy us back, made captive to deliver us, condemned to absolve us. He was made a curse for our blessing, a sin offering for our righteousness, marred that we may be healed. He died for us so that through Him the wrath of God was appeased, darkness made light, fear abated, our debt canceled.

All the weapons of the devil in his battle against us, including the sting of death, have lost their power through the death and resurrection of Christ our Lord. If we can boast with the apostle Paul, it is by the Spirit of Christ. We no longer live, but Christ lives in us; and we are by the same Spirit seated among those who are in heaven, so that for us the world is no more, even while we are in it. We are comforted in tribulation, joyful in sorrow, patient in all things. Let us truly seek to know Jesus Christ, and the infinite riches that are comprised in Him.

—JOHN CALVIN, *Christ the End of the Law: Being the Preface to the Geneva Bible of 1550*, trans. Thomas Weedon (London: William Tegg & Co., 1850), 22, 29–31.

> **John 11:25-26:** Jesus said to her, "I am the resurrection and the life. Whoever believes in me, though he die, yet shall he live, and everyone who lives and believes in me shall never die."

He is risen! He was laid down upon that rocky floor; but only to rest there for a day. For that tomb was His first earthly resting place; all before that was weariness. Having rested there for a short season, He rises; and with renewed strength, into which hereafter no element of weariness can enter, He resumes His work. He has not been carried off either by friend or enemy; He has been raised by the Father, as the righteous One, the fulfiller of His purpose; the finisher of His work; the destroyer of death; the conqueror of him who has the power of death; the Father's beloved Son, in whom He is well pleased.

This true temple has been destroyed, only to be rebuilt in greater magnificence. This true Siloam has only for three days intermitted the flow of its missioned waters, that it might gush forth in larger fullness. This true Sun has only for three days been darkened, that it might be rekindled in its incorruptible glory.

He is risen! Yes; and now we see more fully the meaning of His own words, spoken at a tomb, and over one whom death had bound, "I am the resurrection and the life"; himself at once the raiser and the raised, the life-giver and the living, the possessor and the giver of an infinite life—a higher kind of life than that which the first Adam knew—a life which can force its way into the dungeons of death, transforming them, by its irresistible power, into the dwellings, the palaces, the temples of immortality and glory.

He is risen! He has tasted death, but He has not seen corruption; for He is the Holy One of God, and upon holiness corruption cannot fix itself. As the beloved of the Father, He rises from the dead; for therefore does the Father love Him, because He gives His life for the sheep.

And in this resurrection, we read the Father's testimony to His sonship; the Father's seal set to His completed propitiation; the Father's declaration of satisfaction and delight in the work of Calvary.

—HORATIUS BONAR, *The Everlasting Righteousness; or, How Shall a Man Be Just with God?* (London: James Nisbet and Co., 1873), 132–134.

Hosea 2:14–20:
> "Therefore, behold, I will allure her,
>   and bring her into the wilderness,
>   and speak tenderly to her.
> And there I will give her her vineyards
>   and make the Valley of Achor a door of hope.
> And there she shall answer as in the days of her youth,
>   as at the time when she came out of the land of Egypt.

> "And in that day, declares the LORD, you will call me 'My Husband,' and no longer will you call me 'My Baal.' For I will remove the names of the Baals from her mouth, and they shall be remembered by name no more. And I will make for them a covenant on that day with the beasts of the field, the birds of the heavens, and the creeping things of the ground. And I will abolish the bow, the sword, and war from the land, and I will make you lie down in safety. And I will betroth you to me forever. I will betroth you to me in righteousness and in justice, in steadfast love and in mercy. I will betroth you to me in faithfulness. And you shall know the LORD."

His love is not a forced love that He strives only to bear toward us, but because His Father has commanded Him to be joined to us, it is His nature, His disposition. This disposition is free and natural to Him or He could not be God's Son, nor take after His heavenly Father, unto whom it is natural to show mercy, but not to punish. Mercy pleases Him. Our God is the Father of mercies.

—THOMAS GOODWIN, *The Heart of Christ* (Edinburgh: Banner of Truth, 2011), 60.

He loves life into us.

—JOHN OWEN, *On Communion with God*, in *The Works of John Owen*, ed. W.H. Goold (Edinburgh: Banner of Truth, 1965), 2:63.

Psalm 19:1–4:
The heavens declare the glory of God,
    and the sky above proclaims his handiwork.
Day to day pours out speech,
    and night to night reveals knowledge.
There is no speech, nor are there words,
    whose voice is not heard.
Their voice goes out through all the earth,
    and their words to the end of the world.

The Son of God created the world for this very end, to reveal an image of His excellence. The beauties of nature are pictures or shadows of the excellencies of the Son of God.

When we are delighted with flowery meadows and gentle breezes, we may consider that we are seeing emanations of the sweet benevolence of Jesus Christ. When we behold the fragrant rose and lily, we see His love and purity.

The lush green fields and hillsides, and the singing of birds are the images of His infinite joy and kindness. The stateliness of trees and vineyards are shadows of His infinite beauty and loveliness. The crystal rivers and murmuring streams carry the footprint of His grace and bounty.

When we behold the brightness of the sun, the golden edges of a sunset, or the vibrant colors of a rainbow, we behold the sketches of His glory and goodness, and in the clear blue skies, we see His gentleness.

There is so much in nature wherein we may behold His majesty: the brilliant sun in its strength, the countless stars, the rumble of thunder, the voluminous clouds, towering rocks, and the majestic mountains.

The beautiful light with which the world is filled on a clear day is a mere shadow of His spotless holiness and His delight in communicating himself to us.

—JONATHAN EDWARDS, "Entry 108: Excellency of Christ" in *The "Miscellanies": Entry nos. a-z, aa-zz, 1–500 in The Works of Jonathan Edwards*, vol. 13, ed. Harry S. Stout (New Haven, CT: Yale University Press, 1994), 279.

Philippians 2:5–8: Have this mind among yourselves, which is yours in Christ Jesus, who, though he was in the form of God, did not count equality with God a thing to be grasped, but emptied himself, by taking the form of a servant, being born in the likeness of men. And being found in human form, he humbled himself by becoming obedient to the point of death, even death on a cross.

Inherent in the Father's love is an absolute renunciation: He will not be God for himself alone. He lets go of His divinity and, in this sense, reveals a (divine) God-lessness (of love, of course). The Son's answer to the gift of the Godhead (of equal substance with the Father) can only be eternal thanksgiving to the Father, the Source; a thanksgiving as selfless and unreserved as the Father's original self-surrender. Proceeding from both as their subsistent "We" there breathes the Spirit who is common to both: As the essence of love, He maintains the infinite difference between them, seals it, and, since He is the one Spirit of them both, bridges it.

—HANS URS VON BALTHASAR, *Theo-Drama: The Action*, vol. 4 (San Francisco: Ignatius, 1994), 323–324.

> **Colossians 1:15–16, 19–20:** He is the image of the invisible God, the first-born of all creation. For by him all things were created, in heaven and on earth, visible and invisible, whether thrones or dominions or rulers or authorities—all things were created through him and for him. . . . For in him all the fullness of God was pleased to dwell, and through him to reconcile to himself all things, whether on earth or in heaven, making peace by the blood of his cross.

The first creation of things was made by the power of God the Father through the Word; hence the second creation ought to have been brought about through the Word, by the power of God the Father, in order that restoration should correspond to creation, according to 2 Corinthians 5:19: "In Christ God was reconciling the world to himself."

—THOMAS AQUINAS, *"Summa Theologica" of St. Thomas Aquinas*, trans. Reginaldus de Piperno (London: R. & T. Washbourne, 1922), Book III, Question 3, Article 8.

The incarnation is reconciliation and redemption. In fact, its first goal is to eliminate the evil consequences of the bad use of creaturely freedom, the consequences of the fall, and to restore the fallen Adam. This goal must be the first, because until it is attained, humanity's communion with God cannot be restored. Christ came into the world to save sinners from sin. In coming into the world, Christ enters the realm of sin-poisoned beings. His redemptive suffering begins with His incarnation. Absolutely without human sin, the God-man experiences the sin surrounding Him. Christ experienced sin as an unceasing suffering—from demons and from men.

—SERGIUS BULGAKOV, *The Lamb of God*, trans. Boris Jakim (Grand Rapids, MI: Wm. B. Eerdmans Publishing, 1933, 2008), 345–346.

2 Corinthians 4:3–6: And even if our gospel is veiled, it is veiled to those who are perishing. In their case the god of this world has blinded the minds of the unbelievers, to keep them from seeing the light of the gospel of the glory of Christ, who is the image of God. For what we proclaim is not ourselves, but Jesus Christ as Lord, with ourselves as your servants for Jesus' sake. For God, who said, "Let light shine out of darkness," has shone in our hearts to give the light of the knowledge of the glory of God in the face of Jesus Christ.

For only one who is divine can satisfy the image of God, and only one who is truly human can fulfill that role. Therefore, since it is necessary to find a God-man who retains the integrity of both natures, it is no less necessary that these two integral natures conjoin in one person (just as a body and a rational soul conjoin in one man); for otherwise, it is impossible that one and the same individual be fully divine and fully human.

The acts of Christ's condescension that we speak of do not belong to His divinity; it yet seems improper to infidels that these things should be said of Him even as a man. For we affirm that the divine nature is beyond doubt impassible, and that God cannot at all be brought down from His exaltation, nor toil in anything that He wishes to effect. But we say that the Lord Jesus Christ is very God and very man, one person in two natures, and two natures in one person. When therefore, we speak of God as enduring any humiliation or infirmity, we do not refer to the majesty of that nature, which cannot suffer, but to the feebleness of the human constitution that he assumed. And so there remains no ground of objection against our faith. For in this way we intend no devaluing of the divine nature, but we teach that one person is both divine and human. In the incarnation of God there is no lowering of the Deity, but the nature of man we believe to be exalted.

—ANSELM OF CANTERBURY, *Cur Deus Homo*, 2.7 and 1.8.

> **1 Corinthians 3:11:** For no one can lay a foundation other than that which is laid, which is Jesus Christ.

Christianity stands in a different relationship to the person of Christ than other religions stand to the persons who founded them. Jesus was not the first confessor of the religion named for His name.

He was not the first and the most important Christian. He occupies a wholly unique place in Christianity.

He is not in the usual sense the founder of Christianity, but He is the Christ, the One who was sent by the Father, and who founded His kingdom on earth, and now extends and preserves it to the end of the ages.

Christ is himself Christianity. He stands, not outside, but inside of it. Without His name, person, and work there is no such thing as Christianity.

In one word, Christ is not the one who points the way to Christianity, but the Way itself. He is the only true and perfect Mediator between God and men.

That which the various religions in their belief in a mediator have surmised and hoped is actually and perfectly fulfilled in Christ. In Christianity, Christ occupies a different place than Buddha, Zarathustra, and Muhammad occupy in their respective religions. Christ is not the teacher, not the founder, but the content of Christianity.

—HERMAN BAVINCK, *Our Reasonable Faith, or The Wonderful Works of God*, trans. Henry Zylstra (Grand Rapids, MI: Wm. B. Eerdmans Publishing, 2016), 263, 284.

> **1 Corinthians 1:27–29:** But God chose what is foolish in the world to shame the wise; God chose what is weak in the world to shame the strong; God chose what is low and despised in the world, even things that are not, to bring to nothing things that are, so that no human being might boast in the presence of God.

The lowlier He seemed by reason of His poverty, the greater might the power of His Godhead be shown to be. Hence, in a sermon of the Council of Ephesus we read: "He chose all who were poor and despicable, all who were of small account and hidden from the majority, that we might recognize how His Godhead transformed the earth. For this reason, He chose a poor maid for His mother, a poorer birthplace; for this reason, He lived in want. We learn this from the manger."

—THOMAS AQUINAS, *"Summa Theologica" of St. Thomas Aquinas*, trans. Reginaldus de Piperno (London: R. & T. Washbourne, 1922), Book III, Question 40, Article 3.

His birth in the flesh is the manifestation of human nature: the childbearing of the Virgin is the proof of divine power. The fragility of the babe is shown in the lowliness of his cradle. The greatness of the Most High is proclaimed by the songs of angels. He whom Herod endeavors to destroy is like ourselves in our tender age, but He whom the magi delight to worship on their knees is the Lord of all. For although in the Lord Jesus Christ God and man are one person, yet the source of the humiliation, which is shared by both, is one, and the source of the glory, which is shared by both, is another. For His manhood, which is less than the Father, comes from our side; His Godhead, which is equal to the Father, comes from the Father.

—LEO THE GREAT, Letter 28.4: To Flavian, commonly called "The Tome," in *Letters of Leo the Great*, A Select Library of Nicene and Post-Nicene Fathers of the Christian Church, 2nd ser., vol. 2, trans. Charles Lett Feltoe (New York: The Christian Literature Co., 1895), 41.

Romans 8:35-39: Who shall separate us from the love of Christ? Shall tribulation, or distress, or persecution, or famine, or nakedness, or danger, or sword? As it is written, "For your sake we are being killed all the day long; we are regarded as sheep to be slaughtered." No, in all these things we are more than conquerors through him who loved us. For I am sure that neither death nor life, nor angels nor rulers, nor things present nor things to come, nor powers, nor height nor depth, nor anything else in all creation, will be able to separate us from the love of God in Christ Jesus our Lord.

All His attributes seem but to set out His love.

—THOMAS GOODWIN, *Of Gospel Holiness in the Heart and Life*, in *The Works of Thomas Goodwin*, vol. 7 (Grand Rapids, MI: Reformation Heritage, 2006), 211.

The Gospel teaches us the doctrine of the eternal electing love of God and reveals how God loved those who are redeemed by Christ before the foundation of the world, and how He then gave them to the Son, and the Son loved them as His own.

The Gospel reveals the wonderful love of God the Father to poor sinful, miserable men, in giving Christ not only to love them while in the world, but to love them to the end.

And all this love was given to us while we were wanderers, outcasts, worthless, guilty, and even enemies. The Gospel reveals such love as nothing else reveals. John 15:13: "Greater love has no one than this, that someone lay down his life for his friends."

Romans 5:7–8, "For one will scarcely die for a righteous person—though perhaps for a good person one would dare even to die—but God shows his love for us in that while we were still sinners, Christ died for us."

God in the Gospel revelation appears as clothed with love, as sitting on a throne of mercy and grace. Love is the light and glory that surrounds the throne on which God sits.

—JONATHAN EDWARDS, *Charity and Its Fruits*, in *Ethical Writings*, The Works of Jonathan Edwards, vol. 8, ed. Paul Ramsey (New Haven, CT: Yale University Press, 1749/1989), 143–145.

DAY

51

> **1 Peter 1:13–21:** Therefore, preparing your minds for action, and being sober-minded, set your hope fully on the grace that will be brought to you at the revelation of Jesus Christ. As obedient children, do not be conformed to the passions of your former ignorance, but as he who called you is holy, you also be holy in all your conduct, since it is written, "You shall be holy, for I am holy." And if you call on him as Father who judges impartially according to each one's deeds, conduct yourselves with fear throughout the time of your exile, knowing that you were ransomed from the futile ways inherited from your forefathers, not with perishable things such as silver or gold, but with the precious blood of Christ, like that of a lamb without blemish or spot. He was foreknown before the foundation of the world but was made manifest in the last times for the sake of you who through him are believers in God, who raised him from the dead and gave him glory, so that your faith and hope are in God.

The Father appoints the Redeemer, and himself accepts the price and grants the thing purchased; the Son is the Redeemer by offering himself and is the price; and the Holy Spirit immediately communicates to us the thing purchased by communicating himself, and He is the thing purchased. What Christ purchased for us was communion with God, which consists of partaking of the Holy Spirit. Christ purchased this for us so that we should have the favor of God and might enjoy His love; this love is the Holy Spirit.

Christ purchased for us true spiritual excellency, grace and holiness, the sum of which is love to God, which is the indwelling of the Holy Spirit in the heart. Christ purchased for us spiritual joy and comfort, which is to participate in God's joy and happiness.

—JONATHAN EDWARDS, "Discourse on the Trinity," in *Writings on Trinity, Grace, and Faith*, The Works of Jonathan Edwards, vol. 21, ed. Sang Hyun Lee (New Haven, CT: Yale University Press, 2002), 136.

> **Matthew 5:17–20:** "Do not think that I have come to abolish the Law or the Prophets; I have not come to abolish them but to fulfill them. For truly, I say to you, until heaven and earth pass away, not an iota, not a dot, will pass from the Law until all is accomplished. Therefore whoever relaxes one of the least of these commandments and teaches others to do the same will be called least in the kingdom of heaven, but whoever does them and teaches them will be called great in the kingdom of heaven. For I tell you, unless your righteousness exceeds that of the scribes and Pharisees, you will never enter the kingdom of heaven."

Christ, indeed, wished to conform His conduct to the Law; first, to show His approval of the Old Law; and second, that by obeying the Law He might perfect it and bring it to an end in himself, to show that He ruled over it.

— THOMAS AQUINAS, *"Summa Theologica" of St. Thomas Aquinas*, trans. Reginaldus de Piperno (London: R. & T. Washbourne, 1922), Book III, Question 40, Article 4.

Christ is offered to you as your Savior. There is perfect obedience in Christ. When He came to this world, He came not only to suffer but to do—not only to be a *dying Savior* but also a *doing Savior*—not only to suffer the curse that the first Adam brought upon the world, but to render the obedience that the first Adam had left undone. From *the cradle* to *the cross*, He obeyed the will of God from the heart.

— ROBERT MURRAY M'CHEYNE, *The Sermons of Robert Murray M'Cheyne* (London: Banner of Truth, 1961), 102–103.

> **Matthew 27:28–31, 34–35, 37–44:** And they stripped him and put a scarlet robe on him, and twisting together a crown of thorns, they put it on his head and put a reed in his right hand. And kneeling before him, they mocked him, saying, "Hail, King of the Jews!" And they spit on him and took the reed and struck him on the head. And when they had mocked him, they stripped him of the robe and put his own clothes on him and led him away to crucify him. . . . They offered him wine to drink, mixed with gall, but when he tasted it, he would not drink it. And when they had crucified him, they divided his garments among them by casting lots. . . . And over his head they put the charge against him, which read, "This is Jesus, the King of the Jews." Then two robbers were crucified with him, one on the right and one on the left. And those who passed by derided him, wagging their heads and saying, "You who would destroy the temple and rebuild it in three days, save yourself! If you are the Son of God, come down from the cross." So also the chief priests, with the scribes and elders, mocked him, saying, "He saved others; he cannot save himself. He is the King of Israel; let him come down now from the cross, and we will believe in him. He trusts in God; let God deliver him now, if he desires him. For he said, 'I am the Son of God.'" And the robbers who were crucified with him also reviled him in the same way.

In His head He suffered from the crown of piercing thorns; in His hands and feet, from the driven nails; on His face from the blows and spittle; and over His entire body from the lashes of the whip. Moreover, He suffered in all His bodily senses: in touch, by being scourged and nailed; in taste, by being given vinegar and gall to drink; in smell, by being nailed to the cross in a place reeking with the stench of corpses, "which is called Calvary"; in hearing, by being tormented with the cries of blasphemers and scorners; in sight, by beholding the tears of His mother and of the disciple whom He loved.

—THOMAS AQUINAS, *"Summa Theologica" of St. Thomas Aquinas*, trans. Reginaldus de Piperno (London: R. & T. Washbourne, 1922), Book 3, Question 46, Article 6.

> **1 John 4:10:** In this is love, not that we have loved God but that he loved us and sent his Son to be the propitiation for our sins.

Though a man, He was Mediator; but as the Word He was equal to God, with the Father and with the Holy Spirit, one God. How God has loved us, the Father not sparing His only Son, but delivering Him up for our sinful race! How God has loved us, allowing His Son to become obedient unto death, even the death of the cross. He alone had the power to lay down His life, and the power to take it again; for us He was both Victor and Victim, for us both Priest and Sacrifice, allowing us to become sons of God, reaping the benefit of His selfless act.

—AUGUSTINE OF HIPPO, *The Confessions of St. Augustine, Bishop of Hippo: Book 10*, trans. J. G. Pilkington, M.A. (Edinburgh: T&T Clark, 1876), 286–287.

He could have redeemed us by a single word, just as He created the world. He refused so that we could understand His love. Forgetting His own pain, He prayed for those who crucified Him; at the same time for us, who have crucified Him by our sins. "Forgive them, for they do not know what they are doing." Truly, this love is beyond description. Since the will of the Son was born of the will of the Father, through love for us He was obeying the Father. We can be certain that the Father loves us, for He so loved the world that He gave His Only Begotten Son. This is what being drawn to the Father through the Son means.

—PETER VERMIGLI, *On the Death of Christ, from Philippians*, in *Life, Letters, and Sermons*, vol. 5 of *The Peter Martyr Library*, ed. and trans. John Patrick Donnelly (Kirksville, MO: Thomas Jefferson University Press, 1999), 245.

Matthew 9:20-24: And behold, a woman who had suffered from a discharge of blood for twelve years came up behind him and touched the fringe of his garment, for she said to herself, "If I only touch his garment, I will be made well." Jesus turned, and seeing her he said, "Take heart, daughter; your faith has made you well." And instantly the woman was made well. And when Jesus came to the ruler's house and saw the flute players and the crowd making a commotion, he said, "Go away, for the girl is not dead but sleeping."

Is He then a man, one of us, at whose command, raised in audible and intelligible words, infirmities, diseases, fevers, and other ailments fled away? Was He one of us, whose presence the demons that took possession of men were unable to bear, and terrified, fled away? Was He one of us, by whose order leprosy became obedient, leaving clear skin to those formerly afflicted? And was He one of us, at whose mere touch the issue of blood was stopped? Was He one of us, by whose hand the fluid of the lethargic dropsy fled, causing the swollen body to assume a healthy condition? Was He one of us, who bade the lame to walk? Was it by His work that the maimed stretched forth their hands, and the paralytics rose to their feet, carrying home their beds who had before been borne on the shoulders of others; were the blind were restored to sight, and looked with awe on the day?

—ARNOBIUS OF SICCA, *The Seven Books of Arnobius Adversus Gentes*, trans. Arch Hamilton Bryce and Hugh Campbell (Edinburgh: T&T Clark, 1871), 36.

> **John 14:8–11:** Philip said to him, "Lord, show us the Father, and it is enough for us." Jesus said to him, "Have I been with you so long, and you still do not know me, Philip? Whoever has seen me has seen the Father. How can you say, 'Show us the Father'? Do you not believe that I am in the Father and the Father is in me? The words that I say to you I do not speak on my own authority, but the Father who dwells in me does his works. Believe me that I am in the Father and the Father is in me, or else believe on account of the works themselves."

When the Christian message says with emphasis, "Look to Christ," it does not mean "look away from God," but rather "look to where God really is," for if God is contemplated apart from Christ, then God is not seen as He truly is. Zeal for Christ is zeal for the true God; the exclusive element in the Christian creed: "In no other is there salvation" is simply the exclusiveness of divine truth. Because the truth of God is one, and one only, and because in order to see this truth, we must stand at a certain vantage point, is the reason why we must make such exclusive claims for Christ.

—EMIL BRUNNER, *The Mediator*, trans. Olive Wyon (Philadelphia: Westminster, 1947), 400.

You know what happens when a portrait that has been painted on a panel becomes obliterated through external stains. The artist does not throw away the panel, but the subject of the portrait has to come and sit for it again, and then the likeness is re-drawn on the same material. Even so was it with the all-holy Son of God. He, the Image of the Father, came and dwelt in our midst, in order that He might renew humankind made after Himself, and seek out His lost sheep, even as He says in the Gospel: "I came to seek and to save that which was lost." This also explains His saying: "Except a man be born anew . . ." He was not referring to a man's natural birth from his mother, as they thought, but to the re-birth and re-creation of the soul in the Image of God.

—ATHANASIUS, *On the Incarnation*, trans. T. Herbert Bindley, 2nd ed. revised (London: The Religious Tract Society, 1903), 67.

> **Hebrews 7:23–28:** The former priests were many in number, because they were prevented by death from continuing in office, but he holds his priesthood permanently, because he continues forever. Consequently, he is able to save to the uttermost those who draw near to God through him, since he always lives to make intercession for them. For it was indeed fitting that we should have such a high priest, holy, innocent, unstained, separated from sinners, and exalted above the heavens. He has no need, like those high priests, to offer sacrifices daily, first for his own sins and then for those of the people, since he did this once for all when he offered up himself. For the law appoints men in their weakness as high priests, but the word of the oath, which came later than the law, appoints a Son who has been made perfect forever.

We need not fear that we may emphasize too strongly the true, complete humanity of Christ. It is to our benefit that we should realize it with a certainty that carries no doubt whatsoever. Christ is everything a man is for eternity.

—B. B. WARFIELD, *Selected Shorter Writings of Benjamin B. Warfield*, vol. 1, ed. John E. Meeter (Phillipsburg: P&R Publishing, 2001), 162–163.

Taking a body like our own, subject to the penalty of corruption and death, He gave His over to death in the place of us all and offered it to the Father. By doing this, out of sheer love for us, we all died in Him, abolishing the law of eternal death.

—ATHANASIUS, *On the Incarnation*, trans. Archibald Robertson (London: D. Nutt, 1891), 14–15.

> **Revelation 21:3–4:** And I heard a loud voice from the throne saying, "Behold, the dwelling place of God is with man. He will dwell with them, and they will be his people, and God himself will be with them as their God. He will wipe away every tear from their eyes, and death shall be no more, neither shall there be mourning, nor crying, nor pain anymore, for the former things have passed away."

When the kingdom has fully come, Christ will hand it over to God the Father. The original order will be restored.

But not naturally, as if nothing had ever happened, as if sin had never existed and the revelation of God's grace in Christ had never occurred. Christ gives more than sin stole; grace gives us even more than we had before the fall.

He does not simply restore us to the state of the righteousness of Adam; he makes us, by faith, participants of being unable to sin (1 John 3:9) and of being unable to die (John 11:25–26).

Adam does not again receive the place that he lost by sin. The first man was of the earth, earthly; the second man is the Lord from heaven. Just as we have borne the image of the earthly, so too after the resurrection shall we bear the image of the heavenly man (1 Corinthians 15:45–49).

—HERMAN BAVINCK, "Common Grace," trans. Ray Van Leeuwen, *Calvin Theological Journal* 24 (1988), 59–60.

Hebrews 13:8: Jesus Christ is the same yesterday and today and forever.

Christ does not only perform prophetic, priestly, and kingly activities, but is himself, in His whole person, prophet, priest, and king. Everything He is, says, and does manifests that threefold dignity. In the one activity it is more His prophetic office that is evident, and in another it is His priestly or His kingly office that stands out. It is also true that His prophetic office comes to the fore more in the days of the Old Testament; His priestly office more in His suffering and death; His kingly office more in His state of exaltation.

While it is not possible to separate His offices, the distinction between them is certainly there. To be our Mediator, our Savior, He had to be appointed by the Father and equipped by the Spirit for all three offices.

The truth is that the idea of humanness already encompasses within itself this threefold dignity and activity. Human beings have a head to know, a heart to give of themselves, a hand to govern and to lead; correspondingly, they were in the beginning equipped by God with knowledge and understanding, with righteousness and holiness, with dominion and glory. But the sin that corrupted human beings affected all these capacities, leading to moral degradation, death, and ruin.

In Christ's God-to-humanity relation, He is a prophet; in His humanity-to-God relation He is a priest; in His headship over all humanity He is a king.

Scripture consistently and simultaneously attributes all three offices to Him.

He is always all these things in conjunction, never the one without the other: mighty in speech and action as a king and full of grace and truth in His royal rule.

—HERMAN BAVINCK, *Reformed Dogmatics: Sin and Salvation in Christ*, vol. 3, ed. John Bolt, trans. John Vriend (Grand Rapids, MI: Baker Academic, 2006), 367–368.

Matthew 4:23-25: And he went throughout all Galilee, teaching in their synagogues and proclaiming the gospel of the kingdom and healing every disease and every affliction among the people. So his fame spread throughout all Syria, and they brought him all the sick, those afflicted with various diseases and pains, those oppressed by demons, those having seizures, and paralytics, and he healed them. And great crowds followed him from Galilee and the Decapolis, and from Jerusalem and Judea, and from beyond the Jordan.

I do not inquire or demand to know what god performed such miracles, or at what time he performed them, or whom he relieved; what shattered frame he restored to sound health. This only I long to hear, whether, without the addition of any substance or medical application, He ordered diseases to cease from men at a mere touch; whether He commanded the cause of ill health to be eradicated, and the weak to return to their natural strength. For it is known that Christ, either by applying His hand or by the command of His voice only, opened the ears of the deaf, drove blindness from the eyes, gave speech to the dumb, loosened the rigid joints, gave the power to walk to the paralyzed—was able to heal by a word fever, dropsy, leprosy, and all other kinds of ailments, which some were cursed to endure. What acts like these have the gods done, by whom you allege help has been brought to the sick and the imperiled?

—ARNOBIUS OF SICCA, *The Seven Books of Arnobius Adversus Gentes*, trans. Arch Hamilton Bryce and Hugh Campbell (Edinburgh: T&T Clark, 1871), 38–39.

Isaiah 28:5–6: In that day the Lᴏʀᴅ of hosts will be a crown of glory, and a diadem of beauty, to the remnant of his people, and a spirit of justice to him who sits in judgment, and strength to those who turn back the battle at the gate.

As believers, we see the Bridegroom as beautiful. He is as God, the Word with God; no one could be matched to His beauty. He was beautiful as a babe, born of a virgin, when without losing His divinity, He assumed manhood. Even as a babe, the heavens spoke; the angels sang their praises; a single star directed the wise men to His lowly manger, where He was adored. He was beautiful as a child at His parents' feet, beautiful as He grew, beautiful to those who observed and experienced His miracles; beautiful under persecution; beautiful in laying down His life; beautiful in rising again; beautiful in heaven.

Listen then to the songs of praise of those who worship Him. Let not the weakness of the flesh turn your eyes from the splendor of His beauty! The highest beauty is that of His righteousness and holiness.

—AUGUSTINE OF HIPPO, *Expositions on the Book of Psalms: Psalms 1–150*, vol. 2, A Library of Fathers of the Holy Catholic Church (Oxford; London: F. and J. Rivington; John Henry Parker, 1847–1857), 230.

Psalm 33:1-5: Shout for joy in the Lord, O you righteous!
   Praise befits the upright.
Give thanks to the Lord with the lyre;
   make melody to him with the harp of ten strings!
Sing to him a new song;
   play skillfully on the strings, with loud shouts.
For the word of the Lord is upright,
   and all his work is done in faithfulness.
He loves righteousness and justice;
   the earth is full of the steadfast love of the Lord.

That man should be delivered by Christ's suffering and death was in keeping with both His mercy and His justice. With His justice, because by His death Christ satisfied the penalty for the sin of the human race, and so man was set free; and with His mercy, since man himself could not pay for the sin of all human nature. God gave His Son to pay it.

—THOMAS AQUINAS, *"Summa Theologica" of St. Thomas Aquinas*, trans. Reginaldus de Piperno (London: R. & T. Washbourne, 1922), Book 3, Question 46, Article 1.

The mercy of God, which seems lost to you when you consider the justice of God and the sin of man, is consistent with His holiness. For what can be more merciful than when the sinner, condemned to eternal torment, has nothing by which to redeem himself, and God says, "Take my Only Begotten Son; I give Him for you." And the Son says, "Offer me; I give myself." For this is what the Father and Son say, when they call us to accept them and follow the Christian faith. What can be conceived more just than that He who is worth more than any can conceive should offer to pay the debt for those who cannot?

—ANSELM OF CANTERBURY, *Cur Deus Homo* (Oxford and London: John Henry and James Parker, 1865), 113.

1 Corinthians 1:18–20: For the word of the cross is folly to those who are perishing, but to us who are being saved it is the power of God. For it is written,

"I will destroy the wisdom of the wise,
and the discernment of the discerning I will thwart."

Where is the one who is wise? Where is the scribe? Where is the debater of this age? Has not God made foolish the wisdom of the world?

The Scriptures continually view the suffering and death of Christ from a different perspective and in each case illumine another aspect of it. Like His person, the work of Christ is so multifaceted that it cannot be captured in a single word nor summarized in a single formula.

In the various books of the New Testament, therefore, different meanings of the death of Christ are highlighted, and all of them together help to give us a deep impression and a clear sense of the riches and many-sidedness of our Mediator's work.

So, indeed, one can find in the New Testament various appraisals of the person and work of Christ, which, however, do not exclude but rather supplement one another and enrich our knowledge. Just as in the Old Covenant there were diverse sacrifices, and the promised Messiah was repeatedly presented under different names, so the description of His work carries over into the New Testament and even markedly increases.

The death of Christ is a paschal offering, a covenant offering, a praise offering as well as a sacrifice. It is a ransom and an example; suffering and action; a work and a ministry; a means of justification and sanctification. It is atonement and consecration; redemption and glorification; in a word, the source of our whole redemption.

—HERMAN BAVINCK, *Reformed Dogmatics: Sin and Salvation in Christ*, vol. 3, ed. John Bolt, trans. John Vriend (Grand Rapids, MI: Baker Academic, 2006), 383–384.

> **Luke 18:9-14:** He also told this parable to some who trusted in themselves that they were righteous, and treated others with contempt: "Two men went up into the temple to pray, one a Pharisee and the other a tax collector. The Pharisee, standing by himself, prayed thus: 'God, I thank you that I am not like other men, extortioners, unjust, adulterers, or even like this tax collector. I fast twice a week; I give tithes of all that I get.' But the tax collector, standing far off, would not even lift up his eyes to heaven, but beat his breast, saying, 'God, be merciful to me, a sinner!' I tell you, this man went down to his house justified, rather than the other. For everyone who exalts himself will be humbled, but the one who humbles himself will be exalted."

Now, while these Scriptures lay before me, and sin was laid once again at my door, this word in Luke 18, along with others, encouraged me to pray.

Then the tempter again came after me, suggesting that neither the mercy of God, nor the blood of Christ, did at all concern me, nor could they help me in my sin; therefore it was in vain to pray.

Yet, I thought, I will, nonetheless, pray.

But the tempter said, your sin is unpardonable.

Well, I said, I will pray, nonetheless.

It is no good, said he.

Yet, I determined to pray.

And so, I prayed to God; and while I was at prayer, I uttered words to this effect: "Lord, Satan tells me that neither Your mercy, nor Christ's blood, is sufficient to save my soul. Shall I honor You by believing You will and can? Or listen to him by believing You neither will nor can?" I concluded with, "Lord, I choose to honor You by believing You will and can."

—JOHN BUNYAN, *Grace Abounding to the Chief of Sinners*, Works of John Bunyan, vol. 1 (Bellingham, WA: Logos Bible Software, 2006), 31–32.

> **Ephesians 2:4–7:** But God, being rich in mercy, because of the great love with which he loved us, even when we were dead in our trespasses, made us alive together with Christ—by grace you have been saved—and raised us up with him and seated us with him in the heavenly places in Christ Jesus, so that in the coming ages he might show the immeasurable riches of his grace in kindness toward us in Christ Jesus.

Remember that the God in whose hand are all creatures is your heavenly Father, and He is much more caring of you than you are of yourself.

—JOHN FLAVEL, *Keeping the Heart: How to Maintain Your Love for God* (Fearn, Scotland: Christian Focus, 2012), 57.

My brethren, here is infinite kindness, which the apostle states so clearly in Ephesians 2. It is the full Gospel in words that convey God's extraordinary grace and favor. It describes mercy and love that is extended to us even while we were dead in our sins and lost without hope. Such sweet words to fall on the ears of those who are grasping for hope. It describes our God, rich in mercy, compassionate and understanding. Can we fully comprehend the enormous plan put into place, when God sent His only Son to give His life for the lost and dying? We are made alive in Christ and raised up with Him to be seated in the heavenly places. Such grace displays the sovereignty of God to show favor, so that by grace alone we are saved. His kindness is distinct from mercy, and yet adds to it: "Be kind to one another, tender-hearted, forgiving one another, as God in Christ forgave you" (Ephesians 4:32). Kindness is seen as the root of mercy in Titus 3:4–5: "But when the goodness and loving kindness of God our Savior appeared, he saved us, not because of works done by us in righteousness, but according to his own mercy, by the washing of regeneration and renewal of the Holy Spirit."

—THOMAS GOODWIN, *The Works of Thomas Goodwin*, vol. 2 (Grand Rapids, MI: Reformation Heritage, 2006), 276–277.

DAY

66

> **1 Timothy 2:5–6:** For there is one God, and there is one mediator between God and men, the man Christ Jesus, who gave himself as a ransom for all, which is the testimony given at the proper time.

Jesus Christ in himself is true God, man's loyal partner; Jesus Christ is also true man, God's partner. He is the Lord, made humble for communion with man; He is likewise the Servant, exalted for communion with God. He is the Word spoken from the loftiest transcendence; He is likewise the Word heard in the deepest, darkest immanence. He is both, without their being confused, but also without their being divided; He is wholly the one and wholly the other: God-man.

In this oneness, Jesus Christ is the Mediator, the Reconciler, between God and man. Thus, He comes forward to *man* on behalf of *God* calling for and awakening faith, love, and hope, and to *God* on behalf of *man*, representing man, interceding for him, and satisfying God's holy requirement on his behalf. Thus, He attests and guarantees to man God's free *grace*, and at the same time attests and guarantees to God man's free *gratitude*. Thus, He establishes in His Person the justice of God with regard to man, and also the justice of man before God. He is in His Person the covenant in its fullness, the kingdom of heaven, which is at hand, in which God speaks and man hears, God gives and man receives, God commands and man obeys; God's glory shines in the heights and into the depths, and peace on earth comes to pass among men in whom He is well pleased.

Moreover, exactly in this way, Jesus Christ, as the Mediator and Reconciler between God and man, is also the *Revealer* of them both. We do not need to engage in an investigation to seek out and construct who and what God truly is, and who and what man truly is, but only to read the truth about both where it resides, namely, in the fullness of their togetherness, their covenant that proclaims itself in Jesus Christ.

—KARL BARTH, *The Humanity of God*, trans. Thomas Weiser (Louisville, KY: Westminster John Knox Press, 1960), 46–47.

Romans 11:33–36: Oh, the depth of the riches and wisdom and knowledge of God! How unsearchable are his judgments and how inscrutable his ways!

"For who has known the mind of the Lord,
or who has been his counselor?"
"Or who has given a gift to him
that he might be repaid?"

For from him and through him and to him are all things. To him be glory forever. Amen.

Scripture teaches that God does all things for His own sake and purpose. The final ground and ultimate purpose of Christ's incarnation and satisfaction of justice cannot lie in a creature, in the salvation of the sinner, but in God himself.

For His own sake, the Father sent His Son into the world as an expiation for our sins that His attributes and perfections might be manifested. And there is nothing that so powerfully brings that image of God to the fore as Christ's incarnation, death, and resurrection.

Not just one attribute is brilliantly illumined by these events, but all of them together: His wisdom, grace, love, mercy, long-suffering, righteousness, holiness, and power, to list a few.

As a rule, we hear more about God's grace and justice, but His other attributes must not be forgotten. Christ in His own Person, Word, and work is the perfect comprehensive revelation of God: His servant, His image, His Son. He has made known to us the Father.

If God wanted to reveal himself in His consummate glory, then the creation and re-creation, Christ's incarnation and satisfaction, were necessary. His perfections were already made manifest in creation, but they were more richly and superbly displayed in the re-creation.

—HERMAN BAVINCK, *Reformed Dogmatics: Sin and Salvation in Christ*, vol. 3, ed. John Bolt, trans. John Vriend (Grand Rapids, MI: Baker Academic, 2006), 371.

> **1 Corinthians 15:24–28:** Then comes the end, when he delivers the kingdom to God the Father after destroying every rule and every authority and power. For he must reign until he has put all his enemies under his feet. The last enemy to be destroyed is death. For "God has put all things in subjection under his feet." But when it says, "all things are put in subjection," it is plain that he is excepted who put all things in subjection under him. When all things are subjected to him, then the Son himself will also be subjected to him who put all things in subjection under him, that God may be all in all.

The apostles proclaim the crucified Christ, but also the resurrected and exalted Christ. From the vantage point of the exaltation of Christ, they view and describe His earthly life, suffering, and death.

For the work He now carries out as the exalted Mediator, He laid the foundations in His cross. In His battle with sin, the world, and Satan, the cross has been His only weapon.

By the cross He triumphed in the sphere of justice over all powers that are hostile to God. But in the state of exaltation, consequently, He has also been given the divine right, the divine appointment, the royal power and prerogatives to carry out the work of re-creation in full, to conquer all His enemies, to save all those who have been given Him, and to perfect the entire kingdom of God.

On the basis of His perfect sacrifice made on the cross, He now—in keeping with the will of the Father—distributes all His benefits, not including the physical or magical aftereffect of His earthly life and death.

It is the living and exalted Christ, seated at the right hand of God, who deliberately and with authority distributes these benefits, gathers His elect, overcomes His enemies, and directs the history of the world toward the day of His second coming.

He is still consistently at work in heaven as the Mediator. He not only was but is our chief Prophet, High Priest, and eternal King.

—HERMAN BAVINCK, *Reformed Dogmatics: Sin and Salvation in Christ*, vol. 3, ed. John Bolt, trans. John Vriend (Grand Rapids, MI: Baker Academic, 2006), 3: 473–474.

Matthew 3:13–17: Then Jesus came from Galilee to the Jordan to John, to be baptized by him. John would have prevented him, saying, "I need to be baptized by you, and do you come to me?" But Jesus answered him, "Let it be so now, for thus it is fitting for us to fulfill all righteousness." Then he consented. And when Jesus was baptized, immediately he went up from the water, and behold, the heavens were opened to him, and he saw the Spirit of God descending like a dove and coming to rest on him; and behold, a voice from heaven said, "This is my beloved Son, with whom I am well pleased."

For when the Lord, as a man, was baptized in the Jordan, we were baptized with Him. And when He received the Spirit, we were made recipients as well. He was not merely anointed, as Aaron or David, with oil, but with the Holy Spirit of God. From Him, then, we may receive the unction and the seal of which John spoke. We are also reminded of the words of the prophet Isaiah:

> The Spirit of the Lord GOD is upon me,
> because the LORD has anointed me
> to bring good news to the poor;
> he has sent me to bind up the brokenhearted,
> to proclaim liberty to the captives,
> and the opening of the prison to those who are bound. (Isaiah 61:1)

The Lord himself has said, the Spirit is His, and He sends it, so that the sanctification coming upon the Lord as man may come to all people through Him.

—ATHANASIUS, *Against the Arians*, A Select Library of the Nicene and Post-Nicene Fathers of the Christian Church, 2nd ser., vol. 4, ed. and trans. Philip Schaff and Henry Wace (Buffalo, NY: Christian Literature Publishing Co., 1892), 333–334.

Ephesians 2:8–9: For by grace you have been saved through faith. And this is not your own doing; it is the gift of God, not a result of works, so that no one may boast.

It is a sin-bearer that we need, and our faith cannot be a sin-bearer. Faith can expiate no guilt, can accomplish no appeasement, can pay no penalty, can wash away no stain, can provide no righteousness. It brings us to the cross, where there is atonement, and appeasement, and payment, and cleansing, and righteousness; but the cross itself has no merit or virtue.

Faith is not Christ, nor the cross of Christ. Faith is not the blood, nor the sacrifice. It is not the altar, nor the basin, nor the mercy seat, nor the incense. It does not work itself, but accepts a work done ages ago; it does not wash, but leads us to the fountain opened for sin and uncleanness. . . .

And as faith continues, it is always the beggar's outstretched hand, never the rich man's gold; always the cable, never the anchor; the knocker, not the door, or the palace, or the table; the handmaid, not the mistress; the lattice that lets in the light, not the sun.

Without innate worthiness, faith knits us to the infinite worthiness of Him in whom the Father delights; and knitting us, presents us perfect in the perfection of another. Though it is not the foundation laid in Zion, it brings us to that foundation, and keeps us there, grounded and settled, that we may not be moved away from the hope of the Gospel.

Though it is not the Gospel, the glad tidings, it receives the good news as God's eternal truth, and bids the soul rejoice in it. Though it is not the burnt offering, it stands still and gazes on the ascending flame, which assures us that the wrath that should have consumed the sinner has fallen upon the Substitute.

—HORATIUS BONAR, *The Everlasting Righteousness; or, How Shall a Man Be Just with God?* (Carlisle, PA: Banner of Truth, 1874/1993), 111–113.

> **Hebrews 2:14–18:** Since therefore the children share in flesh and blood, he himself likewise partook of the same things, that through death he might destroy the one who has the power of death, that is, the devil, and deliver all those who through fear of death were subject to lifelong slavery. For surely it is not angels that he helps, but he helps the offspring of Abraham. Therefore he had to be made like his brothers in every respect, so that he might become a merciful and faithful high priest in the service of God, to make propitiation for the sins of the people. For because he himself has suffered when tempted, he is able to help those who are being tempted.

Let us stand still and admire and wonder at the love of Jesus Christ to poor sinners; that Christ should rather die for *us*, than for the *angels*. They were creatures of a more noble extract and might have brought greater revenues of glory to God. That Christ should pass by those golden vessels and make *us* vessels of glory, what an amazing and astonishing love is this! It is the envy of devils and the admiration of angels and saints.

May we love the Lord Jesus Christ with a superlative love. There are none who have suffered so much for you as Christ; there are none who *can* suffer so much for you as Christ. The least measure of the wrath that Christ has sustained for you would have broken the hearts and backs of all created beings.

Certainly the more Christ has suffered for us, the more dear He should be to us; the more bitter His sufferings have been for us, the more sweet His love should be to us, and the more eminent should be our love to Him. Oh, let the suffering Christ lie near your hearts; let Him be your manna, your Tree of Life, your Morning Star. It is better to part with all than with the Pearl of Great Price. Christ is that golden pipe through which the golden oil of salvation runs. How this should inflame our love for Christ!

—THOMAS BROOKS, *The Complete Works of Thomas Brooks*, vol. 5, ed. A. B. Grosart (1866), 203.

> **Acts 7:55-56:** But [Stephen], full of the Holy Spirit, gazed into heaven and saw the glory of God, and Jesus standing at the right hand of God. And he said, "Behold, I see the heavens opened, and the Son of Man standing at the right hand of God."

I believe in Jesus Christ, His only Son, our Lord,
who was conceived by the Holy Spirit
and born of the Virgin Mary.
He suffered under Pontius Pilate,
was crucified, died, and was buried;
He descended to hell.
The third day He rose again from the dead.
He ascended to heaven
and is seated at the right hand of God the Father Almighty.
From there He will come to judge the living and the dead.
 —THE APOSTLES' CREED

It may seem absurd to say that He is in heaven while He still lives on earth. If it is said that this is true about His divine nature, then this expression would mean something else—namely, that while He was a man on earth He was also in heaven. I could point out that no particular place is mentioned here, and that only Christ is distinguished from everyone else as far as His state is concerned, since He is the heir of the kingdom of God, from which the whole human race is banished. However, as very frequently happens, because of the unity of the person of Christ, what correctly applies to one of His natures is also applied to another of His natures, and so we need seek no other solution. So, Christ who is in heaven has clothed himself in our flesh, so that by stretching out His brotherly hand to us He may raise us to heaven with himself.
 —JOHN CALVIN, *John*, in *The Crossway Classic Commentaries* (Wheaton, IL: Crossway, 1994), 74–75.

> **Ephesians 5:1–2, 25–27:** Therefore be imitators of God, as beloved children. And walk in love, as Christ loved us and gave himself up for us, a fragrant offering and sacrifice to God . . . as Christ loved the church and gave himself up for her, that he might sanctify her, having cleansed her by the washing of water with the word, so that he might present the church to himself in splendor, without spot or wrinkle or any such thing, that she might be holy and without blemish.

Only in the cross of Jesus Christ is the love of God to be found.

—DIETRICH BONHOEFFER, "Prayerbook of the Bible" in *Dietrich Bonhoeffer Works*, vol. 5 (Minneapolis: Augsburg Fortress, 2005), 175.

God's high freedom in Jesus Christ is His freedom for love. The divine capacity that operates and exhibits itself in that superiority and subordination is manifestly also God's capacity to bend downward, to attach himself to another and this other to himself, to be together with him. This takes place in that irreversible sequence, but in it is completely real. In that sequence there arises and continues in Jesus Christ the highest communion of God with man. God's deity is thus no prison in which He can exist only in and for himself. It is rather His freedom to be in and for himself but also with and for us, to assert but also to sacrifice himself, to be wholly exalted but also completely humble, not only almighty but also merciful, not only Lord but also servant, not only judge but also the judged, not only man's eternal king but also his brother in time. And all that without forfeiting His deity! All that is the highest proof and proclamation of His deity! He who does and manifestly can do all that, He and no other is the living God. So constituted is His deity, the deity of the God of Abraham, Isaac, and Jacob. In Jesus Christ it is in this way operative and recognizable. If He is the Word of Truth, then the truth is God, is exactly this and nothing else.

—KARL BARTH, *The Humanity of God*, trans. Thomas Weiser (Louisville, KY: Westminster John Knox Press, 1960), 48–49.

> **1 John 3:1-3:** See what kind of love the Father has given to us, that we should be called children of God; and so we are. The reason why the world does not know us is that it did not know him. Beloved, we are God's children now, and what we will be has not yet appeared; but we know that when he appears we shall be like him, because we shall see him as he is. And everyone who thus hopes in him purifies himself as he is pure.

I implore you all, love with me, run the race with me, by believing. Let us long for our heavenly home above; we are strangers here. What shall we see then? The Gospel tells us: "In the beginning was the Word, and the Word was with God." You shall come to the fountain from which a little dew has fallen on you. You shall see the Light, from a ray sent into your dark heart. From its purity, you are being purified. John himself says, "Beloved, we are God's children now, and what we will be has not yet appeared; but we know that when he appears we shall be like him, because we shall see him as he is."

—AUGUSTINE OF HIPPO, "Lectures or Treatise on the Gospel according to St. John," in *St. Augustin: Homilies on the Gospel of John, Homilies on the First Epistle of John, Soliloquies*, A Select Library of the Nicene and Post-Nicene Fathers of the Christian Church, 1st ser., vol. 7, ed. Philip Schaff, trans. John Gibb and James Innes (Buffalo, NY: Christian Literature Co., 1888), 207.

> **Matthew 9:35–38:** And Jesus went throughout all the cities and villages, teaching in their synagogues and proclaiming the gospel of the kingdom and healing every disease and every affliction. When he saw the crowds, he had compassion for them, because they were harassed and helpless, like sheep without a shepherd. Then he said to his disciples, "The harvest is plentiful, but the laborers are few; therefore pray earnestly to the Lord of the harvest to send out laborers into his harvest."

No part of creation stands on its own without Christ. He has filled all things everywhere, while remaining present with His Father. But to show His loving-kindness toward us, He came in humility to visit us in the flesh. Seeing our race of rational creatures perishing, and death reigning over us through corruption; the things He himself had created passing away, and the exceeding wickedness of men increasing to an intolerable level against themselves, under penalty of death, He took pity and had mercy on our frail state, unable to bear that death should win, lest the creature should perish, and His Father's handiwork in men should be wasted—He took upon himself a body, one not different from our own, that He might give himself over to death in order to rescue us from eternal death.

—ATHANASIUS, *On the Incarnation*, trans. T. Herbert Bindley, 2nd ed., revised (London: The Religious Tract Society, 1903), 55.

John 11:38-44: Then Jesus, deeply moved again, came to the tomb. It was a cave, and a stone lay against it. Jesus said, "Take away the stone." Martha, the sister of the dead man, said to him, "Lord, by this time there will be an odor, for he has been dead four days." Jesus said to her, "Did I not tell you that if you believed you would see the glory of God?" So they took away the stone. And Jesus lifted up his eyes and said, "Father, I thank you that you have heard me. I knew that you always hear me, but I said this on account of the people standing around, that they may believe that you sent me." When he had said these things, he cried out with a loud voice, "Lazarus, come out." The man who had died came out, his hands and feet bound with linen strips, and his face wrapped with a cloth. Jesus said to them, "Unbind him, and let him go."

Ignorance is a thing of the flesh, but the Word himself, insofar as He is the Word, knows everything, even before His birth. For it is neither the case that when He became man, He ceased to be God, or that since He is God, He shuns what is human. Rather, the truth is that being God, He assumed flesh for himself, and being in the flesh He made the flesh divine. For just as it was in the flesh that He asked the question "Did I not tell you that if you believed you would see the glory of God?" so it was in the flesh that He raised Lazarus. And He proved to all that He who revives the dead and calls back the soul is aware of the secrets of all things and knew where Lazarus was laid. But He asked a question. Yes, this too the most holy one of God did—the one who endured all things for us—in order that, having taken our ignorance on himself, He might give to us the knowledge of that one true Father of His, and of himself as the one sent on our account for salvation: No grace could be greater than this.

—ATHANASIUS, *Against the Arians*, in *Patrologiae cursus completes*, series graeca, vol. 26, ed. J. P. Migne (Paris: Migne, 1857–1886), 404–405.

Psalm 29:1–4, 9–11:
Ascribe to the Lord, O heavenly beings,
  ascribe to the Lord glory and strength.
Ascribe to the Lord the glory due his name;
  worship the Lord in the splendor of holiness.
The voice of the Lord is over the waters;
  the God of glory thunders,
  the Lord, over many waters.
The voice of the Lord is powerful;
  the voice of the Lord is full of majesty. . . .
The voice of the Lord makes the deer give birth
  and strips the forests bare,
  and in his temple all cry, "Glory!"
The Lord sits enthroned over the flood;
  the Lord sits enthroned as king forever.
May the Lord give strength to his people!
  May the Lord bless his people with peace!

"If God be with us, who can be against us?" I answer, "None, that can deprive us of our inward peace, rest, and quiet." Though there be thunder and lightning, rain and wind, yet a man may be at peace and rest at home.

A man may have much trouble in the world, and yet have rest and quiet in his own spirit: "Peace I leave with you; my peace I give to you. Not as the world gives do I give to you. Let not your hearts be troubled, neither let them be afraid" (John 14:27). No troubles or distresses can deprive a Christian of that inward and blessed peace that Christ purchased for us.

Peace with God and peace of conscience are rare jewels that none can strip us of. The world may wish you peace, but it is only Christ who can give you real peace. The world's peace is commonly an expensive peace, but Christ's peace is free. The world's peace is superficial, but Christ's peace is real and everlasting.

—THOMAS BROOKS, "A Word in Season," in *The Complete Works of Thomas Brooks*, vol. 5, ed. Alexander Balloch Grosart (Edinburgh; London; Dublin: James Nichol; James Nisbet and Co.; G. Herbert, 1867), 510–512.

> **2 Corinthians 5:17–21:** Therefore, if anyone is in Christ, he is a new creation. The old has passed away; behold, the new has come. All this is from God, who through Christ reconciled us to himself and gave us the ministry of reconciliation; that is, in Christ God was reconciling the world to himself, not counting their trespasses against them, and entrusting to us the message of reconciliation. Therefore, we are ambassadors for Christ, God making his appeal through us. We implore you on behalf of Christ, be reconciled to God. For our sake he made him to be sin who knew no sin, so that in him we might become the righteousness of God.

To be entitled to use another's name, when my own name is worthless; to be allowed to wear another's raiment, because my own is torn and filthy; to appear before God in another's person—the person of the Beloved Son—this is the summit of all blessing.

The sin-bearer and I have exchanged names, robes, and persons! I am now represented by Him, my own personality having disappeared; He now appears in the presence of God for me. All that makes Him precious and dear to the Father has been transferred to me.

In one sense I am still the poor sinner, once under wrath; in another I am altogether righteous, and shall be so forever, because of the Perfect One, in whose perfection I appear before God. Nor is this a false pretense or a hollow fiction, which carries no results or blessings with it.

—HORATIUS BONAR, *The Everlasting Righteousness; or, How Shall a Man Be Just with God?* (Carlisle, PA: Banner of Truth, 1874/1993), 44–45.

1 Corinthians 1:30–31: And because of him you are in Christ Jesus, who became to us wisdom from God, righteousness and sanctification and redemption, so that, as it is written, "Let the one who boasts, boast in the Lord."

To understand the benefit of sanctification correctly, we must proceed from the idea that Christ is our holiness in the same sense in which He is our righteousness. He is a complete and all-sufficient Savior.

He does not accomplish His work halfway but saves us truly and completely. He does not rest until, after pronouncing His acquittal in our conscience, He has also imparted full holiness and glory to us.

By His righteousness, accordingly, He does not just restore us to the state of the just who will go scot-free in the judgment of God, in order then to leave us to ourselves to reform ourselves after God's image and to merit eternal life. But Christ has accomplished everything. He bore for us the guilt and punishment of sin, placed himself under the law to secure eternal life for us, and then arose from the grave to communicate himself to us in all His fullness for both our righteousness and sanctification (1 Corinthians 1:30).

The holiness that must completely become ours therefore fully awaits us in Christ.

—HERMAN BAVINCK, *Reformed Dogmatics: Holy Spirit, Church, and New Creation*, vol. 4, ed. John Bolt, trans. John Vriend (Grand Rapids, MI: Baker Academic, 2008), 248.

DAY
80

> **Hebrews 2:14–15:** Since therefore the children share in flesh and blood, he himself likewise partook of the same things, that through death he might destroy the one who has the power of death, that is, the devil, and deliver all those who through fear of death were subject to lifelong slavery.

What could be said that better confirms our faith? Here His infinite love toward us appears; but its overflowing appears in this: that He put on our nature that He might make himself capable of dying, for as God He could not undergo death. And though He refers briefly to the benefits of His death, yet there is in this brevity of words a singularly striking and powerful representation, and that is that He has so delivered us from the tyranny of the devil that we are made safe, and that He has redeemed us from death, that it is no longer to be dreaded.

Through our consciousness of sin, the judgment of God is always visible. From this fear Christ has delivered us, who by undergoing our curse has taken away what is dreaded in death. For though we are not now freed from death, yet in life and in death we have peace and safety when we have Christ going before us.

But if anyone cannot pacify his mind by disregarding death, let him know that he has not grown sufficiently in the faith of Christ, for as extreme fear is owing to ignorance of the grace of Christ, so it is a certain evidence of unbelief.

Death here does not only mean the separation of the soul from the body, but also the punishment inflicted on us by an angry God, so that it includes eternal ruin; for where there is *guilt* before God, there hell reveals itself.

—JOHN CALVIN, *Commentary on the Epistle of Paul the Apostle to the Hebrews*, trans. John Owen (Bellingham, WA: Logos Bible Software, 2010), 71–72.

> **1 Peter 2:9–10:** But you are a chosen race, a royal priesthood, a holy na-
> tion, a people for his own possession, that you may proclaim the excel-
> lencies of him who called you out of darkness into his marvelous light.
> Once you were not a people, but now you are God's people; once you
> had not received mercy, but now you have received mercy.

The King, who himself came to purchase me from my tyrant and His foe;
the King, who laid aside His crown and His royal robes, and left His kingly
palace, and came down himself to save a rebel; the King, who though He
was rich, yet for my sake became poor, that I through His poverty might be
rich—*ought* I to acknowledge Him? Is it even a question? God has called
me unto His kingdom and glory; He has translated me into the kingdom
of the Son of His love. The loyal words shall not falter or fail from my
lips: "You *are* my King!"

God has said to me, "He *is* your Lord; worship Him." Do my lips say,
"My Lord and *my* God"? Does my life say, "Christ Jesus, *my* Lord"—
firmly and personally? Can I share in His last sweet commendation to His
disciples, the more precious because of its divine dignity: "You call me
Master and Lord, *and you say well*, for so I Am"? Have I said, "You are my
King" to Jesus himself, from the depth of my own heart, in unreserved and
unfeigned submission to His scepter? Am I ashamed or afraid to confess
my allegiance in plain English among His friends or before His foes? Is
the seal upon my brow so unmistakable that always and everywhere I am
known to be His subject? Is "You are my King" emblazoned, as it ought
to be, in shining letters on the whole scroll of my life, so that it may be
known and read by all men?

"O my King! Search me and try me and show me the true state of my
case, and then for Your own sake pardon all my past disloyalty, and make
me by Your mighty grace, from this moment, completely loyal, for 'You
are my King.'"

—FRANCES RIDLEY HAVERGAL, *My King and His Service* (Philadelphia: Henry
Altemus, 1892), 10–11.

> **1 Corinthians 1:22–25:** For Jews demand signs and Greeks seek wisdom, but we preach Christ crucified, a stumbling block to Jews and folly to Gentiles, but to those who are called, both Jews and Greeks, Christ the power of God and the wisdom of God. For the foolishness of God is wiser than men, and the weakness of God is stronger than men.

Christ crucified is the sum of the Gospel and contains all the riches of it. Paul was so much taken with Christ, that nothing sweeter than Jesus could drop from his pen and lips. It is observed that he has the name *Jesus* five hundred times in his epistles.

—STEPHEN CHARNOCK, "The Knowledge of Christ Crucified," in *The Complete Works of Stephen Charnock*, vol. 4 (Edinburgh: James Nichol, 1684/1865), 495.

A plain Christ is forever the loveliest Christ. Dress Him up, and you have deformed Him and defamed Him. Bring Him out just as He is, the Christ of God, nothing else but Christ, and Him crucified. Indeed, you cannot have the Christ without the cross; but preach Christ crucified, and you have given Him all the glory that He wants. The Holy Spirit does not reveal in these last times any fresh ordinances, or any novel doctrines, or any new evolutions; but He simply brings to mind the things that Christ himself spoke; He brings Christ's own things to us, and in that way glorifies Him.

Think for a minute of Christ's person as revealed to us by the Holy Spirit. What can more glorify Him than for us to see His person, very God of very God, and yet truly man? What a wondrous being, as human as ourselves, but as divine as God! Was there ever another like to Him? Never.

—CHARLES H. SPURGEON, "The Chief Office of the Holy Spirit," in *Spurgeon on the Holy Spirit* (New Kensington, PA: Whitaker House, 2000), 61.

> **Isaiah 9:6–7:**
> For to us a child is born,
>   to us a son is given;
> and the government shall be upon his shoulder,
>   and his name shall be called
> Wonderful Counselor, Mighty God,
>   Everlasting Father, Prince of Peace.
> Of the increase of his government and of peace
>   there will be no end,
> on the throne of David and over his kingdom,
>   to establish it and to uphold it
> with justice and with righteousness
>   from this time forth and forevermore.
> The zeal of the LORD of hosts will do this.

Some Christians thought that others could not come to heaven if they did not eat the same foods as they ate, but Paul tells them in Romans 14:17 that the kingdom of God consists not in eating and drinking, but "righteousness and peace and joy in the Holy Spirit."

The world's peace is an imaginary peace, but Christ's peace is real. The world's peace is a transient peace, but Christ's peace is permanent. The world's peace is temporary, but Christ's peace is eternal.

When a tyrant threatened one of the ancients that he would "take away his house," he answered, "Yet you cannot take away my peace." Then, "I will banish you from your country." But, "I will carry my peace with me."

The believer is at peace; the controversy between God and him is ended. Christ takes up the quarrel between God and a believer. "We have peace with God through our Lord Jesus Christ" (Romans 5:1).

When our peace is made in the court of heaven, which happens when you first believe, then follows peace in the court of conscience, peace that passes all understanding (see Philippians 4:7).

—THOMAS BROOKS, "A Word in Season," in *The Complete Works of Thomas Brooks*, vol. 5, ed. Alexander Balloch Grosart (Edinburgh; London; Dublin: James Nichol; James Nisbet and Co.; G. Herbert, 1867), 510–512.

Isaiah 42:1–4, 6–7:
Behold my servant, whom I uphold,
   my chosen, in whom my soul delights;
I have put my Spirit upon him;
   he will bring forth justice to the nations.
He will not cry aloud or lift up his voice,
   or make it heard in the street;
a bruised reed he will not break,
   and a faintly burning wick he will not quench;
   he will faithfully bring forth justice.
He will not grow faint or be discouraged
   till he has established justice in the earth;
   and the coastlands wait for his law. . . .
"I am the LORD; I have called you in righteousness;
   I will take you by the hand and keep you;
I will give you as a covenant for the people,
   a light for the nations,
   to open the eyes that are blind,
to bring out the prisoners from the dungeon,
   from the prison those who sit in darkness.

Whatsoever Christ is freed from, I am freed from it. It can no more hurt me than it can hurt Him now in heaven.

> —RICHARD SIBBES, *The Church's Riches by Christ's Poverty*, in *The Works of Richard Sibbes*, vol. 4, ed. Alexander Balloch Grosart (Edinburgh: Banner of Truth, 1983), 405.

One of the great results of Christ's appearing in the world was to proclaim liberty to everyone that would accept it. He offers a most glorious freedom from slavery and bondage. He opens the doors of the prisons and draws people out of the dungeons, redeems out of the captivity to the cruel enemy, frees from drudgery and brings into a perfect and glorious liberty, even the liberty of the sons of God.

> —JONATHAN EDWARDS, "Christian Liberty: A Sermon on James 1:25," in *Sermons and Discourses 1720–1723*, The Works of Jonathan Edwards, vol. 10, ed. Wilson H. Kimnach (New Haven, CT: Yale, 1992), 621.

Isaiah 53:2–5:
He had no form or majesty that we should look at him,
   and no beauty that we should desire him.
He was despised and rejected by men,
   a man of sorrows and acquainted with grief;
and as one from whom men hide their faces
   he was despised, and we esteemed him not.
Surely he has borne our griefs
   and carried our sorrows;
yet we esteemed him stricken,
   smitten by God, and afflicted.
But he was pierced for our transgressions;
   he was crushed for our iniquities;
upon him was the chastisement that brought us peace,
   and with his wounds we are healed.

That Christ should come from the eternal bosom of His Father to a region of sorrow and death; that He should be manifested in the flesh, the Creator made a creature; that He who was clothed with glory should be wrapped with rags of flesh;

He who filled the heavens and earth with His glory should be cradled in a manger that the God of the law should be subject to the law, the God of circumcision be circumcised, the God who made the heavens work at Joseph's lowly trade;

That He who binds the devils in chains should be tempted; He to whom the world belongs, and the fulness thereof, should hunger and thirst; that the God of strength should be weary, the Judge of all flesh condemned, the God of life put to death;

That He who is one with His Father should cry out, "My God, my God, why have You forsaken me?"

That He who held the keys of death and hell should lie imprisoned in the sepulcher of another, having in His lifetime nowhere to lay His head; whose eyes, purer than the sun, should see the darkness of death; who heard nothing but hallelujahs of saints and angels, to hear the blasphemies of the multitude; all this for the sins of the multitude!

—THOMAS BROOKS, *The Works of Thomas Brooks*, vol. 1, ed. Alexander Balloch Grosart (Carlisle, PA: Banner of Truth, 1666/2001), 17–18.

2 Corinthians 5:10: For we must all appear before the judgment seat of Christ, so that each one may receive what is due for what he has done in the body, whether good or evil.

It is specifically Christ who is appointed by the Father to bring about the end of the history of humankind and the world. And He is appointed to this role because He is the Savior, the perfect Savior. The work He completed on earth is only a part of the great work of redemption He has taken upon himself.

And the time He spent here is only a small part of the centuries over which He is appointed as Lord and King. Anointed by the Father from all eternity, He began to engage in His prophetic, priestly, and royal activity immediately after sin came into the world. He continued that activity throughout all the revolving centuries since.

And one day, at the end of time, He will complete it. That which He acquired on earth by His suffering and death He applies from heaven by His Word and the working of His Spirit; and that which He has thus applied, He maintains and defends against all the assaults of Satan, in order to one day, at the end, present it without spot or wrinkle, in total perfection, to His Father who is in heaven.

Accordingly, the return of Christ unto judgment is not an arbitrary addition that can be isolated from His preceding work and viewed by itself. It is a necessary and indispensable component of that work. It brings that work to completion and crowns it.

It is the last and highest step in the state of His exaltation. Because Christ is the Savior of the world, He will someday return as its Judge.

—HERMAN BAVINCK, *Reformed Dogmatics: Holy Spirit, Church, and New Creation,*
vol. 4, ed. John Bolt, trans. John Vriend (Grand Rapids, MI: Baker Academic, 2008), 685.

Romans 8:12–17: So then, brothers, we are debtors, not to the flesh, to live according to the flesh. For if you live according to the flesh you will die, but if by the Spirit you put to death the deeds of the body, you will live. For all who are led by the Spirit of God are sons of God. For you did not receive the spirit of slavery to fall back into fear, but you have received the Spirit of adoption as sons, by whom we cry, "Abba! Father!" The Spirit himself bears witness with our spirit that we are children of God, and if children, then heirs—heirs of God and fellow heirs with Christ, provided we suffer with him in order that we may also be glorified with him.

We must not think that there is one Son, Jesus Christ, God's Son, and another by whom we are called and are sons of God, because it is the same Person, Christ the Son naturally born, while we are sons of God through adoption and joint-heirs through Jesus Christ. Nor should it be thought that God, the Son of God, is someone outside or distant from us, to whom we are likened, made in His image, but that He, God, is undivided, One in essence, and close to each one of us. In Him we truly live and move and have our being.

—MEISTER ECKHART, *Defense Against Charges of Heresy*, trans. Raymond B. Blakney (New York: Harper & Row, 1941), 304.

Proverbs 18:24: A man of many companions may come to ruin, but there is a friend who sticks closer than a brother.

Jesus Christ is mine. I can with the greatest confidence and boldness affirm it. He is my Head, my Husband, my Lord, my Redeemer, my Justifier, my Savior. And I am His. I am as sure that I am His, as I am sure that I live. I am His by purchase and I am His by conquest; I am His by donation and I am His by election; I am His by covenant and I am His by marriage; I am wholly His; I am peculiarly His; I am universally His; I am eternally His.

—THOMAS BROOKS, *Heaven on Earth*, in *The Complete Works of Thomas Brooks*, vol. 2, ed. Alexander Balloch Grosart (Edinburgh: James Nichol, 1866), 320.

Jesus is mine: in Him I have wisdom, righteousness, sanctification, and redemption, a share in all the promises and in all the perfections of God. He will guide me by His counsel, support me by His power, comfort me with His presence, while I am here. And afterwards, when flesh and heart fail, He will receive me to His glory.

—JOHN NEWTON, *Cardiphonia*, in *The Works of John Newton*, vol. 1 (London: Hamilton, Adams & Co., 1824), 488.

> **John 15:1–2, 4:** "I am the true vine, and my Father is the vinedresser. Every branch in me that does not bear fruit he takes away, and every branch that does bear fruit he prunes, that it may bear more fruit. . . . Abide in me, and I in you. As the branch cannot bear fruit by itself, unless it abides in the vine, neither can you, unless you abide in me."

"Unless you abide . . ." We know the meaning of the word *unless*. It expresses some indispensable condition, some inevitable law. "As the branch cannot bear fruit by itself, unless it abides in the vine, neither can you, unless you abide in me." There is but one way for the branch to bear fruit, there is no other possibility, it must abide in unbroken communion with the vine. Not of itself, but only of the vine, does the fruit come. Christ had already said, "Abide in me"; in nature the branch teaches us the lesson so clearly; it is a wonderful privilege to be called and allowed to abide in the heavenly Vine; one might have thought it needless to add these words of warning.

But no—Christ knows so well what a renunciation of self is implied in this: "Abide in me"; how strong and universal the tendency would be to seek to bear fruit by our own efforts; how difficult it would be to get us to believe that actual, continuous abiding in Him is an absolute necessity!

He insists upon the truth: Not of itself can the branch bear fruit; except it abide, it cannot bear fruit. "Neither can you, unless you abide in me." But must this be taken literally? Must I, as exclusively, and manifestly, and unceasingly, and absolutely, as the branch abides in the vine, be equally given up in order to find my whole life in Christ alone? I must indeed.

If I am to be a true branch, if I am to bear fruit, if I am to be what Christ as the Vine wants me to be, my whole existence must be as exclusively devoted to abiding in Him as the natural branch is to abiding in its vine.

—ANDREW MURRAY, "Except Ye Abide," in *The True Vine* (Chicago: Moody Publishers, 2007), 29.

Philippians 2:8–11: And being found in human form, he humbled himself by becoming obedient to the point of death, even death on a cross. Therefore God has highly exalted him and bestowed on him the name that is above every name, so that at the name of Jesus every knee should bow, in heaven and on earth and under the earth, and every tongue confess that Jesus Christ is Lord, to the glory of God the Father.

Christ is to us just what His cross is. All that Christ was in heaven or on earth was put into what He did there. Christ, I repeat, is to us just what His cross is. You do not understand Christ until you understand His cross.

—P. T. FORSYTH, *The Cruciality of the Cross* (London: Hodder and Stoughton, 1909), 44–45.

It sends a spear into the heart of sin that Jesus yielded His heart for our sakes; this nails up the hands and feet of our rebellious lusts, to think that Jesus was crucified for us; this leads us in golden fetters, the happy captives of His mighty grace, when we behold how His love stooped to the curse for us. The weakness of Christ is stronger in its power over our hearts than all His strength could have been. It is by weakness that Christ has achieved His mighty purpose. Today He has left His weakness on the cross, and gone upward to His throne, but there He sits clothed with a glory born of weakness. The eyes of my faith even now behold Him. I am glad I do not see Him more clearly, else I must cease to speak to you, and fall at His feet as dead, so great is His majesty, so glorious His exaltation. That glory in our esteem has sprung out of His weakness, His sorrow, His death. Your brightest coronet, O Christ, is fashioned from the crown of thorns! You are more lovely now than ever You were before! The marks of Your passion have made You altogether lovely in the eyes of Your people!

—CHARLES H. SPURGEON, "The Proof of Our Ministry," in *Metropolitan Tabernacle Pulpit*, vol. 30 (Pasadena, TX: Pilgrim Publications, 1973), 361–372.

Ephesians 2:18-22: For through him we both have access in one Spirit to the Father. So then you are no longer strangers and aliens, but you are fellow citizens with the saints and members of the household of God, built on the foundation of the apostles and prophets, Christ Jesus himself being the cornerstone, in whom the whole structure, being joined together, grows into a holy temple in the Lord. In him you also are being built together into a dwelling place for God by the Spirit.

Great is the wisdom with which the Lord Jesus Christ builds His Church! All is done at the right time, and in the right way. Each stone in its turn is put in its right place.

Sometimes He chooses great stones, and sometimes He chooses small stones. Sometimes the work goes on quickly, and sometimes it goes on slowly. Man is frequently impatient and thinks that nothing is being done.

But humanity's time is not God's time. A thousand years in His sight are but as a single day. The great Builder makes no mistakes. He knows what He is doing. He sees the end from the beginning.

He works by a perfect, unalterable, and certain plan.

—J. C. RYLE, *Holiness: Its Nature, Hindrances, Difficulties and Roots* (London: William Hunt and Co., 1889), 312–312.

Romans 5:1–10: Therefore, since we have been justified by faith, we have peace with God through our Lord Jesus Christ. Through him we have also obtained access by faith into this grace in which we stand, and we rejoice in hope of the glory of God. Not only that, but we rejoice in our sufferings, knowing that suffering produces endurance, and endurance produces character, and character produces hope, and hope does not put us to shame, because God's love has been poured into our hearts through the Holy Spirit who has been given to us. For while we were still weak, at the right time Christ died for the ungodly. For one will scarcely die for a righteous person—though perhaps for a good person one would dare even to die— but God shows his love for us in that while we were still sinners, Christ died for us. Since, therefore, we have now been justified by his blood, much more shall we be saved by him from the wrath of God. For if while we were enemies we were reconciled to God by the death of his Son, much more, now that we are reconciled, shall we be saved by his life.

Christ laid down His life for His enemies; Christ laid down His life for His murderers; Christ laid down His life for those who hated Him; and the spirit of the cross, the spirit of Calvary, is love. When they were mocking Him and deriding Him, what did He say? "Father, forgive them, for they know not what they do" (Luke 23:34). That is love. He did not call down fire from heaven to consume them. There was nothing but love in His heart.

—D. L. MOODY, "The Way to God," in *From the Library of A. W. Tozer: Selections from Writers Who Influenced His Spiritual Journey*, ed. James Stuart Bell (Bloomington, MN: Bethany House, 2011), 185.

1 Peter 2:21-25: For to this you have been called, because Christ also suffered for you, leaving you an example, so that you might follow in his steps. He committed no sin, neither was deceit found in his mouth. When he was reviled, he did not revile in return; when he suffered, he did not threaten, but continued entrusting himself to him who judges justly. He himself bore our sins in his body on the tree, that we might die to sin and live to righteousness. By his wounds you have been healed. For you were straying like sheep, but have now returned to the Shepherd and Overseer of your souls.

We do not hold Christ to be free from every stain merely because He was born of a woman without relations with a man, but because He was sanctified by the Spirit so that the generation was pure and spotless, such as it would have been before Adam's fall. Let us always bear in mind that wherever Scripture refers to the purity of Christ, it refers to His true human nature, since it would be superfluous to say that God is pure. For although the boundless essence of the Word was united with human nature into one person, we do not imagine that He was confined there. The Son of God descended miraculously from heaven, yet without abandoning heaven; was pleased to be conceived miraculously in the Virgin's womb, to live on the earth, and hang upon the cross, yet continuously filled the world even as He had from the beginning.

—JOHN CALVIN, *Institutes of the Christian Religion*, vol. 2, trans. Henry Beveridge (Edinburgh: The Calvin Translation Society, 1845), 20–21 (*Institutes*, 2.13.4).

2 Timothy 1:8–10: Therefore do not be ashamed of the testimony about our Lord, nor of me his prisoner, but share in suffering for the gospel by the power of God, who saved us and called us to a holy calling, not because of our works but because of his own purpose and grace, which he gave us in Christ Jesus before the ages began, and which now has been manifested through the appearing of our Savior Christ Jesus, who abolished death and brought life and immortality to light through the gospel.

Sin produces guilt, pollution, and misery: a breach of the covenant of works, a loss of the image of God, and submission to the domination of corruption. Christ redeemed us from all three by His suffering, His fulfillment of the law, and His conquest of death. Christ's benefits consist in the following: (1) He restores our right relation to God and all creatures (the forgiveness of sins, justification, the purification of our conscience, acceptance as His children, peace with God, and Christian liberty). (2) He renews us after God's image (regeneration in the broad sense, renewal, re-creation, and sanctification). (3) He preserves us for our heavenly inheritance and will someday free us from all suffering and death and grant us eternal blessedness (preservation, perseverance, and glorification).

The first group of benefits is given to us by the illumination of the Holy Spirit, is accepted on our part by faith, changes our consciousness, and sets our conscience free. The second group is conferred on us by the regenerative activity of the Holy Spirit, renews our very being, and redeems us from the power of sin. The third is communicated to us by the preserving, guiding, and sealing activity of the Holy Spirit as the guarantee of our complete redemption, and frees us in soul and body from the domination of misery and death.

—HERMAN BAVINCK, *Reformed Dogmatics: Sin and Salvation in Christ*, vol. 3, ed. John Bolt, trans. John Vriend (Grand Rapids, MI: Baker Academic, 2006), 594–595.

> **Romans 4:5-8:** And to the one who does not work but believes in him who justifies the ungodly, his faith is counted as righteousness, just as David also speaks of the blessing of the one to whom God counts righteousness apart from works: "Blessed are those whose lawless deeds are forgiven, and whose sins are covered; blessed is the man against whom the Lord will not count his sin."

Acceptance and completeness in our standing before God are attributed to the suffering, blood, and death of the divine Substitute. Poor as my faith in Him may be, it places me at once in the position of one to whom "God counts righteousness apart from works." God is willing to receive me on the merits of His perfection; and if I am willing to be thus received, in the perfection of another with whom God is well pleased, the whole transaction is completed. I am justified by His blood. As He is, so am I (even) in this world—even now, with all my imperfections and sins.

All that makes Him precious and dear to the Father has been transferred to me. His excellency and glory are as though they were mine; and I receive the love, the fellowship, and the glory as if I had earned them all. So entirely one am I with the sin-bearer that God treats me not merely as if I had not done the evil I have done, but as if I had done all the good that I have not done, but which my Substitute has done.

—HORATIUS BONAR, *The Everlasting Righteousness; or, How Shall a Man Be Just with God?* (Carlisle, PA: Banner of Truth, 1874/1993), 44–45.

Mark 3:1–6: Again he entered the synagogue, and a man was there with a withered hand. And they watched Jesus, to see whether he would heal him on the Sabbath, so that they might accuse him. And he said to the man with the withered hand, "Come here." And he said to them, "Is it lawful on the Sabbath to do good or to do harm, to save life or to kill?" But they were silent. And he looked around at them with anger, grieved at their hardness of heart, and said to the man, "Stretch out your hand." He stretched it out, and his hand was restored. The Pharisees went out and immediately held counsel with the Herodians against him, how to destroy him.

First there is the pain inflicted on Jesus from the gross manifestation of the hardness of heart of the Jews. Then there is the strong reaction of His indignation that sprang out of this pain. The term by which the former feeling is expressed has at its basis the simple idea of pain. And it is used in the broadest sense of pain, whether physical or mental. It is here emphasizing, however, the sensation itself rather than its expression. It is employed here in a form that puts emphasis on the inward feeling, the discomfort of heart produced by man's inhumanity to man. Jesus' expression of His discomfort was in the angry look directed at the assembly that was unsympathetic toward the plight of the man with the withered hand.

It is not implied that the pain was lasting or the anger longstanding. The glance by which the anger was expressed is seen as fleeting in contrast to the pain that caused it. But the term used for this anger is a term used for resentment set on vengeance. What is ascribed to Jesus in this passage is indignation at perceived wrongdoing, and wishing or intending punishment to the wrongdoer, which forms the core of vindicatory justice. It is a natural reaction of every moral being against perceived wrongdoing.

— B. B. WARFIELD, "On the Emotional Life of Our Lord," in *Biblical and Theological Studies* (New York: Charles Scribner's Sons, 1912), 7.

John 19:30: When Jesus had received the sour wine, he said, "It is finished," and he bowed his head and gave up his spirit.

God the Father is ready to save you. Jesus Christ is ready to receive you. The Holy Spirit is ready to dwell in you. Are you ready?

The "great salvation" is ready for you. The full atonement is made for you. The eternal redemption is obtained for you. Are you ready?

The cleansing fountain is opened for you. The robe of righteousness is wrought for you. The way into the holiest is consecrated for you. Are you ready?

All things that pertain unto life and godliness are given you by His divine power. Exceeding great and precious promises are given to you. The supply of all your needs is guaranteed to you. Strength and guidance, teaching and keeping, are provided for you. Even the good works in which you shall walk are prepared for you. A Father's love and care and a Savior's gift of peace are waiting for you. The feast is spread for you. All these things are ready for you. Are you ready for them?

Even if you did not heed or believe any other words of Jesus, could you— *can* you—doubt His dying words? Surely, they are worthy of all acceptance! What are they?

"It is finished!"

What is finished? "I have finished the work that You gave me to do." And what is that work? Simply the work of our salvation. That is the reason why all things are now ready, because Jesus has finished that all-inclusive work. When a thing is finished, how much is there left to do? The question sounds too absurd with respect to ordinary things. We hardly take the trouble to answer, "Why nothing, of course!" When Jesus has finished the work, how much is there left for you to do? Do you not see? *Nothing*, of course! You have only to accept that work as truly finished and accept His dying declaration that it is so. What further assurance would you have? Is not this enough? Does your heart say Yes or No?

—FRANCES RIDLEY HAVERGAL, *My King and His Service* (Philadelphia: Henry Altemus, 1892), 302–303.

John 1:14: And the Word became flesh and dwelt among us, and we have seen his glory, glory as of the only Son from the Father, full of grace and truth.

"And the Word became flesh," not only when He became a man at His advent, but even from the beginning, when the Word became the Son, not in essence, but in the Father's mind; and yet again when He spoke through the prophets. The Savior is called the offspring of the changeless Word: "In the beginning was the Word, and the Word was with God, and the Word was God" (John 1:1) . . . "And being found in human form, he humbled himself by becoming obedient to the point of death, even death on a cross" (Philippians 2:8). This passage refers not only to the flesh, in which He appeared, but also to His essence, what He was made of. And this essence is that of a Servant.

—CLEMENT OF ALEXANDRIA, *Excerpts from Theodotus*, in *Die griechischen christlichen Schriftsteller der ersten Jahrhunderte 17* (Berlin: Akademice-Verlag, 1897), 112–113.

1 Peter 4:1–6: Since therefore Christ suffered in the flesh, arm yourselves with the same way of thinking, for whoever has suffered in the flesh has ceased from sin, so as to live for the rest of the time in the flesh no longer for human passions but for the will of God. For the time that is past suffices for doing what the Gentiles want to do, living in sensuality, passions, drunkenness, orgies, drinking parties, and lawless idolatry. With respect to this they are surprised when you do not join them in the same flood of debauchery, and they malign you; but they will give account to him who is ready to judge the living and the dead. For this is why the gospel was preached even to those who are dead, that though judged in the flesh the way people are, they might live in the spirit the way God does.

Christ went down into death—voluntary endurance and unutterable anguish.

—B. B. WARFIELD, *Person and Work of Christ* (Oxford: Benediction Classics, 2015), 134.

But, apart from the Apostles' Creed, we must seek for a surer exposition of Christ's descent into hell: and the Word of God furnishes us with one not only holy and pious, but full of wonderful consolation. If Christ had only endured a bodily death, it would not have been effective. In order to stand between us and God's anger, to satisfy His righteous judgment, it was necessary that He should feel the weight of divine vengeance. It was equally necessary that He should engage in close quarters with the powers of hell and the horrors of eternal death. No wonder, then, its being said that He descended into hell, since He endured the death inflicted on the wicked by an angry God. Further, it is frivolous to object to the order in which an event that precedes burial should be placed after it. It shows us that not only was the body of Christ given up as the price of redemption, but that He paid a greater price in that He bore in His soul the tortures of a condemned and forsaken man.

—JOHN CALVIN, *Institutes of the Christian Religion*, vol. 2, trans. Henry Beveridge (Edinburgh: The Calvin Translation Society, 1845), 59–60 (*Institutes* 2.16.10).

> **1 Corinthians 15:21–22:** For as by a man came death, by a man has come also the resurrection of the dead. For as in Adam all die, so also in Christ shall all be made alive.

The first man, being of earth and from the earth, had the option of doing good or evil residing in his own power and was master of his own propensity toward one or the other. Carried away by temptation, and inclining toward disobedience, he fell back into mother earth from whom he derived his nature, and mastered now by corruption and death, bequeathed sin's penalty to humankind.

As evil increased among men, the intellect choosing vice over goodwill, sin became king, and the human nature uninhabitable by the Holy Spirit. Since the first Adam did not preserve the grace that had been vouchsafed to him by God, God the Father destined for us the second Adam from heaven. For He sent His own Son, whose nature is changeless, in our likeness, in order that, just as through the disobedience of the first Adam we became liable to divine wrath, so through the obedience of the second we might both escape the curse and do away with the devastation that proceeded from it. And when the Word of God became man, He received the Holy Spirit from the Father, as one of us, not receiving something peculiarly for himself, for He was the giver of the Spirit. He received it so that, as a human being who knew no sin, He might impart His nature to those who would receive Him.

John the Baptist, having baptized Jesus, said, "The Holy Spirit descended on him in bodily form, like a dove; and a voice came from heaven, 'You are my beloved Son; with you I am well pleased'" (Luke 3:22). The Spirit deserted humankind on account of sin, but the one who knew no sin became one of us so that He might allow the Spirit to remain with us. For us, therefore, through himself, He receives the Spirit and renews in our nature the ancient blessing.

—CYRIL OF ALEXANDRIA, *Commentary on John*, in *Patrologiae cursus completes*, series graeca, vol. 73, ed. J. P. Migne (Paris: Migne, 1857–1886), 205, 208.

Isaiah 53:10–12: Yet it was the will of the LORD to crush him; he has put him to grief; when his soul makes an offering for guilt, he shall see his offspring; he shall prolong his days; the will of the LORD shall prosper in his hand. Out of the anguish of his soul he shall see and be satisfied; by his knowledge shall the righteous one, my servant, make many to be accounted righteous, and he shall bear their iniquities . . . because he poured out his soul to death and was numbered with the transgressors; yet he bore the sin of many, and makes intercession for the transgressors.

But that Christ on His cross did rise and fall,
sin had eternally benighted all.
Yet dare I almost be glad? I do not see
that spectacle of too much weight for me.
Who sees in God's face that his self-life must die,
what a death were it then to see God die?
It made His own world, nature, shrink.
It made His footstool crack, and the sun wink.
Could I behold those hands which span the poles
and tune all spheres at once, pierced with those holes?
Could I behold that endless height;
zenith to us and our antipodes, humbled below us?
Or that blood which is the seat of all our souls,
if not of His, made dirt of dust, or that flesh
which was worn by God for His apparel, ragged and torn?
If on these things I dare not look, dare I
on His distressed mother cast mine eye,
who was God's partner here, and furnished thus
half of that sacrifice which ransomed us?
Though these things as I write be from mine eye,
they are present yet unto my memory,
for it looks toward them, and You look toward me,
O Savior, as You hang upon the tree.
I turn my back to You, but to receive correction,
until Your mercies bid You leave. Or, think me worth
Your anger, punish me. Restore Your image by Your grace,
that You may know me, and I will turn my face.

—JOHN DONNE, "Good Friday," 1613, "Riding Westward," in *Poems of John Donne*, vol. 1, ed. E. K. Chambers (London: Lawrence & Bullen, 1896), 172–173.

> **John 10:2–5, 14, 27–29:** "He who enters by the door is the shepherd of the sheep. To him the gatekeeper opens. The sheep hear his voice, and he calls his own sheep by name and leads them out. When he has brought out all his own, he goes before them, and the sheep follow him, for they know his voice. A stranger they will not follow, but they will flee from him, for they do not know the voice of strangers. . . . I am the good shepherd. I know my own and my own know me. . . . My sheep hear my voice, and I know them, and they follow me. I give them eternal life, and they will never perish, and no one will snatch them out of my hand. My Father, who has given them to me, is greater than all, and no one is able to snatch them out of the Father's hand."

In order to learn the new song, you must hear the melody of the voice of Christ in the Gospel.

You have heard that the glorious Gospel is where you will learn the song, and that it is Christ that must teach it. And this is the way that He teaches it: by causing the soul to hear the melody of His own voice in the Gospel.

It is Christ that speaks to us in the Gospel. Many hear His words, but they perceive no sweetness in them. They perceive no pleasantness in His voice, in the doctrines and invitations and promises of the Gospel. It is all a flavorless thing and a dead letter to them.

But to the godly, Christ's mouth is found to be most sweet. You must perceive the sweetness of His voice. You must see the glory of the doctrines, and the kindness of those invitations, and the exceeding preciousness of the promises.

—JONATHAN EDWARDS, "They Sing A New Song" (Revelation 14:3), in *Sermons and Discourses, 1739–1742*, The Works of Jonathan Edwards, vol. 22, ed. Harry S. Stout, Nathan O. Hatch, and Kyle P. Farley (New Haven, CT; London: Yale University Press, 2003), 243–244.

2 Corinthians 5:20-21: Therefore, we are ambassadors for Christ, God making his appeal through us. We implore you on behalf of Christ, be reconciled to God. For our sake he made him to be sin who knew no sin, so that in him we might become the righteousness of God.

To release me from the curse, Christ was called a curse. He who destroyed my curse, taking away my sin, takes away the sin of the world. He became, as it were, the new Adam to take the place of the first Adam. He made my disobedience His own as Head of the whole body. If I remain disobedient and rebellious, both by denial of God and my own sins, Christ bears that reproach on my account. But when I have submitted all things to Him through faith in Him and am living a reformed life by His grace and help, then He also will have fulfilled His submission, bringing me, whom He has saved, to God. For this, according to my view, is the subjection of Christ; namely, the fulfilling of the Father's will. But as the Son subjects all to the Father, so does the Father to the Son; the One by His work, the other by His good pleasure. He, then, who commits to God those whom He has saved, makes our condition His own. When Christ on the cross called out to His Father, "My God, My God, why have You forsaken me?" it was not He who was forsaken, as some have thought. God the Father was turning His back on sin, our sin. Christ was in His own Person, representing us. For we were the forsaken, despised, and lost without hope. By the sufferings of the Lamb of God, we were saved and made acceptable to the Father by faith.

—GREGORY OF NAZIANZUS, *Select Orations of St. Gregory Nazianzen*: Oration 30:5, A Select Library of Nicene and Post-Nicene Fathers of the Christian Church, 2nd ser., vol. 7, trans. Charles Gordon Browne and James Edward Swallow (New York: The Christian Literature Co., 1894), 311.

> **John 18:36:** Jesus answered, "My kingdom is not of this world. If my kingdom were of this world, my servants would have been fighting, that I might not be delivered over to the Jews. But my kingdom is not from the world."

Christ said to His Father, "You loved me before the foundation of the world." At that mysterious date, not of time, but of everlasting love, God chose us in Him. Before the world began, God, who cannot lie, gave the promise of eternal life to Him for us, and made with Him for us a covenant ordered in all things. The leading provisions of that covenant were a Lamb for our atonement and a King for our government—a dying and a living Savior. This God the Father did for us, and His own divine interest is strongly indicated in the words "God will provide *himself* a Lamb" and "I have provided *me* a King." The source of the kingship of Christ is God himself, in the eternal counsels of His love. It is one of the grand thoughts of God.

God has appointed His King "to be ruler over Israel *and* over Judah." In doing so He gives His children a great bond of union. For "one King shall be King to them all," and He shall "gather together in one the children of God that were scattered abroad." Satan scatters, but Jesus gathers. Shall we then allow the enemy to have his way, and tempt us to keep apart and aloof from those over whom our beloved King reigns? Let us try today to remember this and make it practical in all our contacts with His children.

Why has God made Jesus King? Who would have guessed the answer? "*Because* the Lord loved His people." The very thought of the kingship of Christ sprang from the everlasting love of God to His people. Make that statement a personal reality: "His people," that is, *you and me*. God made Jesus King over you because He loved you, and with nothing less than the love He had for His Son. Which is the more wonderful—the love that devised such a gift, or the gift that was devised by such love! Oh, to realize the glorious value of it! May we who by His grace know something of God's gift of His Son as our Savior, learn more day by day of the preciousness of the gift of His anointed One as our King!

—FRANCES RIDLEY HAVERGAL, *My King and His Service* (Philadelphia: Henry Altemus, 1892), 5–6.

> **Mark 14:61–63:** But he remained silent and made no answer. Again the high priest asked him, "Are you the Christ, the Son of the Blessed?" And Jesus said, "I am, and you will see the Son of Man seated at the right hand of Power, and coming with the clouds of heaven." And the high priest tore his garments and said, "What further witnesses do we need?"

Though it was a shocking exhibition, and highly incompatible with the majesty of the Son of God to be dragged before the judgment seat of a profane man and to be tried on the charge of a capital offense, as a criminal in chains, yet we ought to remember that our salvation consists in the doctrine of the cross: "We preach Christ crucified, a stumbling block to Jews and folly to Gentiles" (1 Corinthians 1:23).

For the Son of God chose to stand bound before an earthly judge and there to receive the sentence of death in order that we, delivered from condemnation, may not fear to approach freely the throne of God. If, therefore, we consider what advantage we reap from Christ having been tried before Pilate, the disgrace of so unworthy a subjection will be immediately washed away. None are offended at the condemnation of Christ except those who are either proud hypocrites or despisers of God and who are not ashamed of their own iniquity.

So then, the Son of God stood as a criminal before a mortal man, and there permitted himself to be accused and condemned that we may stand boldly before God. His enemies endeavored to fix upon Him everlasting infamy, but we ought rather to look at the end to which the providence of God directs us. For if we can fathom how dreadful is the judgment seat of God, and that we could never have been acquitted there unless Christ had been pronounced guilty on earth, we will never be ashamed of glorying in His chains. Relying on Him as our intercessor, we may come into the presence of God with joy. Christ was silent before His accusers in order that we might boldly cry, "Abba! Father!" (see Romans 8:15).

—JOHN CALVIN, *Commentary on a Harmony of the Evangelists, Matthew, Mark, and Luke*, vol. 3, trans. William Pringle (Edinburgh: The Calvin Translation Society, 1845), 274–275.

1 Corinthians 15:21–22: For as by a man came death, by a man has come also the resurrection of the dead. For as in Adam all die, so also in Christ shall all be made alive.

God, the Word made flesh in Christ, assumed the human nature common to all men, for He would have all men to be saved, and so, according to the harmony of nature, in which the work of grace is reflected, He has worked out our salvation. Whatever God the Father has bestowed on Him, He has given to all men in Him. For what would He not give, who gave His Only Begotten Son, and Holy Spirit?

—MEISTER ECKHART, *Defense Against Charges of Heresy*, trans. Raymond B. Blakney (New York: Harper & Row, 1941), 292.

For that which He has not assumed He has not healed; but that which is united to His Godhead is also saved. If Adam's fall was not complete, then Christ's work to save humankind would only be a partial salvation. But if the whole of Adam's nature fell, it must be covered by the whole nature of Him who was begotten, and so be saved completely. Let no one begrudge us our complete salvation or clothe the Savior only with a partial humanity. For if His manhood is without spirit (the Arians teach this, that they may attribute His passion to the Godhead), which gives life to the body, He could not have suffered. And if He has a spirit but not a mind, how is He a man, for man is not a mindless animal. So it follows that He suffered and died as a man with a spirit, mind, and body, and so could save man from his sins. He perfectly represented us in His death on the cross for our sins.

—GREGORY OF NANZIANZUS, *Letters of St. Gregory Nazianzen: to Cledonius the Priest Against Apollinarius*, A Select Library of Nicene and Post-Nicene Fathers of the Christian Church, 2nd ser., vol. 7, trans. Charles Gordon Browne and James Edward Swallow (New York: The Christian Literature Co., 1894), 440.

John 6:42: They said, "Is not this Jesus, the son of Joseph, whose father and mother we know? How does he now say, 'I have come down from heaven'?"

On two occasions we are told that Jesus felt that occurrences He witnessed were extraordinary and experienced the appropriate emotion of wonder regarding them (Matthew 8:10; Luke 7:9; Mark 6:6). Once desire is attributed to Him (Luke 22:15). And once our Lord speaks of himself as being conceivably the subject of shame (Mark 8:38). These show a being who reacts as we might react to the incidents that arise in daily interaction with men, and whose reactions bear all the characteristics of the corresponding emotions we are familiar with in our experience. Perhaps it may be well explicitly to note that our Lord's emotions fulfilled themselves, as ours do, in physical reactions. He who hungered (Matthew 4:2), thirsted (John 19:28), was weary (John 4:6), who knew both physical pain and pleasure, expressed also in bodily affections the emotions that stirred His soul. That He did so is seen by the simple circumstance that these emotions were observed and recorded. But the physical expression of emotions is also frequently attested. Not only do we read that He wept (John 11:35; Luke 19:41), sighed (Mark 7:34), and sighed deeply (Mark 8:12), but we read also of His angry glare (Mark 3:5), His annoyed speech (Mark 10:14), His chiding words (e.g., Mark 3:12), the undercurrent of His rage (e.g., John 11:33, 38), the open exultation of His joy (Luke 10:21), the loud cry that escaped Him in His moment of desolation (Matthew 27:46). Nothing is lacking to make the impression strong that we have before us in Jesus a human being like ourselves.

—B. B. WARFIELD, "On the Emotional Life of Our Lord," in *Biblical and Theological Studies* (New York: Charles Scribner's Sons, 1912), 16–17.

Psalm 90:2: Before the mountains were brought forth, or ever you had formed the earth and the world, from everlasting to everlasting you are God.

Hebrews 13:8: Jesus Christ is the same yesterday and today and forever.

The doctrine of creation and the doctrine of the incarnation has constituted a problem in connection with the immutability of God. It should be maintained that the divine nature did not undergo any essential change in the incarnation. It remained impassible, that is, incapable of suffering and death, free from ignorance, and insusceptible to weakness and temptation. It is well to stress the fact that the incarnation was a personal act. It is more accurate to say that the Son of God became incarnate than to say the divine nature assumed human flesh. The result of the incarnation was that the divine Savior could be ignorant and weak, could be tempted, and could suffer and die, not in His divine nature, but by virtue of His possession of a human nature.

—LOUIS BERKHOF, *Systematic Theology* (Grand Rapids, MI: Wm. B. Eerdmans Publishing, 1996), 323–332.

For although the boundless essence of the Word was united with human nature into one person, we do not imagine that He was confined therein. The Son of God descended miraculously from heaven, yet without abandoning heaven; was pleased to be conceived miraculously in the Virgin's womb, to live on the earth, and hang upon the cross, and yet always filled the world as from the beginning.

—JOHN CALVIN, *Institutes of the Christian Religion*, vol. 2, trans. Henry Beveridge (Edinburgh: The Calvin Translation Society, 1845), 20–21 (*Institutes*, 2.13.4).

Luke 4:31–37, 40–41: And he went down to Capernaum, a city of Galilee. And he was teaching them on the Sabbath, and they were astonished at his teaching, for his word possessed authority. And in the synagogue there was a man who had the spirit of an unclean demon, and he cried out with a loud voice, "Ha! What have you to do with us, Jesus of Nazareth? Have you come to destroy us? I know who you are—the Holy One of God." But Jesus rebuked him, saying, "Be silent and come out of him!" And when the demon had thrown him down in their midst, he came out of him, having done him no harm. And they were all amazed and said to one another, "What is this word? For with authority and power he commands the unclean spirits, and they come out!" And reports about him went out into every place in the surrounding region. . . . Now when the sun was setting, all those who had any who were sick with various diseases brought them to him, and he laid his hands on every one of them and healed them. And demons also came out of many, crying, "You are the Son of God!" But he rebuked them and would not allow them to speak, because they knew that he was the Christ.

Jesus in His own person is the embodied sovereignty of God. He lives out that sovereignty in the flesh. He manifests the kingdom of God by enthroning the creation-will of God and demonstrating His lordship over Satan. Jesus conducts himself as Lord and true King, ruling over demons, ruling over nature at its fiercest, ruling over sickness, conquering death itself. With the coming of Jesus, the kingdom is not merely immanent; it gains the larger scope of invasion. Jesus points to His release of the victims of Satan, and to His own devastation of demons and the demonic, as attesting that "the kingdom of God has come upon you" (Matthew 12:28). He reveals God's royal power through salvation.

—CARL F. H. HENRY, "Reflections on the Kingdom of God," *Journal of the Evangelical Theological Society* 35, no. 1 (March 1992), 42.

Ephesians 3:14–19: For this reason I bow my knees before the Father, from whom every family in heaven and on earth is named, that according to the riches of his glory he may grant you to be strengthened with power through his Spirit in your inner being, so that Christ may dwell in your hearts through faith—that you, being rooted and grounded in love, may have strength to comprehend with all the saints what is the breadth and length and height and depth, and to know the love of Christ that surpasses knowledge, that you may be filled with all the fullness of God.

Wine is a symbol of earthly joy, and who has had but one sip of the love of Christ does not know this true wine of the kingdom to be better than the greatest joy the world can give! How much more will we comprehend and experience this wine of heaven when deeper and fuller drafts are our daily portion as we follow on to know the love that passes knowledge!

1. The breadth of Christ's love is contrasted with the narrowness of earthly love. Perhaps it is not so much by looking at His love for all the redeemed, which no man can number, that we realize that it reaches and includes *even me*.

2. The length of His love, contrasted with the shortness of earthly love, is indeed immeasurable, for His love is everlasting; and when inconceivable ages have passed, we shall be no nearer the end of it.

3. The height of God's love, contrasted with the lowliness of all that is represented by the world's love and joy, breaks through and leads us up into the free sky above, expanding to the very throne of God. He proved His love to be strong as death, and when all God's waves and billows went over Him, the many waters could not quench it.

4. The depth, contrasted with the shallowness of the world's best love reaches the depth of our fall, the depth of our sin, the depth of our need that only His love can fill.

—FRANCES RIDLEY HAVERGAL, *My King and His Service* (Philadelphia: Henry Altemus, 1892), 214–216.

Revelation 7:16–17: "They shall hunger no more, neither thirst anymore; the sun shall not strike them, nor any scorching heat. For the Lamb in the midst of the throne will be their shepherd, and he will guide them to springs of living water, and God will wipe away every tear from their eyes."

Though Christ is now at the right hand of God, exalted as King of heaven, and Lord of the universe, yet since He still has a human nature, He still excels in humility. Though the man Christ Jesus is the highest of all creatures in heaven, yet He as much excels them all in humility as He does in glory and dignity.

And though He now appears in such glorious majesty and dominion in heaven, yet He appears as a lamb in His humility with mild and sweet treatment of His saints there. For He is a lamb still, even on the throne of His exaltation. And He that is the Shepherd of the whole flock is himself a Lamb and goes before them in heaven as such: "For the Lamb in the midst of the throne will be their shepherd, and he will guide them to springs of living water, and God will wipe away every tear from their eyes" (Revelation 7:17). He still manifests His lamb-like excellencies in His dealings with His saints on earth in admirable patience, love, gentleness, and compassion, instructing, supplying, supporting, and comforting them, often coming to them, and manifesting himself to them by His Spirit, so that He may eat with them, and they with Him, admitting them to sweet communion with Him, enabling them with boldness and confidence to come to Him, and comfort their hearts in Him. And in heaven Christ still appears, as it were, with the marks of His wounds upon Him, and so appears as a lamb as it had been slain.

—JONATHAN EDWARDS, "The Excellency of Christ," *Sermons and Discourses, 1734–1738*, The Works of Jonathan Edwards, vol. 19, ed. M. X. Lesser and Harry S. Stout (New Haven, CT; London: Yale University Press, 2001), 581.

Revelation 5:11–14: Then I looked, and I heard around the throne and the living creatures and the elders the voice of many angels, numbering myriads of myriads and thousands of thousands, saying with a loud voice,

"Worthy is the Lamb who was slain,
to receive power and wealth and wisdom and might
and honor and glory and blessing!"

And I heard every creature in heaven and on earth and under the earth and in the sea, and all that is in them, saying,

"To him who sits on the throne and to the Lamb
be blessing and honor and glory and might forever
and ever!"

And the four living creatures said, "Amen!" and the elders fell down and worshiped.

We are never finished with the cross, nor ever shall be. Its wonders will be always new, always filled with awe and joy. "The Lamb who was slain" will be the theme of our praise above. Why should such a name be given to Him in a book such as the Revelation, which in one sense carries us far beyond the cross, were it not that we shall always realize its connection with our salvation, always look to it even in the midst of glory, always learning from it some new lesson regarding the work of Him in whom we have redemption through His blood, even the forgiveness of sins, according to the riches of His grace? What will they who here on earth speak of themselves as being done with the cross say to being brought face-to-face with the Lamb who was slain in the age of absolute perfection, the age of the heavenly glory?

—HORATIUS BONAR, *The Everlasting Righteousness; or, How Shall a Man Be Just with God?* (Carlisle, PA: Banner of Truth, 1874/1993), 61.

> **2 Corinthians 1:20–22:** For all the promises of God find their Yes in him. That is why it is through him that we utter our Amen to God for his glory. And it is God who establishes us with you in Christ, and has anointed us, and who has also put his seal on us and given us his Spirit in our hearts as a guarantee.

It would be presumptuous for us to hold that God is favorably disposed to us, had we not His own testimony, and had He not shown by invitation, His desire that we know His will. It has already been seen that Christ is the only pledge of true love, for without Him all things, both above and below, speak of hatred and wrath. We have also seen, that since the knowledge of the divine goodness cannot be of importance unless it leads us to confide in it, we must exclude a knowledge mingled with doubt—a knowledge which, far from being firm, is continually wavering. But the human mind, when blinded and darkened, is far from being able to rise to a proper knowledge of the divine will; nor can the heart, fluctuating with perpetual doubt, rest secure in such knowledge. Hence, in order that the Word of God may gain full credit, the mind must be enlightened, and the heart confirmed, from some other quarter. We have a full definition of faith if we say that it is a firm and sure knowledge of divine favor toward us, founded on the truth of the promise in Christ, and revealed to our minds and sealed on our hearts by the Holy Spirit.

—JOHN CALVIN, *Institutes of the Christian Religion*, vol. 2, trans. Henry Beveridge (Edinburgh: The Calvin Translation Society, 1845), 103–104 (*Institutes*, 3.2.7).

Gratuitous remission of sins can never be separated from the Spirit of regeneration; for this would be as it were to rend Christ asunder.

—JOHN CALVIN, *Commentary on the Epistle of Paul the Apostle to the Romans*, trans. John Owen (Bellingham, WA: Logos Bible Software, 2010), 290.

We maintain that in this way a person is reconciled in Christ to God the Father, by no merit of their own, by no value of works, but by gratuitous mercy. When we embrace Christ by faith, we come, as it were, into communion with Him.

—JOHN CALVIN, "Calvin's Reply to Sadoleto," in *A Reformation Debate*, ed. John Olin (Grand Rapids, MI: Baker, 1966/1539), 66–67.

Colossians 3:3–4: For you have died, and your life is hidden with Christ in God. When Christ who is your life appears, then you also will appear with him in glory.

Once in Christ, we shall never be out of Christ.

—J. C. RYLE, *Practical Religion: Being Plain Papers on the Daily Duties, Experience, Dangers, and Privileges of Professing Christians* (Carlisle, PA: Banner of Truth, 1878/2013), 374.

The union of the heart of a believer to Christ is begun when his heart is drawn to Christ at conversion, when he first discovers God's excellence; and with this drawing of his heart to Christ, a vital union with Him is established; and through this union the believer becomes a living branch of the true vine, a member of Christ's mystical body, living by a kind of participation in Christ's own life.

But while the saints are in the body, there is still a great distance between Christ and them: there are remainders of alienation, and the vital union is imperfect; and so, consequently, is the communication of spiritual life: there is much between Christ and a believer to keep them apart, much indwelling sin, temptation, and carnal objects to keep the soul separated from Christ, hindering a perfect union.

But when the soul leaves the body, all these hindrances shall be removed, every separating wall shall be broken down, and every impediment taken out of the way; all distance shall cease; the heart shall be wholly and perfectly drawn, firmly and forever bound to Him by a perfect view of His glory.

And the vital union shall then be brought to perfection: the soul shall live perfectly in Christ, being perfectly filled with His Spirit, animated by His influences; living as it were by Christ's life, without spiritual death or carnal life. Departed souls of saints are with Christ, as they enjoy a glorious and immediate union and communion with Him.

—JONATHAN EDWARDS, "True Saints, When Absent from the Body, Are Present with the Lord," in *Sermons and Discourses 1743–1758*, The Works of Jonathan Edwards, vol. 25, ed. Wilson H. Kimnach and Harry S. Stout (New Haven, CT: Yale University Press, 2006), 231–233.

1 John 4:2-3: By this you know the Spirit of God: every spirit that confesses that Jesus Christ has come in the flesh is from God, and every spirit that does not confess Jesus is not from God. This is the spirit of the antichrist, which you heard was coming and now is in the world already.

Some say that it was God the Word, not the man, whose call roused Lazarus from the tomb, and that it was not God who grew weary in His journey but the assumed man, and that this was the one who hungered and thirsted, was crucified and died. Those who believe this have gone completely astray from the truth and do not know the mystery of His complete union with the flesh.

For we do not say that there were two sons or two Christs, but one Christ and Son, who on the one hand is God the Only Begotten, born before time from God the Father, His substantial Word, and on the other hand is the very same One who was born in the flesh from the Virgin Mary. Let no one divide Him in two, claiming there are two sons, but confess Him as one and the same, as the Word of God become man, and assert everything to this understanding of Him, words and deeds alike. For since the same One was at the same time both God and man, He speaks both what belongs to God and what belongs to man, and likewise His acts are both human and divine.

—CYRIL OF ALEXANDRIA, "Answer to Tiberius," in *Select Letters*, ed. and trans. Lionel R. Wickham (Oxford: Claredon Press, 1983), 155.

Revelation 21:9–14: Then came one of the seven angels who had the seven bowls full of the seven last plagues and spoke to me, saying, "Come, I will show you the Bride, the wife of the Lamb." And he carried me away in the Spirit to a great, high mountain, and showed me the holy city Jerusalem coming down out of heaven from God, having the glory of God, its radiance like a most rare jewel, like a jasper, clear as crystal. It had a great, high wall, with twelve gates, and at the gates twelve angels, and on the gates the names of the twelve tribes of the sons of Israel were inscribed—on the east three gates, on the north three gates, on the south three gates, and on the west three gates. And the wall of the city had twelve foundations, and on them were the twelve names of the twelve apostles of the Lamb.

Above all, the time of Christ's second coming is the time of the consummation of the church's marriage with the Lamb, and the time of the complete and most perfect joy of the wedding.

On that resurrection morning, when the Sun of Righteousness shall appear in the heavens, shining in all His brightness and glory, He will appear as a bridegroom.

He shall come in the glory of His Father, with all His holy angels. And at that glorious appearing of the great God, and our Savior Jesus Christ, shall the whole elect Church, complete in every individual member and each member with the whole man, both body and soul, and both in perfect glory, ascend up to meet the Lord in the air, to be from that point on forever with the Lord.

That will indeed be a joyful meeting of this glorious bridegroom and bride. Then the bridegroom will appear in all His glory without any veil.

—JONATHAN EDWARDS, "The Church's Marriage to Her Sons, and to Her God," in *Sermons and Discourses, 1743–1758*, The Works of Jonathan Edwards, vol. 25, ed. Wilson H. Kimnach and Harry S. Stout (New Haven, CT; London: Yale University Press, 2006), 183–184.

John 8:12: Again Jesus spoke to them, saying, "I am the light of the world. Whoever follows me will not walk in darkness, but will have the light of life."

I could not do without Thee, O Savior of the lost!
Whose precious blood redeemed me at such tremendous cost.
Thy righteousness, Thy pardon, Thy precious blood must be
My only hope and comfort, My glory and my plea!
I could not do without Thee! I cannot stand alone,
I have no strength or goodness, no wisdom of my own.
But Thou, beloved Savior, art all in all to me,
And weakness will be power, if leaning hard on Thee.
I could not do without Thee! For oh! The way is long,
And I am often weary, and sigh replaces song.
How could I do without Thee? I do not know the way.
Thou knowest and Thou leadest and will not let me stray.
I could not do without Thee, O Jesus, Savior dear!
Even when my eyes are resting, I know that Thou art near.
How dreary and how lonely this changeful life would be,
Without the sweet communion and secret rest with Thee!
I could not do without Thee! No other friend can read
The spirit's strange deep longings, interpreting its need.
No human heart could enter each dim recess of mine,
And soothe and hush and calm it, O blessed Lord, but Thine!
I could not do without Thee! For years are fleeting fast,
And soon, in solemn loneliness, the river must be passed.
But Thou wilt never leave me, and though the waves roll high,
I know Thou wilt be near me and whisper, "It is I."

—FRANCES RIDLEY HAVERGAL, *Under the Surface* (London: J. Nisbet & Co., 1876), 64–66.

Ephesians 5:29–30: For no one ever hated his own flesh, but nourishes and cherishes it, just as Christ does the church, because we are members of his body.

The Mediator must be true God and true man. This will become clearer if we reflect on the fact that the work to be performed by the Mediator was of no common description: It was to restore us to the divine favor, so as to make us, instead of sons of men, sons of God; instead of heirs of hell, heirs of a heavenly kingdom. Who could do this unless the Son of God were to become the Son of man, and so receive what is ours in order to transfer to us what is His, making what is His by nature to become ours by grace? Relying on this fact, we trust that we are the sons of God because the natural Son of God assumed a body like ours, flesh of our flesh, bone of our bones, that He might be one with us. He decided to take what was peculiar to us, that He might in turn extend to us what was peculiarly His own. Hence that holy brotherhood that He spoke of with His own lips: "I am ascending to my Father and your Father, to my God and your God" (John 20:17).

In this way, we have a sure inheritance in the heavenly kingdom, because the only Son of God, to whom it entirely belonged, has adopted us as His children; "and if children, then heirs—heirs of God and fellow heirs with Christ" (Romans 8:17). Moreover, it was especially necessary that He who was to be our Redeemer should be truly God and man. It was His to swallow up death: Who but Life could do so? It was His to conquer sin: Who but Righteousness itself? Therefore, God, in His infinite mercy, having determined to redeem us, became himself our Redeemer in the person of His Only Begotten Son.

—JOHN CALVIN, *Institutes of the Christian Religion*, vol. 2, trans. Henry Beveridge (Edinburgh: The Calvin Translation Society, 1845), 3–4 (*Institutes*, 2.12.2).

1 Peter 2:21-25: For to this you have been called, because Christ also suffered for you, leaving you an example, so that you might follow in his steps. He committed no sin, neither was deceit found in his mouth. When he was reviled, he did not revile in return; when he suffered, he did not threaten, but continued entrusting himself to him who judges justly. He himself bore our sins in his body on the tree, that we might die to sin and live to righteousness. By his wounds you have been healed. For you were straying like sheep, but have now returned to the Shepherd and Overseer of your souls.

Matthew 16:24-25: Then Jesus told his disciples, "If anyone would come after me, let him deny himself and take up his cross and follow me. For whoever would save his life will lose it, but whoever loses his life for my sake will find it."

Neither desire nor any other virtue has value or life except through the Only Begotten Son, Christ crucified, since the soul has drawn love from Him and is enabled to follow in His footsteps. In this way, and in no other, is suffering of value: It satisfies the price of sin. With gentle, uniting love born from the sweet knowledge of God's goodness, and from the contrition the heart experiences in the knowledge of its own sin in God's unspeakable love for you, He chose to create you anew in grace. God washed you and made you a new creation by the blood the Only Begotten Son poured out for you.

—SAINT CATHERINE OF SIENA, *The Dialogue*, trans. Giuliana Cavallini (New Jersey: Paulist Press, 1980), 29.

1 Corinthians 1:18–25: For the word of the cross is folly to those who are perishing, but to us who are being saved it is the power of God. For it is written,

"I will destroy the wisdom of the wise,
and the discernment of the discerning I will thwart."

Where is the one who is wise? Where is the scribe? Where is the debater of this age? Has not God made foolish the wisdom of the world? For since, in the wisdom of God, the world did not know God through wisdom, it pleased God through the folly of what we preach to save those who believe. For Jews demand signs and Greeks seek wisdom, but we preach Christ crucified, a stumbling block to Jews and folly to Gentiles, but to those who are called, both Jews and Greeks, Christ the power of God and the wisdom of God. For the foolishness of God is wiser than men, and the weakness of God is stronger than men.

In the person of Christ were "hidden all the treasures of wisdom and knowledge" (Colossians 2:3). Some gifts of wisdom were distributed at creation, but its true treasures were opened in redemption, the highest degree of wisdom God exerted in the world. Christ is called the "the power of God and the wisdom of God" (1 Corinthians 1:24). Christ is the wisdom of God in essence, and the Gospel is that wisdom worked out in practice, as it is the power of God to subdue the heart to himself.

The wisdom of God is wonderfully apparent in redemption. His wisdom in creation overwhelms the eye; understanding His wisdom in how He rules the world amazes the curious observer, seeing how He orchestrates events to His will. The works of creation are the footsteps of His wisdom; the work of redemption is the face of His wisdom.

—STEPHEN CHARNOCK, *The Existence and Attributes of God*, vol. 1 (Grand Rapids, MI: Baker, 1682/2000), 552–553.

> **Colossians 2:1-3:** For I want you to know how great a struggle I have for you and for those at Laodicea and for all who have not seen me face to face, that their hearts may be encouraged, being knit together in love, to reach all the riches of full assurance of understanding and the knowledge of God's mystery, which is Christ, in whom are hidden all the treasures of wisdom and knowledge.

The one true goal or resting place, where doubt and weariness, the sting of a pricking conscience, and the longings of an unsatisfied soul would all be quieted is Christ himself.

Not the church, but Christ.

Not doctrine, but Christ.

Not traditions, but Christ.

Not ceremonies, but Christ:

Christ the God-man, giving His life for ours, sealing the everlasting covenant, and making peace for us through the blood of His cross.

Christ the divine storehouse of all light and truth, "In whom are hidden all the treasures of wisdom and knowledge."

Christ the infinite vessel, filled with the Holy Spirit, the Enlightener, the Teacher, the Life Giver, the Comforter, so that "from his fullness we have all received, grace upon grace" (John 1:16).

This alone is the wretched soul's refuge, its rock to build upon, its home to abide in, until the great tempter is bound, and every conflict ended in victory.

—HORATIUS BONAR, *Words to Winners of Souls* (Philipsburg, NJ: P&R, 1860/1995), 6.

John 1:1–5, 14: In the beginning was the Word, and the Word was with God, and the Word was God. He was in the beginning with God. All things were made through him, and without him was not any thing made that was made. In him was life, and the life was the light of men. The light shines in the darkness, and the darkness has not overcome it. . . . And the Word became flesh and dwelt among us, and we have seen his glory, glory as of the only Son from the Father, full of grace and truth.

What a wonder is it, that two natures infinitely distant, should be more intimately united than anything in the world and yet without any confusion!

That the same person should have both *glory* and *grief*; an *infinite joy* in the Deity and an *inexpressible sorrow* in the humanity.

That a *God* upon a *throne* should be an *infant* in a *cradle*.

That the thundering *Creator* be a weeping *babe* and a suffering *man*.

These are such expressions of *mighty power*, as well as *condescending love*, that they astonish men upon earth, and angels in heaven.

—STEPHEN CHARNOCK, "On the Power of God," in *The Existence and Attributes of God*, vol. 2 (New York: Robert Carter & Brothers, 1853), 63–64.

The glory and beauty of the blessed Jehovah, which is most worthy in itself to be the object of our admiration and love, is there exhibited in the most emotionally powerful manner that can be conceived of, as it appears shining in all its luster, in the face of an incarnate, infinitely loving, meek, compassionate, dying Redeemer.

All the virtues of the Lamb of God, His humility, patience, meekness, submission, obedience, love, and compassion, are exhibited to our view, in a way that moves our hearts more powerfully than anything else that can be imagined.

—JONATHAN EDWARDS, *Religious Affections*, revised edition, The Works of Jonathan Edwards, vol. 2, ed. John E. Smith and Harry S. Stout (New Haven, CT: Yale University Press, 2009), 123–124.

> **John 14:31; 15:9–10:** I do as the Father has commanded me, so that the world may know that I love the Father. . . . As the Father has loved me, so have I loved you. Abide in my love. If you keep my commandments, you will abide in my love, just as I have kept my Father's commandments and abide in his love.

We may be surprised to note that Jesus' love to God the Father is only once explicitly mentioned in Scripture (John 14:31), but in this single mention it is shown as the motive of His entire saving work, particularly of His offering up His life. When the time of that offering was at hand, Jesus explained: "I will no longer talk much with you, for the ruler of this world is coming. He has no claim on me, but I do as the Father has commanded me" (John 14:30–31). The motive of Jesus' earthly life and death is more commonly presented as His love for sinful men. Here, His motive is presented as loving obedience to God the Father. He had come to do His Father's will, and He would do it to the bitter end. He declares His purpose to be under the impulse of love; obedience even to death on the cross.

As His love for His Father was the source of His obedience, and the motivation of His faithfulness to the work that had been committed to Him, so He declares that the love of His followers, imitating His love for them, was to be the source of their obedience. Further, through their obedience would come all the good that can come to human beings, including their love for one another. Self-sacrificing love is the essence of the Christian life, its incentive being the self-sacrificing love of Christ himself.

—B. B. WARFIELD, "On the Emotional Life of Our Lord," in *Biblical and Theological Studies* (New York: Charles Scribner's Sons, 1912), 4–5.

Ephesians 3:6: This mystery is that the Gentiles are fellow heirs, members of the same body, and partakers of the promise in Christ Jesus through the gospel.

We are now to examine how we obtain the enjoyment of those blessings that the Father has conferred on His Only Begotten Son, not for His own private use, but to enrich the poor and needy. And first it must be said that while there is separation between Christ and us, all that He suffered and performed for the salvation of humankind is useless and unavailing to us. To communicate what He received from His Father, He must, therefore, become ours and dwell within us. On this account He is called our Head, the firstborn among many brethren, and we in turn are said to be grafted into Him, and to put on Christ, for as I have observed, whatever He possesses is nothing to us until we are united to Him. But though it is true that we obtain this by faith, since we see that the communication of Christ, offered in the Gospel, is not embraced by all, reason itself teaches us to proceed further, and to inquire into the power of the Spirit, by which we are introduced to the enjoyment of Christ and all His benefits.

—JOHN CALVIN, *Institutes of the Christian Religion*, trans. John Allen (Philadelphia: Presbyterian Board of Publication, 1813), 485 (*Institutes*, 3.1.1).

> **Matthew 27:62–66:** The next day, that is, after the day of Preparation, the chief priests and the Pharisees gathered before Pilate and said, "Sir, we remember how that impostor said, while he was still alive, 'After three days I will rise.' Therefore order the tomb to be made secure until the third day, lest his disciples go and steal him away and tell the people, 'He has risen from the dead,' and the last fraud will be worse than the first." Pilate said to them, "You have a guard of soldiers. Go, make it as secure as you can." So they went and made the tomb secure by sealing the stone and setting a guard.

They took the body down from the cross, and one of the few rich men among the first Christians obtained permission to bury it in a rock tomb in his garden. The Romans then set a military guard lest there should be an attempt to recover the body. There was a certain symbolism in these natural proceedings: It was typical that the tomb should be sealed with the secrecy of ancient Eastern sepulture and guarded by the authority of the Caesars. For in this type of cavern the whole of that great and glorious humanity we call antiquity was buried. It was the culmination of a portion of human history. The mythologists and the philosophers were buried there, the gods and the heroes and the sages. In the great Roman era, they had lived. But as they could only live, so they could only die; and they were dead.

On the third day, the friends of Christ, coming at daybreak to the place, found the tomb empty and the stone rolled away. By varying degrees, they each realized the new wonder; but even they hardly realized that the world had essentially died that night. What they were looking at was the dawning of a new day, and in a semblance of the gardener, God walked again in the garden, not in the cool of the evening, but in the bright dawn.

—G. K. CHESTERTON, "The Everlasting Man," in *The Collected Works of G. K. Chesterton*, vol. 2 (San Francisco: Ignatius, 1986), 344–345.

> **Romans 8:29–30:** For those whom he foreknew he also predestined to be conformed to the image of his Son, in order that he might be the firstborn among many brothers. And those whom he predestined he also called, and those whom he called he also justified, and those whom he justified he also glorified.

Christ given to us by the kindness of God is grasped and possessed by faith, by means of which we obtain in particular a twofold benefit; first, being reconciled by the righteousness of Christ, God becomes, instead of a Judge, a gracious Father; and secondly, being sanctified by His Spirit, we cultivate blamelessness and purity of life. For unless you understand first of all what your position is before God, and the nature of His judgment concerning you, you have no foundation on which to establish your salvation nor one on which to build piety toward God.

—JOHN CALVIN, *Institutes of the Christian Religion*, vol. 2, trans. Henry Beveridge (Edinburgh: The Calvin Translation Society, 1845), 302 (*Institutes*, 3.11.1).

Christ, therefore, justifies no man without also sanctifying him. These blessings are conjoined by a perpetual and inseparable tie. Those whom He enlightens by His wisdom He redeems; whom He redeems He justifies; whom He justifies He sanctifies. But as the question relates only to justification and sanctification, to them let us confine ourselves. Though we distinguish between them, they are inseparably understood in Christ. Would you obtain justification in Christ? You must previously possess Christ. But you cannot possess Him without being made a partaker of His sanctification, for Christ cannot be divided. Since the Lord, therefore, does not grant us the enjoyment of these blessings without bestowing himself, He bestows both at once, but never the one without the other. And so we are justified not *without* works and yet not *by* works, since through our sharing in Christ, who justifies us, sanctification is included.

—JOHN CALVIN, *Institutes of the Christian Religion*, vol. 2, trans. Henry Beveridge (Edinburgh: The Calvin Translation Society, 1845), 386 (*Institutes*, 3.16.1).

1 John 4:8: Anyone who does not love does not know God, because God is love.

For what further need has God of the mysteries of love? God himself is love. Just a look into the heart of the Father reveals His love for humankind in sending His Only Begotten Son to the earth. In His ineffable essence He is the Father, full of compassion, mercy, love, and understanding of His creation. The Father is loving: and the great proof of this is He whom He begot of himself; and the fruit brought forth by love is love.

For this reason, the Son also came down, clothing himself, as it were, with humanity, voluntarily subjecting himself to the experiences of humanity, that by bringing himself to the measure of our weakness, He might correspondingly bring us to the measure of His strength. And being offered up and giving himself as a ransom, He left for us a New Covenant: My love I give unto you. How great is it? For each of us He gave His life. This He demands from us in return for one another.

—CLEMENT OF ALEXANDRIA, "Who Is the Rich Man Who Shall Be Saved?" #37 in *Ante-Nicene Fathers*, vol. 2, trans. William Wilson (Buffalo, NY: Christian Literature Publishing Co., 1885), 601.

Romans 10:9–17: Because, if you confess with your mouth that Jesus is Lord and believe in your heart that God raised him from the dead, you will be saved. For with the heart one believes and is justified, and with the mouth one confesses and is saved. For the Scripture says, "Everyone who believes in him will not be put to shame." For there is no distinction between Jew and Greek; for the same Lord is Lord of all, bestowing his riches on all who call on him. For "everyone who calls on the name of the Lord will be saved." How then will they call on him in whom they have not believed? And how are they to believe in him of whom they have never heard? And how are they to hear without someone preaching? And how are they to preach unless they are sent? As it is written, "How beautiful are the feet of those who preach the good news!" But they have not all obeyed the gospel. For Isaiah says, "Lord, who has believed what he has heard from us?" So faith comes from hearing, and hearing through the word of Christ.

If our Lord is so good to us to have His Word still preached to us, we have by that fact a sure and infallible sign that He is near at hand to us, and that He seeks our salvation, and that He calls us to himself as though He were speaking to us, and as if we were seeing Him in the flesh before us.

Jesus Christ extends His arms to receive us as often as the Gospel is preached to us and heard by us.

—JOHN CALVIN, *Sermons on Ephesians*, trans. Arthur Golding (Carlisle, PA: Banner of Truth, 1974), 368.

Romans 3:21–26: But now the righteousness of God has been manifested apart from the law, although the Law and the Prophets bear witness to it— the righteousness of God through faith in Jesus Christ for all who believe. For there is no distinction: for all have sinned and fall short of the glory of God, and are justified by his grace as a gift, through the redemption that is in Christ Jesus, whom God put forward as a propitiation by his blood, to be received by faith. This was to show God's righteousness, because in his divine forbearance he had passed over former sins. It was to show his righteousness at the present time, so that he might be just and the justifier of the one who has faith in Jesus.

In the cross of Christ, as in a magnificent theater, the inestimable goodness of God is displayed before the whole world. In all the creatures, indeed, both high and low, the glory of God shines.

But nowhere has God's glory shone more brightly than in the cross, in which there has been an astonishing change of things, the condemnation of all people has been manifested, sin has been blotted out, salvation has been restored to humanity. In short, the whole world has been renewed, and everything restored to good order.

—JOHN CALVIN, *Commentary on the Gospel According to John*, vol. 2, trans. William Pringle (London: The Calvin Translation Society, 1847; reprint, Grand Rapids, MI: Baker, 1981), 73.

I could never myself believe in God, if it were not for the cross. In the real world of pain, how could one worship a God who was immune to it? In imagination I have turned instead to that lonely, twisted, tortured figure on the cross, nails through hands and feet, back lacerated, limbs wrenched, brow bleeding from thorn-pricks, mouth dry and intolerably thirsty, plunged in godforsaken darkness.

That is the God for me! He laid aside His immunity to pain. He entered our world of flesh and blood, tears and death. He suffered for us. Our sufferings become more manageable in light of His.

—JOHN STOTT, *The Cross of Christ* (Downers Grove, IL: IVP, 1986), 335–336.

> **John 3:16–17:** For God so loved the world, that he gave his only Son, that whoever believes in him should not perish but have eternal life. For God did not send his Son into the world to condemn the world, but in order that the world might be saved through him.

"For God so loved the world, that he gave his only Son." If the great and superabundant love of God the Father is what our Lord has toward the world, it is recognized in the fact that His Son exposed himself to misfortune for the sake of the world and on its account. It would therefore appear a small thing and of little worth if what was given for our sake is not the Son but merely a creature. Moreover, the term *only begotten* would be fictitious and untrue, for how could the Son, if He is one of the creatures, be thought of as the Only Begotten? But since the love of God the Father is incomparable, it follows that the one given for the sake of the world is His one and only Son. For this is what makes the deed so precious, that He is not one of the creatures, but the Only Begotten of the Father.

—CYRIL OF ALEXANDRIA, *Thesaurus on the Trinity*, in *Patrologiae cursus completes*, series graeca, vol. 75, ed. J. P. Migne (Paris: Migne, 1857–1886), 544.

> **John 14:8–11:** Philip said to him, "Lord, show us the Father, and it is enough for us." Jesus said to him, "Have I been with you so long, and you still do not know me, Philip? Whoever has seen me has seen the Father. How can you say, 'Show us the Father'? Do you not believe that I am in the Father and the Father is in me? The words that I say to you I do not speak on my own authority, but the Father who dwells in me does his works. Believe me that I am in the Father and the Father is in me, or else believe on account of the works themselves."

The Son being manifest in the flesh, expresses and utters what was in the heart of all Three.

—THOMAS GOODWIN, *A Discourse of Election*, in *The Works of Thomas Goodwin*, vol. 9 (Grand Rapids, MI: Reformation Heritage, 2006), 148.

They are inseparable in Divine Majesty, for the Father is not without the Son, nor the Son without the Father, nor the Father and Son without the Holy Spirit, nor the Holy Spirit without them. These three Persons are one God in the one and perfect divinity of majesty, and the unity of their divinity is unbreakable; the Divinity cannot be torn apart, for it remains unbreakable, without change. But the Father is declared through the Son, the Son through creation, and the Holy Spirit through the Son incarnate. How? It is the Father who begot the Son before the ages; the Son through whom all things were made by the Father when creatures were created; and the Holy Spirit who, in the likeness of a dove, appeared at the baptism of the Son of God before the end of time.

—HILDEGARD OF BINGEN, *Scivias* (Minneapolis: Paulist Press, 1990), 161–162.

Luke 22:17–20: And he took a cup, and when he had given thanks he said, "Take this, and divide it among yourselves. For I tell you that from now on I will not drink of the fruit of the vine until the kingdom of God comes." And he took bread, and when he had given thanks, he broke it and gave it to them, saying, "This is my body, which is given for you. Do this in remembrance of me." And likewise the cup after they had eaten, saying, "This cup that is poured out for you is the new covenant in my blood."

Concerning the cup, we thank You, our Father, for the holy vine of David Your servant, which you made known to us through Jesus Your Servant. To you be the glory forever. Concerning the broken bread, we thank You, our Father, for the life and knowledge which You made known to us through Jesus Your Servant. To You be the glory forever. Just as this broken bread was scattered over the mountains and was gathered together and became one, so let your church be gathered from the ends of the earth into Your kingdom. Yours is the glory and the power through Jesus Christ forever.

—*THE DIDACHE*, 9:2–4.

Q. What does it mean to eat the crucified body of Christ and to drink His poured-out blood?

A. It means to accept with a believing heart the entire suffering and death of Christ and thereby to receive forgiveness of sins and eternal life.

But it means more. Through the Holy Spirit, who lives both in Christ and in us, we are united more and more to Christ's blessed body. And so, although He is in heaven and we are on earth, we are flesh of His flesh and bone of His bone. And we forever live on and are governed by one Spirit, as the members of our body are by one soul.

—THE HEIDELBERG CATECHISM, Q. and A. 76.

Romans 1:16: For I am not ashamed of the gospel, for it is the power of God for salvation to everyone who believes, to the Jew first and also to the Greek.

Since Christ embraced the cross itself, dare I
His image, th' image of His cross, deny?
Would I have profit by the sacrifice,
And dare the chosen altar to despise?
It bore all other sins, but is it fit
That it should bear the sin of scorning it?
Who from the picture would avert his eye,
How would he fly his pains, who there did die?
From me no pulpit, nor misgrounded law,
Nor scandal taken, shall this cross withdraw,
It shall not, for it cannot; for the loss
Of this cross were to me another cross.
Better were worse, for no affliction,
No cross is so extreme, as to have none.
For when that cross ungrudged unto you sticks,
Then are you to yourself a crucifix.
As perchance carvers do not faces make,
But that away, which hid them there, do take;
Let crosses, so, take what hid Christ in thee,
And be His image, or not His, but He.

—JOHN DONNE, "The Cross," in *Poems of John Donne*, vol. 1,
ed. E. K. Chambers (London: Lawrence & Bullen, 1896), 167–169.

> **Deuteronomy 18:15–19:** "The LORD your God will raise up for you a prophet like me from among you, from your brothers—it is to him you shall listen—just as you desired of the LORD your God at Horeb on the day of the assembly, when you said, 'Let me not hear again the voice of the LORD my God or see this great fire any more, lest I die.' And the LORD said to me, 'They are right in what they have spoken. I will raise up for them a prophet like you from among their brothers. And I will put my words in his mouth, and he shall speak to them all that I command him. And whoever will not listen to my words that he shall speak in my name, I myself will require it of him.'"

When you hear the Gospel, declaring that Jesus Christ was sent to earth by His Father, giving His life as a ransom for many, it ought to be obvious to you that the riches of God and the promise of eternal life are found in Him alone, Jesus Christ whom He has sent, established as the beginning and the end of our salvation.

Christ is seen in Isaac, the beloved son of His father who was offered as a sacrifice but did not succumb to the power of death. He is seen also in Jacob, the watchful shepherd, having great care for His sheep. We see Him in Joseph, the good and compassionate brother, who in His position of power was not ashamed to acknowledge His brothers. He is the great bishop Melchizedek, who offered an eternal sacrifice once for all. He is as the sovereign lawgiver Moses, writing His law on the tables of our hearts by His Spirit. He is as the faithful captain and guide Joshua, leading us to the Promised Land. He is as the victorious and noble king David, by His hand subduing rebellious powers. He is as the magnificent and triumphant king Solomon, governing His kingdom in peace and prosperity. He is as the strong and powerful Samson, by His death overwhelming all His enemies.

And we are by the same Spirit seated among those who are in heaven, so that for us the world is no more, even while we are in it.

This is what we should in short seek in the whole of Scripture: truly to know Jesus Christ, and the infinite riches that are comprised in Him and are offered to us by Him from God the Father. If one were to sift thoroughly the Law and the Prophets, he would not find a single word which would not draw and bring us to Him.

—JOHN CALVIN, *Christ the End of the Law: Being the Preface to the Geneva Bible of 1550*, trans. Thomas Weedon (London: William Tegg & Co., 1850), 28–33.

Psalm 16:5–11:
The LORD is my chosen portion and my cup;
    you hold my lot.
The lines have fallen for me in pleasant places;
    indeed, I have a beautiful inheritance.
I bless the LORD who gives me counsel;
    in the night also my heart instructs me.
I have set the LORD always before me;
    because he is at my right hand, I shall not be shaken.
Therefore my heart is glad, and my whole being rejoices;
    my flesh also dwells secure.
For you will not abandon my soul to Sheol,
    or let your holy one see corruption.
You make known to me the path of life;
    in your presence there is fullness of joy;
    at your right hand are pleasures forevermore.

He had joy, but it was not the shallow joy of mere pagan delight in living, nor the delusive joy of a hope destined to failure, but the deep exultation of a conqueror setting captives free. This joy underlay all His sufferings and shed its light along the whole thorn-strewn path that was trodden by His torn feet. We hear but little of it, however, as we hear but little of His sorrows: the narratives are not given to descriptions of the mental state of the great One whose work they illustrate. We hear just enough of it to assure us of its presence underlying and giving its color to all His life (see Luke 4:21; John 5:11, 27). If our Lord was "the Man of Sorrows," He was more profoundly still "the Man of Joy."

—B. B. WARFIELD, "On the Emotional Life of Our Lord," in *Biblical and Theological Studies* (New York: Charles Scribner's Sons, 1912), 13.

> **John 14:25–26; 15:26:** "These things I have spoken to you while I am still
> with you. But the Helper, the Holy Spirit, whom the Father will send in
> my name, he will teach you all things and bring to your remembrance
> all that I have said to you. . . . But when the Helper comes, whom I will
> send to you from the Father, the Spirit of truth, who proceeds from the
> Father, he will bear witness about me."

But in the case of the divine nature, we learn that whatever the Father
does, the Son joins Him in His work, and that the Son does not have any
special operation apart from the Holy Spirit; but every operation we can
name that extends from God to the creation has its origin from the Father,
proceeds through the Son, and is perfected in the Holy Spirit.

—GREGORY OF NYSSA, *On Not Three Gods*, A Select Library of the Nicene and
Post-Nicene Fathers of the Christian Church, 2nd ser., vol. 5, ed. Philip Schaff and
Henry Wace (Buffalo, NY: Christian Literature 1893), 34.

The Father gives to the Son; and the Son communicates with the Holy
Spirit. For it is Jesus himself, not I, who says, All things are delivered unto
me of my Father." And of the Holy Spirit, He says, "When the Spirit of
Truth shall come, He shall glorify me; for He shall receive of mine, and
shall show it unto you." The Father through the Son, with the Holy Spirit,
bestows all things; the gifts of the Father are none other than those of the
Son, and those of the Holy Spirit, for there is one salvation, one power,
one faith; one God, the Father; one Lord, His Only Begotten Son; One
Holy Spirit, the Comforter. And it is enough for us to know these things;
but enquire not curiously into His nature or substance, for had it been
written, we would have spoken of it; what is not written, let us not venture
into; for it is sufficient for our salvation to know that there is the Father,
the Son, and the Holy Spirit.

—CYRIL OF JERUSALEM, "The Catechetical Lectures of S. Cyril, Archbishop of
Jerusalem," in *A Library of Fathers of the Holy Catholic Church, Anterior to the Divi-
sion of the East and West*, vol. 2, trans. Members of the English Church (Oxford: John
Henry Parker, 1839), 215.

John 14:1: "Let not your hearts be troubled. Believe in God; believe also in me."

We believe in one God,
    the Father Almighty,
    maker of heaven and earth,
    of all things visible and invisible.
And in one Lord Jesus Christ,
    the only Son of God,
    begotten from the Father before all ages,
        God from God,
        Light from Light,
        true God from true God,
    begotten, not made,
    of the same essence as the Father.
    Through Him all things were made.
For us and for our salvation
        He came down from heaven.
        He became incarnate by the Holy Spirit and the Virgin Mary,
        and was made human.
        He was crucified for us under Pontius Pilate.
        He suffered and was buried.
        The third day He rose again, according to the Scriptures.
        He ascended to heaven
        and is seated at the right hand of the Father.
        He will come again with glory
        to judge the living and the dead.
        His kingdom will never end.
And we believe in the Holy Spirit,
    the Lord, the giver of life.
    He proceeds from the Father and the Son,
    and with the Father and the Son is worshiped and glorified.
    He spoke through the prophets.
    We believe in one holy catholic and apostolic church.
    We affirm one baptism for the forgiveness of sins.
    We look forward to the resurrection of the dead,
    and to life in the world to come. Amen.
    —THE NICENE CREED

Romans 11:36–12:1: For from him and through him and to him are all things. To him be glory forever. Amen. I appeal to you therefore, brothers, by the mercies of God, to present your bodies as a living sacrifice, holy and acceptable to God, which is your spiritual worship.

It is you that God entertained thoughts of restoring after your miserable fall into dreadful depravity and corruption, and into danger of the dreadful misery that unavoidably follows upon it.

It is for you, in particular, that God gave His Son; yes, His only Son, and sent Him into the world.

It is for you that the Son of God so freely gave himself.

It is for you that He was born, died, rose again and ascended, and intercedes.

It is to you that the free application of the fruit of these things is made, all done perfectly and altogether freely, without any deserving on your part, without any of your righteousness or strength.

Therefore, let your life be spent in praises to God.

When you praise Him in prayer, let it not be with coldness and indifference.

When you praise Him in your closet, let your whole soul be involved.

When you praise Him in singing, do not merely make a noise, without any stirring of the heart, without any internal melody. Surely, you have reason to shout and cry, "Grace, grace, be the top stone of the temple!"

Certainly, you do not lack mercy and bounty to praise God; you only lack a heart of love to praise Him.

Surely, if the angels are astonished at God's mercy to you, and even they shout with joy and admiration at the sight of God's grace to you, you, on whom this grace is bestowed, have much more reason to shout.

—JONATHAN EDWARDS, "Glorious Grace," in *Sermons and Discourses, 1720–1723,* The Works of Jonathan Edwards, vol. 10, ed. Wilson H. Kimnach (New Haven, CT; London: Yale University Press, 1992), 399.

Acts 4:11–12: "This Jesus is the stone that was rejected by you, the builders, which has become the cornerstone. And there is salvation in no one else, for there is no other name under heaven given among men by which we must be saved."

Q. Why is the Son of God called Jesus, meaning "Savior"?

A. Because He saves us from our sins, and because salvation should not be sought and cannot be found in anyone else.

Q. Do those who look for their salvation in saints, in themselves, or elsewhere really believe in the only Savior, Jesus?

A. No. Although they boast of being His, by their actions they deny the only Savior, Jesus.

Either Jesus is not a perfect Savior, or those who in true faith accept this Savior have in Him all they need for their salvation.

Q. Why do you call Him "Our Lord"?

A. Because—not with gold or silver, but with His precious blood—He has set us free from sin and from the tyranny of the devil, and has bought us, body and soul, to be His very own.

—THE HEIDELBERG CATECHISM, Q. and A. 29, 30, 34.

John 15:13: Greater love has no one than this, that someone lay down his life for his friends.

There is no love so great and so wonderful as that which is in the heart of Christ.

He is one who delights in mercy.

He is ready to pity those who are in suffering and sorrowful circumstances.

He is one who delights in the happiness of His creatures.

The love and grace that Christ has manifested does as much exceed all that which is in this world as the sun is brighter than a candle.

Parents are often full of kindness toward their children, but there is no kindness like that of Jesus Christ.

—JONATHAN EDWARDS, "Children Ought to Love the Lord Jesus Christ Above All (Matthew 10:37)," in *Sermons and Discourses, 1739–1742*, The Works of Jonathan Edwards, vol. 22, ed. Harry S. Stout, Nathan O. Hatch, and Kyle P. Farley (New Haven, CT; London: Yale University Press, 2003), 171.

Luke 9:23–24: And he said to all, "If anyone would come after me, let him deny himself and take up his cross daily and follow me. For whoever would save his life will lose it, but whoever loses his life for my sake will save it."

This self-love of ours so blinds us that we make the smallest faults in the world to be akin to heinous and unpardonable sins. We have this evil so deeply rooted in our hearts that if we are told of our duty, it only half moves us. For this reason, the apostle Paul here sets the example of God before us. He has forgiven us through His only Son. Without delay He sent our Lord Jesus Christ, who spared not himself when it was a question of our redemption and salvation.

What, then, can break down the hardness of our hearts, what can mortify all our excessive passions, what can correct our cruelty, bring low our pride and high-mindedness, and sweeten all our bitterness? It is this: to contemplate what God has done for us. "For God so loved the world, that he gave his only Son, that whoever believes in him should not perish but have eternal life" (John 3:16).

What has moved God to show himself so merciful toward us? Nothing else but our wretchedness and helplessness. Seeing that He who is so good has nevertheless had compassion on the state in which we were plunged, what shall we do?

Ought we not to have more compassion for one another when we find in ourselves that which we pardon in our neighbor? God can find no infirmity in himself; how then can He be moved to forgive us? Because He is the fountain of goodness and mercy.

When I see what grieves me in my neighbor, if I examine myself, I shall find what is similar there, and more. Ought not all these things to lead me to show more compassion and forgiveness?

The way to make it easy for us to forgive many faults and to bear with many vices that may displease us is to fix our eyes upon the inestimable love that God has poured out on us in the person of His Son Jesus Christ.

—JOHN CALVIN, *Sermons on Ephesians*, trans. Arthur Golding (Carlisle, PA: Banner of Truth, 1974), 483–485.

Matthew 17:1-8: And after six days Jesus took with him Peter and James, and John his brother, and led them up a high mountain by themselves. And he was transfigured before them, and his face shone like the sun, and his clothes became white as light. And behold, there appeared to them Moses and Elijah, talking with him. And Peter said to Jesus, "Lord, it is good that we are here. If you wish, I will make three tents here, one for you and one for Moses and one for Elijah." He was still speaking when, behold, a bright cloud overshadowed them, and a voice from the cloud said, "This is my beloved Son, with whom I am well pleased; listen to him." When the disciples heard this, they fell on their faces and were terrified. But Jesus came and touched them, saying, "Rise, and have no fear." And when they lifted up their eyes, they saw no one but Jesus only.

"Jesus only!" In the shadow
Of the cloud so chill and dim
We are clinging, loving, trusting,
He with us, and we with Him
All unseen, though ever nigh
"Jesus only"—all our cry.

"Jesus only!" In the glory,
When the shadows all are flown,
Seeing Him in all His beauty,
Satisfied with Him alone.
May we join His ransomed throng,
"Jesus only!"—all our song!

—FRANCES RIDLEY HAVERGAL, *Under the Surface*
(London: J. Nisbet & Co., 1876), 66–67.

Psalm 24:7–10:
Lift up your heads, O gates!
  And be lifted up, O ancient doors,
  that the King of glory may come in.
Who is this King of glory?
  The LORD, strong and mighty,
  the LORD, mighty in battle!
Lift up your heads, O gates!
  And lift them up, O ancient doors,
  that the King of glory may come in.
Who is this King of glory?
  The LORD of hosts,
  he is the King of glory!

Lord, who created man in wealth and store,
  Though foolishly he lost the same,
    Decaying more and more,
      Till he became
        Most poor:
          With Thee
          O let me rise
        As larks, harmoniously,
      And sing this day Thy victories:
Then shall the fall further the flight in me.

—GEORGE HERBERT, "Easter Wings 1," in *Herbert:
Poems, Everyman Library* (New York: Knopf, 2004), 25.

Christ as the God-man has become the God of providence in whose hand
is the kingdom, to "reign until he has put all his enemies under his feet."
In a word, the term *Lord* seems to have been specifically given to Christ not
because it is a term of function rather than of dignity, but because along
with the dignity it emphasizes function.

—B. B. WARFIELD, *The Works of Benjamin B. Warfield*, vol. 3, (New York: Oxford
University Press, 1927–1932. Reprint, Grand Rapids, MI: Baker, 1981), 274–276.

> **1 Corinthians 8:6:** Yet for us there is one God, the Father, from whom are all things and for whom we exist, and one Lord, Jesus Christ, through whom are all things and through whom we exist.

John points out that all things, whether angels or archangels, thrones or dominions, were established and created by Him who is God over all, through His Word. For when He had spoken of the Word of God as having been in the Father, he added, "All things were made through him, and without him was not any thing made that was made" (John 1:3). David also, when he had listed His praises, adds by name all the things I have mentioned, both the heavens and all the powers therein: "For He commanded and they were created" (Psalm 148:5). Whom, therefore, did He command? The Word, no doubt, by whom, He says, the heavens were established, and all their power by the breath of His mouth. But stating that Christ did himself make all things freely, and as He pleased, again David says, "He has made whatever he pleased."

But the things established are distinct from Him who has established them, and what has been made from Him who has made them. For Christ himself is uncreated, both without beginning and end, and lacking nothing. He is sufficient in himself; and He grants to all others this very thing: existence; but the things that have been made by Him have had a beginning. So that He who made all things can alone, together with His Word, properly be termed God and Lord; but the things that have been made cannot have the same term applied to them, neither do they have a right to assume the name that belongs to the Creator.

—IRENAEUS, *Against Heresies*, in *Ante-Nicene Fathers*, vol. 1, ed. Alexander Roberts, James Donaldson, and A. Cleveland Coxe, trans. Alexander Roberts and William Rambaut (Buffalo, NY: Christian Literature Publishing Co., 1885), 421–422 (*Against Heresies*, 3.8.3).

1 Corinthians 2:2: For I decided to know nothing among you except Jesus Christ and him crucified.

Our faith is a Person. The Gospel that we preach is a Person. And go wherever we may, we have something solid and tangible to preach. If you had asked the twelve disciples, in their day, "What do you believe in?" they would not have needed to go round about with a long reply, but they would have pointed to their Master, and they would have said, "We believe Him."

"But what are your doctrines?" "There they stand incarnate." "But what is your practice?" "There stands our practice. He is our example." "What, then, do you believe?" Hear the glorious answer of the apostle Paul: "We preach Christ crucified."

Our creed, our body of divinity, our whole theology is summed up in the person of Christ Jesus. The apostle preached doctrine; but the doctrine was Christ. He preached practice; but the practice was all in Christ.

—CHARLES H. SPURGEON, C. H. *Spurgeon's Autobiography, vol. 3* (1856–1878).

For Christ alone makes all other doctrines suddenly vanish. Hence there is nothing that Satan so much as endeavors to accomplish as obscuring the view of Christ, because he knows that to do so opens the way to every kind of lie. Thus, the only means of retaining as well as restoring pure doctrine is to place Christ in plain view with all His blessings, that His excellence may be truly perceived.

—JOHN CALVIN, *Commentaries on the Epistles of Paul the Apostle to the Philippians, Colossians, and Thessalonians*, trans. William Pringle (Grand Rapids, MI: Baker, 2003), 145–146.

> **2 Peter 1:10–12:** Therefore, brothers, be all the more diligent to confirm your calling and election, for if you practice these qualities you will never fall. For in this way there will be richly provided for you an entrance into the eternal kingdom of our Lord and Savior Jesus Christ. Therefore I intend always to remind you of these qualities, though you know them and are established in the truth that you have.
>
> **John 12:31–32:** "Now is the judgment of this world; now will the ruler of this world be cast out. And I, when I am lifted up from the earth, will draw all people to myself."

Here is something which is truly important, and something which is basic and fundamental to the whole Christian position. The order in which these things are put is absolutely vital. The apostle does not ask us to do anything until he has first of all emphasized and repeated what God has done for us in Christ.

How often have men given the impression that to be a Christian means that you display in your life a kind of general belief of faith, and then you add to it virtue and knowledge and charity! To them, the Christian message is an exhortation to us to live a certain type of life, and an exhortation to put these things into practice.

But that is an utter travesty of the Gospel. The Christian Gospel in the first place does not ask us to do anything. It first of all proclaims and announces to us what God has done for us.

The first statement of the Gospel is not an exhortation to action or to certain conduct or behavior. Before man is called upon to do anything, he must have received something. Before God calls upon a man to put anything into practice, He has made it possible for man to put it into practice.

—D. MARTYN LLOYD-JONES, *Expository Sermons on 2 Peter* (Carlisle, PA: Banner of Truth, 1983), 23–24.

> **Romans 8:33–34:** Who shall bring any charge against God's elect? It is God who justifies. Who is to condemn? Christ Jesus is the one who died—more than that, who was raised—who is at the right hand of God, who indeed is interceding for us.

From this doctrine our faith derives manifold advantages. First, it perceives that the Lord, by His ascension to heaven, has opened access to the heavenly kingdom, which Adam had shut. For having entered it in our flesh, as it were in our name, it follows, as the apostle says, that we are in a manner now seated in heavenly places, not entertaining a mere hope of heaven, but possessing it by faith. Secondly, faith perceives that His seat beside the Father is not without great advantage to us. Having entered the temple not made with hands, He constantly appears as our advocate and intercessor in the presence of the Father; directs attention to His own righteousness, so as to turn it away from our sins; so reconciles Him to us, as by His intercession to pave for us a way of access to His throne, presenting it to miserable sinners, to whom it would otherwise be an object of dread, as replete with grace and mercy.

Thirdly, it discerns His power, on which depend our strength, might, resources, and triumph over hell, "When he ascended on high he led a host of captives, and he gave gifts to men" (Ephesians 4:8). Spoiling His foes, He gave gifts to His people, and daily loads them with spiritual riches. He thus occupies His exalted seat, that, thence transferring His virtue unto us, He may quicken us to spiritual life, sanctify us by His Spirit, and adorn His Church with various graces, by His protection preserve it safe from all harm, and by the strength of His hand curb the enemies raging against His cross and our salvation; so that He may possess all power in heaven and earth, until He has utterly routed all His foes, who are also ours, and completed the structure of His Church. Such is the true nature of the kingdom, such is the power, which the Father has conferred upon Him, until He arrives to complete the last act by judging the quick and the dead.

—JOHN CALVIN, *Institutes of the Christian Religion*, vol. 1, trans. Henry Beveridge (Edinburgh: The Calvin Translation Society, 1845), 450 (*Institutes*, 2.16.16).

Colossians 1:15-20: He is the image of the invisible God, the firstborn of all creation. For by him all things were created, in heaven and on earth, visible and invisible, whether thrones or dominions or rulers or authorities— all things were created through him and for him. And he is before all things, and in him all things hold together. And he is the head of the body, the church. He is the beginning, the firstborn from the dead, that in everything he might be preeminent. For in him all the fullness of God was pleased to dwell, and through him to reconcile to himself all things, whether on earth or in heaven, making peace by the blood of his cross.

If Christ means anything at all, it is simply and solely because through Him God is revealed, the eternal unchangeable God, in His very being.

> —EMIL BRUNNER, *The Mediator*, trans. Olive Wyon (Philadelphia: Westminster, 1947), 400.

In former times, it was indeed said that humans were made in the image and likeness of God, but no one knew what this meant. For up to this point the Word that humans looked like was invisible, so we could not see God's likeness in humanity. When, however, the Word of God was made flesh, He confirmed both matters: He showed us the true image, becoming that which was His image, and He strengthened and restored the likeness, making humans like the invisible Father through the visible Word.

> —IRENAEUS, *Against Heresies*, in *Ante-Nicene Fathers*, vol. 1, ed. Alexander Roberts, James Donaldson, and A. Cleveland Coxe, trans. Alexander Roberts and William Rambaut (Buffalo, NY: Christian Literature Publishing Co., 1885), 544 (*Against Heresies*, 5.16.2).

> **Galatians 2:17-21:** But if, in our endeavor to be justified in Christ, we too were found to be sinners, is Christ then a servant of sin? Certainly not! For if I rebuild what I tore down, I prove myself to be a transgressor. For through the law I died to the law, so that I might live to God. I have been crucified with Christ. It is no longer I who live, but Christ who lives in me. And the life I now live in the flesh I live by faith in the Son of God, who loved me and gave himself for me. I do not nullify the grace of God, for if righteousness were through the law, then Christ died for no purpose.

The manger and the cross are never far apart.

—MARTIN LUTHER, quoted in Roland H. Bainton, *Martin Luther's Christmas Book* (Minneapolis: Augsburg Publishing House, 1997), 5.

Begin where Christ began—in the womb of the Virgin, in the manger, at His mother's breast. For this purpose He came down, was born, lived among men, suffered, was crucified, and died, so that in every way possible He might present himself to our sight. He wanted us to fix the gaze of our hearts upon himself and thus to prevent us from endeavoring to reach heaven on our own and from our random speculating about the Divine Majesty.

Whenever you consider the doctrine of justification and wonder how or where or in what condition to find a God who justifies or accepts sinners, then you must know that there is no other God besides this Man Jesus Christ. Embrace Him, cleave to Him with your whole heart, setting aside all speculations about the Divine Majesty: For he that is a searcher of God's majesty shall be overwhelmed by His glory.

—MARTIN LUTHER, *Commentary on Galatians* (London: James Duncan, 1830), 15.

> **Romans 5:6–8:** For while we were still weak, at the right time Christ died for the ungodly. For one will scarcely die for a righteous person—though perhaps for a good person one would dare even to die—but God shows his love for us in that while we were still sinners, Christ died for us.

The very point of the Christian view of the cross is that God does not wait for someone else to pay the price of sin, but in His infinite love has himself paid the price for us—God himself, in the person of the Son, loved us and gave himself for us; God himself, in the person of the Father, who so loved the world that He gave His Only Begotten Son.

It is a strange thing that when people talk about the love of God, they show by every word they utter that they have no concept of the depth of God's love.

If you want to find an instance of true gratitude for the infinite grace of God, do not go to those who think of God's love as something that cost nothing, but go rather to those who in agony of soul have faced the awful fact of the guilt of sin, and then have come to know with a trembling wonder that the miracle of all miracles has been accomplished, and that the eternal Son has died in their stead.

—J. GRESHAM MACHEN, "What the Bible Teaches About Jesus," in *Selected Shorter Writings*, ed. D. G. Hart (Phillipsburg: Presbyterian and Reformed, 2004), 31–32.

> **1 Corinthians 3:21–23:** So let no one boast in men. For all things are yours, whether Paul or Apollos or Cephas or the world or life or death or the present or the future—all are yours, and you are Christ's, and Christ is God's.

By virtue of the believer's union with Christ, he really does possess all things. That we know plainly from Scripture. But it may be asked, how does he possess all things? And what does he gain from it? How is a true Christian so much richer than other men?

To answer this, I will tell you what I mean by possessing all things. God is Three-in-One, Father, Son, and Holy Spirit. All that He is, and all that He has, and all that He does and has done, includes the whole universe: earth and heaven, angels, sun, moon, and stars, land and sea, humankind and animals, all the silver and gold—belong to the Christian as much as the money in his pocket, the clothes on his back, the house he lives in, and the food he eats; yes, more properly his, more advantageously his, than if he could command all things mentioned to be available as he pleased at any time, but by virtue of his union with Christ, who does possess all things, so he possesses it all. It is all his.

—JONATHAN EDWARDS, "Union with Christ," in *The "Miscellanies": Entry nos. a-z, aa-zz, 1–500*, The Works of Jonathan Edwards, vol. 13, ed. Harry S. Stout (New Haven, CT: Yale University Press, 1994), 183–184.

Ephesians 3:14–19: For this reason I bow my knees before the Father, from whom every family in heaven and on earth is named, that according to the riches of his glory he may grant you to be strengthened with power through his Spirit in your inner being, so that Christ may dwell in your hearts through faith—that you, being rooted and grounded in love, may have strength to comprehend with all the saints what is the breadth and length and height and depth, and to know the love of Christ that surpasses knowledge, that you may be filled with all the fullness of God.

Let us adore Him for His great love, the love that has a height, and depth, and length, and breadth, beyond the grasp of our poor understanding:

> a love that moved Him to empty himself, to take on the form of a servant, and to be obedient unto death, even the death of the cross;
>
> a love that pitied us in our lost condition, that found us when we did not seek Him, that spoke peace to our souls in the day of our distress;
>
> a love that bears with all our present weaknesses, mistakes, backslidings, and shortcomings;
>
> a love that is always watchful, always ready to guide, to comfort, and to heal;
>
> a love that will not be wearied, cannot be conquered, and is incapable of change;
>
> a love that will, in the end, prevail over all opposition, will perfect that which concerns us, and will not leave us until it has brought us perfect in holiness and happiness, to rejoice in His presence in glory.

The love of Christ: it is the wonder, the joy, the song of angels. And the sense of it shed abroad in our hearts makes life pleasant and death welcome.

—JOHN NEWTON, *The Works of John Newton*, vol. 2, ed. Richard Cecil (London: Hamilton, Adams & Co., 1824), 179–181.

Hebrews 1:1–3, 5–6: Long ago, at many times and in many ways, God spoke to our fathers by the prophets, but in these last days he has spoken to us by his Son, whom he appointed the heir of all things, through whom also he created the world. He is the radiance of the glory of God and the exact imprint of his nature, and he upholds the universe by the word of his power. After making purification for sins, he sat down at the right hand of the Majesty on high. . . . For to which of the angels did God ever say, "You are my Son, today I have begotten you"? Or again, "I will be to him a father, and he shall be to me a son"? And again, when he brings the firstborn into the world, he says, "Let all God's angels worship him."

Q. Why is He called God's Only Begotten Son when we also are God's children?

A. Because Christ alone is the eternal, natural Son of God. We, however, are adopted children of God—adopted by grace through Christ.

Q. What does it mean that He "was conceived by the Holy Spirit and born of the Virgin Mary"?

A. That the eternal Son of God, who is and remains true and eternal God, took to himself, through the working of the Holy Spirit, from the flesh and blood of the Virgin Mary, a truly human nature so that He might also become David's true descendant, like His brothers and sisters in every way except for sin.

Q. How does the holy conception and birth of Christ benefit you?

A. He is our Mediator, and in God's sight He covers with His innocence and perfect holiness my sinfulness in which I was conceived.

—THE HEIDELBERG CATECHISM, Q. and A. 33, 35, 36.

Philippians 2:5-8: Have this mind among yourselves, which is yours in Christ Jesus, who, though he was in the form of God, did not count equality with God a thing to be grasped, but emptied himself, by taking the form of a servant, being born in the likeness of men. And being found in human form, he humbled himself by becoming obedient to the point of death, even death on a cross.

The Gospel leads us to love Christ as the crucified Savior. He is the Savior and Lord who suffered the greatest humilities, was put to the most humiliating death, even though He was the Lord of glory.

This, in many ways, teaches His followers humility and leads them to a humble love of Christ.

For by God's sending His Son into the world to suffer such a humiliating death, He did, as it were, pour contempt on all the earthly glory that men tend to be proud of, in that He gave His Son, the Head of all the elect, to appear in circumstances so far from earthly glory, circumstances of the greatest earthly humility.

Hereby the humbling of God appeared, and hereby Christ, above all others, showed His humility in that He was willing to be abased, and in humbling himself became obedient to the point of death, even death on a cross. And hereby Christ our Lord and Master showed His contempt of earthly glory, and those things upon which men pride themselves.

If we therefore conduct ourselves as the followers of the crucified Christ, we shall walk humbly before God and men all the days of our lives.

—JONATHAN EDWARDS, *Charity and Its Fruits*, in *Ethical Writings*, The Works of Jonathan Edwards, vol. 8, ed. Paul Ramsey (New Haven, CT: Yale University Press, 1749/1989), 247–248.

> **Matthew 9:2-7:** And behold, some people brought to him a paralytic, lying on a bed. And when Jesus saw their faith, he said to the paralytic, "Take heart, my son; your sins are forgiven." And behold, some of the scribes said to themselves, "This man is blaspheming." But Jesus, knowing their thoughts, said, "Why do you think evil in your hearts? For which is easier, to say, 'Your sins are forgiven,' or to say, 'Rise and walk'? But that you may know that the Son of Man has authority on earth to forgive sins"—he then said to the paralytic, "Rise, pick up your bed and go home." And he rose and went home.

That Christ is the very God, it is manifestly declared, in that Paul attributes equally unto Him that which he attributes to the Father; namely, divine power, as the giving of grace, the forgiveness of sins, peace of conscience, eternal life, victory over sin, death, the devil, and hell.

This would not be lawful for him to do, even sacrilege, except that Christ were very God. Again, no man gives to others what he himself does not have to give. But seeing that Christ gives grace, peace, and the Holy Spirit, delivers from the power of the devil, sin, and death, it is certain that He has infinite and divine power, equal in all points to the power of the Father. Neither does Christ give grace and peace, as the apostles gave and brought the same unto men by preaching the Gospel; but He gives as Author and Creator. The Father created and gives life, grace, peace, and all other good things. The self-same things the Son creates and gives. To give grace, peace, everlasting life; to forgive sins, to make righteous, to quicken, to deliver from death and the devil, are not the works of any creature, but of the Divine Majesty alone. The angels can neither create nor give these things; therefore, these works pertain only to the glory of the Sovereign Majesty, the Maker of all things: and seeing Paul attributes the self-same power of creating and giving all these things unto Christ equally with the Father, it must follow that Christ is verily and naturally God.

—MARTIN LUTHER, *Commentary on Galatians* (London: James Duncan, 1830), 17–18.

John 11:32–36: Now when Mary came to where Jesus was and saw him, she fell at his feet, saying to him, "Lord, if you had been here, my brother would not have died." When Jesus saw her weeping, and the Jews who had come with her also weeping, he was deeply moved in his spirit and greatly troubled. And he said, "Where have you laid him?" They said to him, "Lord, come and see." Jesus wept. So the Jews said, "See how he loved him!"

When Christ saw the people in misery, His bowels yearned within Him; the works of grace and mercy in Christ came from His bowels first. Whatsoever Christ did, He did it out of love, grace, and mercy—from His very bowels.

—RICHARD SIBBES, "The Church's Riches by Christ's Poverty," in *The Works of Richard Sibbes*, vol. 4, ed. Alexander Balloch Grosart (Edinburgh: Banner of Truth, 1983), 523.

Jesus wept with those who wept. And it was compassion that brought Him into the world and induced Him not only to shed tears but to shed His blood.

He poured out His blood as water on the earth, out of compassion to the poor, miserable children of men.

We do not read of anyone who, when Christ was on earth, came to Him with a heavy heart or under any kind of sorrow or distress, who was not met with kindness and compassion.

He has the same compassion now after He ascended into glory. There is still the same encouragement for the bereaved to go to Him and lay their sorrows before Him.

Afflicted persons tend to speak of their sorrows to those who have experienced affliction and know what sorrow is. But there is none on earth or in heaven that has ever experienced the sorrow of Christ.

Therefore, He knows how to comfort the sorrowful. Christ is fully able to give the help that is needed for the problem presented. His power and His wisdom are sufficient, His compassion unfailing.

—JONATHAN EDWARDS, "The Sorrows of the Bereaved Spread Before Jesus," in *The Works of Jonathan Edwards*, vol. 2, ed. Edward Hickman (Carlisle, PA: Banner of Truth, 1834/1998), 966–967.

John 6:32–35: Jesus then said to them, "Truly, truly, I say to you, it was not Moses who gave you the bread from heaven, but my Father gives you the true bread from heaven. For the bread of God is he who comes down from heaven and gives life to the world." They said to him, "Sir, give us this bread always." Jesus said to them, "I am the bread of life; whoever comes to me shall not hunger, and whoever believes in me shall never thirst."

We may taste that the Lord is gracious; but if we do not find a longing for it in our hearts, we will not be able to hold on to it in our minds. Christ is the meat, the bread, the food of our souls. Nothing is in Him of a higher spiritual nourishment than His love, which we should always desire. In this love He is glorious.

—JOHN OWEN, "Meditations and Discourses Concerning the Glory of Christ," in *The Works of John Owen*, vol. 1, ed. William Goold (Edinburgh: Banner of Truth, 1965), 338.

Cast your eyes among all created beings, survey the universe, observe strength in one thing, beauty in a second, faithfulness in a third, wisdom in a fourth; but you shall find none greater than Jesus Christ. He is bread to the hungry, water to the thirsty, a garment to the naked, healing to the wounded. Whatever the soul desires is found in Him. He is "wisdom from God, righteousness and sanctification and redemption" (1 Corinthians 1:30).

—JOHN FLAVEL, *The Whole Works of the Reverend John Flavel*, vol. 2 (London; Edinburgh; Dublin: W. Baynes and Son; Waugh and Innes; M. Keene, 1820), 216.

Matthew 26:36–39: Then Jesus went with them to a place called Gethsemane, and he said to his disciples, "Sit here, while I go over there and pray." And taking with him Peter and the two sons of Zebedee, he began to be sorrowful and troubled. Then he said to them, "My soul is very sorrowful, even to death; remain here, and watch with me." And going a little farther he fell on his face and prayed, saying, "My Father, if it be possible, let this cup pass from me; nevertheless, not as I will, but as you will."

In these crucial moments, our Lord expressed the ultimate depths of human anguish, and by the intensity of His mental suffering, owned the right to the title Man of Sorrows. The scope of His suffering was broad, embracing the series of painful emotions that run from consternation and dismay, through despondency, which is almost despair, to a sense of complete desolation. In view of this mental anguish, the physical torture of the crucifixion retires into the background, and we may well believe that our Lord, though He died on the cross, yet died of a broken heart.

And through His agony, His demeanor to His disciples, His enemies, His judges, and His executioners was instinctive with calm self-mastery. The cup that was put to His lips was bitter: None of its bitterness was lost to Him as He drank it, but He drank it as His own cup, which was His own will, because it was His Father's will, to drink. "Shall I not drink the cup that the Father has given me?" (John 18:11). It was in this spirit, not of unwilling subjection to unavoidable evil, but of voluntary endurance of unutterable anguish for adequate ends, that He passed into and through all His sufferings. His very passion was His own action. He had power to lay down His life, and it was by His own power that He laid it down, and by His own power that He trod the whole pathway of suffering that led to the actual laying down of His life. Nowhere is He the victim of circumstances or the helpless sufferer. Everywhere and always, it is He who possesses the mastery both of circumstances and of himself.

—B. B. WARFIELD, "On the Emotional Life of Our Lord," in *Biblical and Theological Studies* (New York: Charles Scribner's 1912), 15.

Psalm 116:5–6: Gracious is the LORD, and righteous; our God is merciful. The LORD preserves the simple; when I was brought low, he saved me.

In Jesus Christ, infinite highness and infinite lowness meet. Christ, as He is God, is infinitely great and high above all. He is higher than the kings of the earth, for He is King of kings, and Lord of lords. He is higher than the heavens, and higher than the highest angels of heaven.

So great is He that all men, all kings and princes, are as worms of the dust before Him; all nations are as a drop in the bucket; even the angels are as nothing before Him.

He is so high that He is infinitely above any need of ours; above our reach, and above our conception, so that we cannot understand Him (see Proverbs 30:4).

He is sovereign Lord of all. He rules over the whole universe and does whatever pleases Him. His knowledge is without bounds. His wisdom is perfect, and none can outthink Him. His power is infinite, and none can resist Him. His riches are immense and inexhaustible. His majesty is without measure.

And yet He is of infinite humility. No one is so low or inferior, but that Christ's humility is gracious to them.

He condescends not only to the angels, humbling himself to behold the things that are done in heaven, but He also condescends to such poor creatures as men, and that not only to take notice of princes and kings, but those also of lowest rank and degree.

"God chose what is low and despised in the world, even things that are not, to bring to nothing things that are" (1 Corinthians 1:28).

—JONATHAN EDWARDS, "The Excellency of Christ," in *The Works of Jonathan Edwards*, vol. 1, ed. Edward Hickman (Carlisle, PA: Banner of Truth, 1834/1998), 680–681.

> **John 11:21–27:** Martha said to Jesus, "Lord, if you had been here, my brother would not have died. But even now I know that whatever you ask from God, God will give you." Jesus said to her, "Your brother will rise again." Martha said to him, "I know that he will rise again in the resurrection on the last day." Jesus said to her, "I am the resurrection and the life. Whoever believes in me, though he die, yet shall he live, and everyone who lives and believes in me shall never die. Do you believe this?" She said to him, "Yes, Lord; I believe that you are the Christ, the Son of God, who is coming into the world."

Christ's death is the Christian's life. Christ's cross is the Christian's title to heaven. Christ lifted up and put to shame on Calvary is the ladder by which Christians enter into the holiest and are at length landed in glory.

It is true that we are sinners—but Christ has suffered for us.

It is true that we deserve death—but Christ has died for us.

It is true that we are guilty debtors—but Christ has paid our debts with His own blood.

This is the real Gospel! This is the good news! On this let us lean while we live.

To this let us cling when we die. Christ has been lifted up on the cross, and has thrown open the gates of heaven to all believers.

—J. C. RYLE, *Expository Thoughts on John*, vol. 1 (Carlisle, PA: Banner of Truth, 1869/2012), 141–143.

> **Psalm 103:10–12:**
> He does not deal with us according to our sins,
>   nor repay us according to our iniquities.
> For as high as the heavens are above the earth,
>   so great is his steadfast love toward those who fear him;
> as far as the east is from the west,
>   so far does he remove our transgressions from us.

I take refuge in Christ, who has given himself for my sins; therefore, Satan, you shall not prevail against me, or go about terrifying me, by setting forth the greatness of my sins, and so bring upon me heaviness, distrust, despair, hatred, contempt, and even blasphemy of God. By saying I am a sinner, you give me armor and weapons against you, so that with your own sword I may cut your throat, for you put me in mind of God's love toward me, a wretched and damned sinner: "For God so loved the world, that he gave his only Son, that whoever believes in him should not perish but have eternal life" (John 3:16). And as often as you point out that I am a sinner, you call to my remembrance the benefit of Christ my Redeemer, upon whose shoulders, and not my own, lie all my sins, for "The LORD has laid on him the iniquity of us all" (Isaiah 53:6). Therefore, when you say I am a sinner, you do not terrify me, but comfort me above measure.

Whoever knows these truths shall easily avoid all the snares of the devil, who, by putting man in mind of his sins, drives him to despair and destroys him, unless he withstands him with these truths, and this heavenly wisdom, whereby sin, death, and the devil are overcome. But the man who does not put away the remembrance of his sins, but keeps it still, and torments himself with his own imaginings, thinking either to help himself by his own strength or to delay the time until his conscience may be quieted, falls into Satan's snares, miserably afflicts himself, and at length is overcome with temptation, for the devil will never cease to accuse his conscience. This sly serpent knows how to present Jesus Christ, our Mediator and Savior, as a lawgiver, judge, and condemner.

—MARTIN LUTHER, *Commentary on Galatians* (London: James Duncan, 1830), 22–24.

1 Timothy 1:15–17: The saying is trustworthy and deserving of full acceptance, that Christ Jesus came into the world to save sinners, of whom I am the foremost. But I received mercy for this reason, that in me, as the foremost, Jesus Christ might display his perfect patience as an example to those who were to believe in him for eternal life. To the King of the ages, immortal, invisible, the only God, be honor and glory forever and ever. Amen.

I believe that Jesus Christ is the chief among ten thousand; that He came into the world to save the chief of sinners, by making an atonement for sin by His death, by being perfectly obedient to the law on our behalf; that He is now exalted on high to give repentance and remission of sins to all that believe; and that He lives forever to make intercession for us.

—JOHN NEWTON, *Letters of John Newton* (Carlisle, PA: Banner of Truth Trust, 1869/2007), 21.

I know that He died for me; for had He been pleased to destroy me (it would have been just if He had), He would not have shown me such things as these.

I know that I am His child because He teaches me to say, "Abba, Father."

I know that I am His because He has enabled me to choose Him for myself. For such a choice and desire could never have taken place in my heart if He had not placed it there himself.

By nature, I was too blind to know Him, too proud to trust Him, too obstinate to serve Him, too base-minded to love Him. The enmity I was filled with against His government, righteousness, and grace was too strong to be subdued by any power but His own.

The love I have for Him is but a faint and feeble spark, but it is an emanation from himself.

He kindled it, and He keeps it alive.

And because it is His work, I trust that many waters shall not quench it.

—JOHN NEWTON, *The Works of John Newton*, vol. 1 (London: Hamilton, Adams & Co., 1824), 643–644.

Galatians 3:13–14: Christ redeemed us from the curse of the law by becoming a curse for us—for it is written, "Cursed is everyone who is hanged on a tree"— so that in Christ Jesus the blessing of Abraham might come to the Gentiles, so that we might receive the promised Spirit through faith.

God does not show mercy as a judge, but as a sovereign. Therefore, when He in His mercy sought the salvation of sinners, the question was how to make an agreement between the exercise of the mercy of God as a sovereign, and of His strict justice as a judge. And this was done by the sufferings of Christ, in which sin was punished fully and the justice of God answered. Christ suffered enough for the punishment of the sins of the greatest sinner that ever lived. So that God, when He judges, may act according to a rule of strict justice and yet acquit the sinner, if he is in Christ. Justice cannot require any more for any man's sin than the sufferings of one of the persons of the Trinity, which Christ suffered.

—JONATHAN EDWARDS, *Sinners in the Hands of an Angry God and Other Writings* (Thomas Nelson Inc., 2000), 47.

It is in this way, as the One who himself suffers judgment, that He becomes our Judge. It is in this way that He places our faith in question, taking it away, disregarding it as our own work. For what remains of our faith when we hear Him cry, "My God, my God, why hast thou forsaken me?" If the Son of God can confirm faith only by allowing it to be taken from Him, what can this mean for us but the revelation that our faith, as our own work, is a lost work? Yet it is not we, but Jesus Christ who has borne the turning away of God's face, and our own responsibility can only be to acknowledge it as borne by Him, and to accept its validity against all the claims of our own work.

—KARL BARTH, *Church Dogmatics*, vol. 2, pt. 1, ed. G. W. Bromiley and T. F. Torrance, trans. T. H. L. Parker and J. L. M. Haire (London: T&T Clark, 2004), 253.

Matthew 22:34–46: But when the Pharisees heard that he had silenced the Sadducees, they gathered together. And one of them, a lawyer, asked him a question to test him. "Teacher, which is the great commandment in the Law?" And he said to him, "You shall love the Lord your God with all your heart and with all your soul and with all your mind. This is the great and first commandment. And a second is like it: You shall love your neighbor as yourself. On these two commandments depend all the Law and the Prophets." Now while the Pharisees were gathered together, Jesus asked them a question, saying, "What do you think about the Christ? Whose son is he?" They said to him, "The son of David." He said to them, "How is it then that David, in the Spirit, calls him Lord, saying,

"'The Lord said to my Lord,
"Sit at my right hand,
"until I put your enemies under your feet"'?

"If then David calls him Lord, how is he his son?" And no one was able to answer him a word, nor from that day did anyone dare to ask him any more questions.

With the scribes our Lord debated. Clothed in their Scripture, He cast them down in controversy. With the breastplate of truth, the Psalms, He was girded. He questioned them and was questioned, and victorious was He whose shield was the Torah, and Isaiah His sword and spear, and the prophets the arrows for His bow. His names silently renounce the Stranger, for Jesus is Messiah, and our Lord and our God.

—EPHREM THE SYRIAN, *Hymns on Virginity*, in *Hymns*, trans. Kathleen McVey (New York: Paulist Press, 1989), 426.

> **Mark 8:27–29:** And Jesus went on with his disciples to the villages of Cae-
> sarea Philippi. And on the way he asked his disciples, "Who do people say
> that I am?" And they told him, "John the Baptist; and others say, Elijah;
> and others, one of the prophets." And he asked them, "But who do you
> say that I am?" Peter answered him, "You are the Christ."

Christ is the one and only Son of God, not two: yet in two respects He is the Son of God. As He is the eternal Word, He is by nature the Son of the Father. As He is a man, the same Son also, yet not by nature, or by adoption, but only by personal union: "And the angel answered her, 'The Holy Spirit will come upon you, and the power of the Most High will overshadow you; therefore the child to be born will be called holy—the Son of God'" (Luke 1:35). "This is my beloved Son . . ." (Matthew 3:17). This phrase in Scripture, agreeing to this Union, is the communion of properties, which is a true and real claim, even as far as it arises of the true and real union of natures.

—WILLIAM PERKINS, *A Golden Chain*, in *The Works of William Perkins*, vol. 6, ed. Joel R. Beeke and Derek W. H. Thomas (Grand Rapids, MI: Reformation Heritage Books, 2018), chap. 16 "On the Distinction of Both Natures."

"Who do people say that I am?" He asks. The reason for this acknowledging himself as Son of Man here is to prevent their thinking that He is asking them about what cannot be seen. They answer: "John the Baptist, Elijah, one of the prophets (Jeremiah.)" And again, "But who do you say that I am?" "You are the Christ," says Peter. And at once He blesses him. You see, He was not asking in ignorance, but wished to show that the teaching that proclaims the true Son to the church is from the Father. His purpose was to press Peter into saying what he had learned from the Father.

—EPIPHANIUS, *Anacoratus*, in *Patrologiae cursus completes*, series graeca, vol. 43, ed. J. P. Migne (Paris: Migne, 1857–1886), 88.

John 5:43–47: "I have come in my Father's name, and you do not receive me. If another comes in his own name, you will receive him. How can you believe, when you receive glory from one another and do not seek the glory that comes from the only God? Do not think that I will accuse you to the Father. There is one who accuses you: Moses, on whom you have set your hope. For if you believed Moses, you would believe me; for he wrote of me. But if you do not believe his writings, how will you believe my words?"

It is now the proper time to show that the very name of Jesus, as also that of Christ, was honored by the prophets of old. Moses himself was the first to declare the glorious title of the "Christ," delivering types and images, according to the oracle of God that declared to him, "See that you make everything according to the pattern that was shown you on the mountain" (Hebrews 8:5)—the same man whom, when blessing a high priest of God, expected him to represent Christ. And in this way, the dignity of the priesthood surpasses all superiority among men, with the additional honor and glory that he attaches to the name of Christ. Only Christ being, of course, a divine being.

—EUSEBIUS, *The Ecclesiastical History of Eusebius Pamphilus, Bishop of Cesarea, in Palestine*, trans. Christian Frederick Crusé (Philadelphia: J. B. Lippincott & Co., 1860), 21–22.

> **Matthew 4:8–11:** Again, the devil took him to a very high mountain and showed him all the kingdoms of the world and their glory. And he said to him, "All these I will give you, if you will fall down and worship me." Then Jesus said to him, "Be gone, Satan! For it is written,
>
> "'You shall worship the Lord your God
> and him only shall you serve.'"
>
> Then the devil left him, and behold, angels came and were ministering to him.

Christian doctrine teaches us how Christ came into the world to deliver us from the fruits of Satan's envy toward us. The devil, being miserable himself, was envious of humankind's happiness and could not bear to see our first parents in their happy state in Eden, and therefore tried his best to ruin them, and he accomplished it. The Gospel teaches how Christ came into the world to destroy the works of the devil and deliver us from the misery that his envy has brought us.

—JONATHAN EDWARDS, *Charity and Its Fruits*, in *Ethical Writings*, The Works of Jonathan Edwards, vol. 8, ed. Paul Ramsey (New Haven, CT: Yale University Press, 1749/1989), 224.

The heart cannot be troubled except with the weapons of food, riches, or glory and in a word, a human being cannot succumb to the devil unless he has been wounded beforehand by one of these assailants. Therefore, it was these three arguments that the devil brought before the Savior. First, he urged Him to turn the stones into bread, then he promised Him the whole world if He would just fall down and worship him, and third, he said that if He would pay heed to him, He would be glorified by receiving no injury from such a fall. The Lord, showing himself greater than these things, commanded the devil to get behind Him, teaching us through this, that unless we refute these three arguments, it is not possible to drive away the devil.

—EVAGRIUS OF PONTUS, *On Thoughts*, in *Sources Chrétiennes*, vol. 438, ed. H. de Lubac, J. Daniélou, and C. Mondésert (Paris: Editions du Cerf, 1941, 1998), 150, 152.

> **1 Peter 1:3, 6–7:** Blessed be the God and Father of our Lord Jesus Christ! According to his great mercy, he has caused us to be born again to a living hope through the resurrection of Jesus Christ from the dead.... In this you rejoice, though now for a little while, if necessary, you have been grieved by various trials, so that the tested genuineness of your faith—more precious than gold that perishes though it is tested by fire—may be found to result in praise and glory and honor at the revelation of Jesus Christ.

Christmas Day

Because You have given Jesus Christ Your only Son to be born on this day for us, who by the operation of the Holy Spirit was made man through the Virgin Mary, His mother, and that without sin, to make us clean from all sin.

Easter Day

We are chiefly bound to praise You for the glorious resurrection of Your Son Jesus Christ our Lord, for He is the Passover Lamb who was offered for us, and has taken away the sin of the world, who by His death has destroyed death, and by His rising to life again has restored to us everlasting life.

Ascension

Through Your dear beloved Son, Jesus Christ our Lord, who after His most glorious resurrection appeared to all His apostles, and in their sight ascended into heaven to prepare a place for us, that where He is, henceforth might we also ascend and reign with Him in glory.

—SCOTT H. HENDRIX AND BERNARD MCGINN, ed., *Early Protestant Spirituality*, trans. Scott H. Hendrix, *The Classics of Western Spirituality* (New York; Mahwah, NJ: Paulist Press, 2009), 297.

1 Corinthians 11:26–29: For as often as you eat this bread and drink the cup, you proclaim the Lord's death until he comes. Whoever, therefore, eats the bread or drinks the cup of the Lord in an unworthy manner will be guilty concerning the body and blood of the Lord. Let a person examine himself, then, and so eat of the bread and drink of the cup. For anyone who eats and drinks without discerning the body eats and drinks judgment on himself.

Almighty God, our heavenly Father, who by Your tender mercies gave Your Only Begotten Son Jesus Christ to suffer death upon the cross for our redemption, who made by the offering of himself a full, perfect, and sufficient sacrifice and satisfaction for the sins of the whole world. And through His holy Gospel commands us to continue the perpetual memory of His precious death, until His coming again. Hear us, O merciful Father, we beseech You, and grant that we Your creatures, receiving the bread and wine, according to Your Son our Savior Jesus Christ's holy institution, and in remembrance of His death and passion, may be partakers of His most blessed body and blood. Who in the same night that He was betrayed, took bread, and when He had given thanks, broke it, and gave it to His disciples, saying: "Take, eat, this is my body which is given for you; do this in remembrance of me." Likewise, after supper He took the cup, and when He had given thanks, He gave it to them, saying, "Drink all of this, for this is my blood of the New Testament, which is shed for you and for many, for the remission of sins: Do this as often as you drink it in remembrance of me."

—CONSECRATION PRAYER OF THE EUCHARIST, *Book of Common Prayer*,
in Scott H. Hendrix and Bernard McGinn, ed., *Early Protestant Spirituality*, trans.
Scott H. Hendrix, The Classics of Western Spirituality (New York; Mahwah, NJ: Paulist Press, 2009), 299.

Romans 6:3–8: Do you not know that all of us who have been baptized into Christ Jesus were baptized into his death? We were buried therefore with him by baptism into death, in order that, just as Christ was raised from the dead by the glory of the Father, we too might walk in newness of life. For if we have been united with him in a death like his, we shall certainly be united with him in a resurrection like his. We know that our old self was crucified with him in order that the body of sin might be brought to nothing, so that we would no longer be enslaved to sin. For one who has died has been set free from sin. Now if we have died with Christ, we believe that we will also live with him.

The good Lord healed this twofold death of ours through His single bodily death, and through the one resurrection of His body He gave us a twofold resurrection. By means of His bodily death, He destroyed him who had the power over our souls and bodies in death and rescued us from his tyranny over both.

—GREGORY OF PALAMAS, *The Homilies of St. Gregory Palamas*, ed. Christopher Veniarmin (South Canaan, PA: Saint Tikhon's Seminary, 2004), 197.

Christ's baptism prefigured our own, and by this means He freed himself from the obligations of the Law. He gave a practical demonstration of the Gospel, chose His disciples, inaugurated the teaching of a new doctrine, and revealed the way of a new life, different from that which the Law requires, and consistent with His doctrine. He taught that we should conduct ourselves accordingly toward our fellow believers because we also, once baptized, present before others a prophetic picture of the world to come. We die with Him in baptism, and our resurrection is modeled after His.

—THEODORE OF MOPSUESTIA, "Catechetical Homily," in *Les homélies catéché-tiques de Théodore de Mopsueste: reproduction phototypique du ms. Mingana* Syr. 561, ed. Raymond Tonneau and Robert Deveresse (Birmingham, AL: Selly Oak Colleges' Library, 1949), *Vatican City: Biblioteca Apostolica Vaticana*, 153.

> **Revelation 12:9–10:** And the great dragon was thrown down, that ancient serpent, who is called the devil and Satan, the deceiver of the whole world—he was thrown down to the earth, and his angels were thrown down with him. And I heard a loud voice in heaven, saying, "Now the salvation and the power and the kingdom of our God and the authority of his Christ have come, for the accuser of our brothers has been thrown down, who accuses them day and night before our God."

Christ, seeing that the heavenly portion He had deposited in the human body was being devoured by the evil that consumes the soul, and seeing the Evil One rule over human beings, in order to raise up His own, no longer left the care of human corruption to other physicians. Rather, He emptied himself of the glory He shares with God, His Father, born without a human father. Yet He was no stranger, since it was because of you and me that this immortal One came in mortal form, born through His virgin mother, that in His wholeness He might save us wholly.

Adam had fallen through the sinful tasting of the forbidden fruit. And for this reason, Christ took on flesh and came as both God and mortal, bringing together into one entity two natures, the one concealed, the other obvious to other humans. But when He had been heralded by the great light at His birth, and preceded in His teaching by John the Baptist, proclaiming Christ in the midst of the wilderness, He was revealed to those who were far off and those who were near, a cornerstone joining both. He bestowed on mortals the twofold cleansing of His blood and of the Spirit. For the blood of Christ my Lord was poured out, a payment for primal ills, a recompense for sins in the flesh. If I had not been a mutable, mortal man, all I should have needed was the command of God to care for me, save me, and exalt me to great honor. But as it is, God did not create you or me as gods, but rather as unstable beings prone to lean either way.

—GREGORY OF NAZIANZUS, "On the Testaments of the Coming Christ," in *St. Gregory of Nazianzus: Poemata Arcana*, trans. D. A. Sykes (Oxford: Clarendon Press, 1967), 42–46.

John 1:12–13: But to all who did receive him, who believed in his name, he gave the right to become children of God, who were born, not of blood nor of the will of the flesh nor of the will of man, but of God.

Godly souls can derive great confidence and delight from the sacrament of Communion as a testimony that they form one body with Christ, so that everything that is His they may call their own. Hence it follows that we can be confidently assured that eternal life, of which He himself is heir, is ours, and that the kingdom of heaven, into which He has entered, can no more be taken from us than from Him. Equally true is the fact that we cannot be condemned for our sins, and are free from the guilt of which He absolves us, since He has been pleased that these sins should be imputed to himself as if they were His own. This is the wondrous exchange made by His boundless goodness. Having become with us the Son of Man, He has made us with himself sons of God. By His own descent to the earth He has prepared our ascent to heaven. Having received our mortality, He has bestowed on us His immortality. Having undertaken our weakness, He has made us strong in His strength. Having submitted himself to our poverty, He has transferred to us His riches. Having taken upon himself the burden of unrighteousness with which we were oppressed, He has clothed us with His righteousness. To all these gifts we have full access, enabling us to conclude that they are as truly given to us as if Christ were bodily present with us.

—JOHN CALVIN, *Institutes of the Christian Religion*, vol. 3, trans. Henry Beveridge (Edinburgh: The Calvin Translation Society, 1845), 390–391 (*Institutes*, 4.17.2–3).

John 1:18: No one has ever seen God; the only God, who is at the Father's side, he has made him known.

He in whom we are beloved is Christ, the delight of His heavenly Father and the "express image of His person." He could have given us nothing more excellent, nothing dearer, even if He had given the whole universe.

—FRANCIS TURRETIN, *Institutes of Elenctic Theology*, vol. 1, ed. James T. Dennison Jr., trans. George Musgrave Giger (Phillipsburg: P&R Publishing, 1992–1997), 242. (3.20.6)

He calls Him the image of the invisible God, meaning by this, that it is in Him alone that God, who is otherwise invisible, is manifested to us, in accordance with what is said in John 1:18: "No one has ever seen God; the only God, who is at the Father's side, he has made him known." For Christ is called the image of God on this ground: that He makes God in a manner visible to us. The sum is this: that God in himself, that is, in His pure majesty, is invisible, and not to the eyes of the body merely, but also to the understandings of men, and that He is revealed to us in Christ alone, that we may behold Him as in a mirror. For in Christ He shows us His righteousness, goodness, wisdom, power—in short, His entire self. We must, therefore, beware of seeking Him elsewhere, for everything that would set itself up as a representation of God, apart from Christ, will be an idol.

—JOHN CALVIN, *Commentaries on the Epistles to the Philippians, Colossians, and Thessalonians: with Four Homilies or Sermons on Idolatry, and an Exposition of Psalm 87*, trans. John Pringle (Edinburgh: The Calvin Translation Society, 1851), 149–150.

Hebrews 4:15: For we do not have a high priest who is unable to sympathize with our weaknesses, but one who in every respect has been tempted as we are, yet without sin.

The sensitivity of His soul and the depth of feeling that flowed through His being are seen in a clear light. And while they tore His heart and, in the end, broke the bonds which bound His spirit to its tenement of clay, they never took the helm of life or overthrew either the judgment of His calm understanding or the completeness of His perfect trust in His Father. If He cried out in agony for deliverance, it was the cry of a child to His Father, whom He trusted always and with all, and with the explicit condition: "Not my will but Your will be done." If the sense of desolation invaded His soul, He yet confidently commended His departing spirit into His Father's hands (Luke 23:46).

As we survey the emotional life of our Lord as depicted by the Gospels, let us not permit it to slip out of sight that we are not only observing the proofs of the truth of His humanity, and not merely regarding the most perfect example of a human life that history affords, but are contemplating the atoning work of the Savior in its fundamental elements. The cup that He drank to its bitter dregs was not His cup but our cup; and He needed to drink it only because He was set upon our salvation.

—B. B. WARFIELD, "On the Emotional Life of Our Lord," in *Biblical and Theological Studies* (New York: Charles Scribner's Sons, 1912), 15, 19.

1 Corinthians 15:47–49: The first man was from the earth, a man of dust; the second man is from heaven. As was the man of dust, so also are those who are of the dust, and as is the man of heaven, so also are those who are of heaven. Just as we have borne the image of the man of dust, we shall also bear the image of the man of heaven.

For we do not sever Jesus the Man from the Godhead, but we teach the unity and identity of Person, who of old was not man but God, and the Only Son before all ages, unmingled with body or anything corporeal; but who in these last days has assumed Manhood also for our salvation; passible in His flesh, impassible in His Godhead; limited in the body, unlimited in the Spirit; at once earthly and heavenly, tangible and intangible, comprehensible and incomprehensible; that by One and the same Person, who was perfect Man and also God, the entire humanity fallen through sin might be created anew.

For the words "The Second Man is the Lord from Heaven; As is the Heavenly, such are they that are Heavenly; No man hath ascended up into Heaven save He which came down from Heaven, even the Son of Man which is in Heaven," and the like, are to be understood as said to describe the union of the Begotten Son with the heavenly Father; just as "All things were made by Christ, and Christ dwelleth in your hearts" is said, not only speaking of the visible nature of man, but that Christ's nature can dwell in us, uniting us to Him and to the Father.

—GREGORY OF NANZIANZUS, *Letters of St. Gregory Nazianzen: To Cledonius the Priest Against Apollinarius*, A Select Library of Nicene and Post-Nicene Fathers of the Christian Church, 2nd ser., vol. 7, trans. Charles Gordon Browne and James Edward Swallow (New York: The Christian Literature Co., 1894), 439–440.

> **James 1:2–4:** Count it all joy, my brothers, when you meet trials of various kinds, for you know that the testing of your faith produces steadfastness. And let steadfastness have its full effect, that you may be perfect and complete, lacking in nothing.

We should know that the happiness that is promised to us in Christ does not consist in outward advantages alone—such as leading a joyful and peaceful life, abounding in wealth, being safe from all harm, and enjoying the pleasures of the flesh—but rather refers more properly to the spiritual life. In the world, the prosperity and well-being of a people consists partly in the abundance of temporal things and domestic peace, and partly in protection against outside attacks. Christ enriches His people with all things necessary to their eternal salvation, fortifying them with courage to stand up against the attacks of the enemy of their souls. From this we infer that He rules, inwardly and outwardly, more for us than for himself. And being replenished, insofar as God knows to be expedient, with the gifts of the Spirit, of which we are naturally lacking. We may feel from their first fruits that we are truly united to God. Then, trusting in the power of the same Spirit, may not doubt that we shall always be victorious against the devil, the world, and everything that can do us harm.

Not being earthly or carnal, and therefore subject to corruption, but spiritual, the kingdom of Christ raises us to eternal life, so that we can patiently live under earthly discomforts, content with the fact that our King will never abandon us, but will supply our basic necessities until our warfare on earth is ended and we are called home to be forever with Him. The nature of His kingdom is such that He communicates to us whatever He receives of His Father, so that we can contend fearlessly with the devil, sin, and death. And as He replenishes us liberally with His gifts, we can in turn bring forth fruit unto His glory.

—JOHN CALVIN, *Institutes of the Christian Religion*, vol. 2, trans. Henry Beveridge (Edinburgh: The Calvin Translation Society, 1845), 41 (*Institutes*, 2.15.4).

John 1:14: And the Word became flesh and dwelt among us, and we have seen his glory, glory as of the only Son from the Father, full of grace and truth.

It is sometimes suggested that the Son of God assumed at the incarnation not human nature as manifests itself in an individual, but human nature in general, that is, generic or universal. The idea it is meant to express is not a clear one. In any case, the idea receives no support from a survey of the emotional life of our Lord as it is presented to us in the Gospel narratives. The impression of a distinct individuality, acting in accordance with its specific character, is strong in these narratives. Whether our Lord's human nature is considered generic or individual, it certainly functioned in the days of His flesh as if it were individual; and we have the same reason for pronouncing it an individual human nature that we have for pronouncing any human nature of whose functioning we have knowledge.

The series of emotions attributed to our Lord in the Gospel narratives, in their variety and their complex but harmonious interaction, illustrate this balanced comprehensiveness of His individuality. Various as they are, they do not inhibit one another; compassion and indignation rise together in His soul; joy and sorrow meet in His heart and kiss each other. Strong as they are—not mere joy but exultation, not mere irritated annoyance but raging indignation, not mere passing pity but the deepest movements of compassion and love, not mere surface distress but an exceeding sorrow even unto death—they never overmaster Him. He remains ever in control.

—B. B. WARFIELD, "On the Emotional Life of Our Lord," in *Biblical and Theological Studies* (New York: Charles Scribner's Sons, 1912), 17–18.

DAY
178

Romans 5:6–8: For while we were still weak, at the right time Christ died for the ungodly. For one will scarcely die for a righteous person—though perhaps for a good person one would dare even to die—but God shows his love for us in that while we were still sinners, Christ died for us.

Jesus Christ is the meaning of divine agape; where He is ignored, the love of God is also ignored. And when Christ's death for sinners is considered unimportant, God's love in Christ loses its central focus. In the New Testament, the high point of the divine agape is found on Mount Calvary.

—CARL F. H. HENRY, *God, Revelation, and Authority*, vol. 6. (Waco, TX: Word, 1976–1983), 356.

It is not only a wonder that God the Father gave His Only Begotten Son, but that He gave Him in such a way that His Beloved should be cruelly slain!

More transcendent still is that He gave Him up for those who hated Him. Note how high a price He sets upon us! If when we hated Him, and were His enemies, He gave His Son, what will He not do now, when we are reconciled by Him through grace?

—JOHN CHRYSOSTOM, *Homilies of St. John Chrysostom, Archbishop of Constantinople, on the Epistle of St. Paul the Apostle to the Ephesians*, A Select Library of the Nicene and Post-Nicene Fathers of the Christian Church, 1st ser., vol. 13, ed. Philip Schaff, trans. William John Copeland and Gross Alexander (Buffalo, NY: Christian Literature Co., 1889), 53.

2 Corinthians 4:3–6: And even if our gospel is veiled, it is veiled to those who are perishing. In their case the god of this world has blinded the minds of the unbelievers, to keep them from seeing the light of the gospel of the glory of Christ, who is the image of God. For what we proclaim is not ourselves, but Jesus Christ as Lord, with ourselves as your servants for Jesus' sake. For God, who said, "Let light shine out of darkness," has shone in our hearts to give the light of the knowledge of the glory of God in the face of Jesus Christ.

Christ models human nature made beautiful by the very will and law of God (John 1:14; 2 Corinthians 4:6). He alone truly keeps His promises, and in doing so fulfills God's righteousness redemptively for repentant sinners, whether Jew or Gentile. By His resurrection, the crucified Jesus reverses the undeserved death of the cross; He is victor over the pretensions of self-assertive sinners and over the hollow authority of arbitrary rulers. By vindicating righteousness, He validates all legitimate rights. Jesus Christ mediates the new and final covenant between God and man: Once again human rights and responsibilities are seen to stem from the justice and justification of God who openly declares His will for humankind.

—CARL F. H. HENRY, *God, Revelation, and Authority*, vol. 6. (Waco, TX: Word, 1976–1983), 432.

The pearl of great price, the Lord Jesus, is the quintessence of all good things. To give us Christ is more than if God had given us all the world.

He can make more worlds, but He has no more Christs to bestow.

He is such a gold mine that the angels cannot reach His depths (Ephesians 3:8).

Through Christ we have justification, adoption, and coronation.

The sea of God's mercy in giving us Christ should swallow up all our wants.

—THOMAS WATSON, *The Lord's Prayer* (Carlisle, PA: Banner of Truth Trust, 1662/1999), 206.

> **Isaiah 53:4–5:**
> Surely he has borne our griefs
>   and carried our sorrows;
> yet we esteemed him stricken,
>   smitten by God, and afflicted.
> But he was pierced for our transgressions;
>   he was crushed for our iniquities;
> upon him was the chastisement that brought us peace,
>   and with his wounds we are healed.

In Christ's human nature there are two things to be considered, the real flesh and the affections or feelings. The apostle then teaches us that He had not only put on the real flesh of man but also all the feelings that belong to man, and he also shows why this is beneficial.

The Son of God undertook our infirmities because all knowledge without feeling the need for healing is cold and lifeless. But he teaches us that Christ was made subject to human affections, that He might be a merciful and faithful high priest.

The Son of God had no need of experience that He might know the emotions of mercy. But we could not be persuaded that He is merciful and ready to help us had He not become acquainted by experience with our miseries. But this was one of the many favors God gave us.

Therefore, whenever any evil afflicts us, let us always remember that nothing happens to us but what the Son of God himself has experienced in order that He might empathize with us; nor let us doubt that He is present with us as though He suffered with us.

Acquaintance with our sorrows and suffering so inclines Christ to compassion that He is continually imploring God's aid for us. In a word, by taking on our common nature, He might introduce us, together with himself, into the sanctuary of God.

—JOHN CALVIN, *Commentaries on the Epistle of Paul the Apostle to the Hebrews*, trans. John Owen (Edinburgh: The Calvin Translation Society, 1853), 74–76.

Matthew 14:23: And after he had dismissed the crowds, he went up on the mountain by himself to pray. When evening came, he was there alone.

Mark 6:46: And after he had taken leave of them, he went up on the mountain to pray.

Luke 6:12: In these days he went out to the mountain to pray, and all night he continued in prayer to God.

Mark 1:35: And rising very early in the morning, while it was still dark, he departed and went out to a desolate place, and there he prayed.

The completeness of Jesus' trust in God, illustrated in His unconditional "Nevertheless, not my will, but yours, be done" (Luke 22:42), and echoed in His "Father, into your hands I commit my spirit" (Luke 23:46), finds endless illustration in the Gospels. Trust is never, however, explicitly attributed to Him. Except in the scoffing language with which He was assailed as He hung on the cross, "He trusts in God; let God deliver him now, if he desires him" (Matthew 27:43), the term *trust* is never mentioned in connection with His relationship to God. Nor is the term *faith* used. Nor are many of what we may call the fundamental religious affections directly attributed to Him, although He is depicted as literally living, moving, and having His being in God. His profound feeling of dependence on God, for example, is illustrated in every conceivable way, not least in the constant habit of prayer, which the Gospel writers ascribe to Him. But we are never directly told that He felt this dependence on God or "feared God" or felt the emotions of reverence and awe in the divine presence. We are repeatedly told that He returned thanks to God, but we are never told that He experienced the emotion of gratitude. The narrative brings Jesus before us as acting under the impulse of religious emotions, but it does not comment on the emotions themselves.

—B. B. WARFIELD, "On the Emotional Life of Our Lord," in *Biblical and Theological Studies* (New York: Charles Scribner's Sons, 1912), 16.

Matthew 11:28-30: "Come to me, all who labor and are heavy laden, and I will give you rest. Take my yoke upon you, and learn from me, for I am gentle and lowly in heart, and you will find rest for your souls. For my yoke is easy, and my burden is light."

There is this to encourage and embolden the poor sinner: Christ is man as well as God; He is a creature, as well as the Creator, and He is the most humble and lowly in heart of any creature in heaven or on earth. This may make the poor, unworthy creature bold in coming to Him.

You do not need to hesitate one moment, but you may run to Him, and cast yourself upon Him. You will certainly be graciously and meekly received by Him. Though He be a lion, He will only be a lion to your enemies. He will be a lamb to you.

Any one of you that is a father or mother will not despise one of your own children who comes to you in distress. Oh, how much less danger is there of Christ despising you, if in your heart you come to Him!

—JONATHAN EDWARDS, "The Excellency of Christ," in *Sermons and Discourses, 1734–1738*, The Works of Jonathan Edwards, vol. 19, ed. M. X. Lesser and Harry S. Stout (New Haven, CT; London: Yale University Press, 2001), 583–584.

> **Mark 1:40–42:** And a leper came to him, imploring him, and kneeling said to him, "If you will, you can make me clean." Moved with pity, he stretched out his hand and touched him and said to him, "I will; be clean." And immediately the leprosy left him, and he was made clean.

A leper comes to Christ. He begs to be made clean and is healed with a touch by the power of the Word. He is commanded to be silent, yet to show himself to the priest and to offer the gift that Moses required to serve as a testimony. In the leper, then, is exhibited the healing of the multitude who hear and believe and come down from the mountain with the Lord. They are marked with the foul defilement of the body, and on hearing the proclamation of the kingdom, they beg to be healed. They are simply touched, as was the first leper, and are healed by the power of the Word; and as this healing may not be offered more than it is sought, silence is commanded, and they are bidden to show themselves to the priests. This is so that they may be seen to have been announced beforehand, according to the Law, and that the power of the Word may be perceived where the Law was weak. The one who is made clean is also to offer to God a recognition of the healing that he has received, but that gift is not to be from his ancestors: the person, having been cleansed of his bodily sins, must provide the sacrifice to God, because the laws of Moses were not efficacious to save, but only declarative.

—HILARY OF POITIERS, *Commentary on Matthew*, in *Patrologiae cursus completes.*, *series latina*, vol. 9, ed. J. P. Migne (Paris: Migne, 1844–1864), 954–955.

Romans 5:1–2, 9–11, 15–21: Therefore, since we have been justified by faith, we have peace with God through our Lord Jesus Christ. Through him we have also obtained access by faith into this grace in which we stand, and we rejoice in hope of the glory of God. . . . Since, therefore, we have now been justified by his blood, much more shall we be saved by him from the wrath of God. For if while we were enemies we were reconciled to God by the death of his Son, much more, now that we are reconciled, shall we be saved by his life. More than that, we also rejoice in God through our Lord Jesus Christ, through whom we have now received reconciliation. . . . But the free gift is not like the trespass. For if many died through one man's trespass, much more have the grace of God and the free gift by the grace of that one man Jesus Christ abounded for many. And the free gift is not like the result of that one man's sin. For the judgment following one trespass brought condemnation, but the free gift following many trespasses brought justification. For if, because of one man's trespass, death reigned through that one man, much more will those who receive the abundance of grace and the free gift of righteousness reign in life through the one man Jesus Christ. Therefore, as one trespass led to condemnation for all men, so one act of righteousness leads to justification and life for all men. For as by the one man's disobedience the many were made sinners, so by the one man's obedience the many will be made righteous. Now the law came in to increase the trespass, but where sin increased, grace abounded all the more, so that, as sin reigned in death, grace also might reign through righteousness leading to eternal life through Jesus Christ our Lord.

This is the great mystery of the Gospel in the blood of Christ, that those who sin every day should have peace with God all their days.

—JOHN OWEN, "An Exposition of Psalm 130," in *The Works of John Owen: Temptation and Sin*, vol. 6, ed. William H. Goold (Carlisle, PA: Banner of Truth Trust, 1668/1967), 339.

> **Romans 5:17:** For if, because of one man's trespass, death reigned through that one man, much more will those who receive the abundance of grace and the free gift of righteousness reign in life through the one man Jesus Christ.

Christ caused humanity to cleave to and to become one with God. For unless a human being had overcome the enemy of humanity, the enemy would not have been legitimately vanquished. And again, unless it had been God incarnate who had freely given salvation, we could never have possessed it securely. And unless humanity had been joined to God, we could never have become partakers of incorruptibility. For it was incumbent upon the Mediator between God and humanity, by His relationship to both, to bring both to friendship and concord, and present humanity to God, while He revealed God to humanity. For, in what way could we partake of the adoption of children, unless we had received from Him through the Son that fellowship that refers to himself, unless His Word, having been made flesh, had entered into communion with us? Wherefore also He passed through every stage of life, restoring to all communion with God.

For it behooved Him who was to destroy sin and redeem humanity that He should himself be made a man, tempted by the devil, held by death, risen from the dead, so that humanity could escape eternal death. For as by the disobedience of the one human, born of the earth, many were made sinners, and forfeited life, so was it necessary that by the obedience of one, born of a virgin by the power of God, many should be justified and receive salvation. And so, the Word of God was made flesh. If He only appeared as flesh, His works were not true. But as He appeared, so He was: God became a man that He might defeat sin, deprive death of its power, and revive humanity; therefore, His works are true.

—IRENAEUS, *Against Heresies*, in *Ante-Nicene Fathers*, vol. 1, ed. Alexander Roberts, James Donaldson, and A. Cleveland Coxe, trans. Alexander Roberts and William Rambaut (Buffalo, NY: Christian Literature Publishing Co., 1885), 448 (*Against Heresies*, 3.18.7).

Genesis 2:7: Then the LORD God formed the man of dust from the ground and breathed into his nostrils the breath of life, and the man became a living creature.

O Beloved, Your way of knowing is amazing! The way You recognize every creature even before it appears. The way You gaze into the face of every human being and see all Your works gazing back at You. O what a miracle to be awake inside Your breathing.

Because a woman brought death, a bright maiden overcame it, and so the highest blessing in all of creation lies in the form of a woman, since God has become man in a sweet and blessed Virgin.

O You who are ever giving life to all life, moving all creatures, root of all things, washing them clean, wiping out their mistakes, healing their wounds. You are our true life, luminous, wonderful, awakening the heart from its ancient sleep.

—HILDEGARD OF BINGEN, Symphonia: *A Critical Edition of the Symphonia armonie celestium revelationum* (Symphony of the Harmony of Celestial Revelations), trans. Barbara Newman (Ithaca: Cornell University, 1998).

> **John 11:33–37:** When Jesus saw her weeping, and the Jews who had come with her also weeping, he was deeply moved in his spirit and greatly troubled. And he said, "Where have you laid him?" They said to him, "Lord, come and see." Jesus wept. So the Jews said, "See how he loved him!" But some of them said, "Could not he who opened the eyes of the blind man also have kept this man from dying?"

What need was there to weep for one whom He was going to raise from the dead before long? Jesus wept as an example to us of sympathy and humanity to one's own kind. Jesus wept in order that He might give the lesson of weeping to those who weep in deeds rather than in words. "Jesus wept." He wept but did not grieve. To be without tears He rejected as harsh and inhuman, but addiction to grief He avoided as base and unmanly. Rather, He wept, giving sympathy its due place. He comes to the cave and contemplates the stone lying across the tomb. He orders the Jews standing by to roll away the stone from the mouth of the cave. Now, this is the man who says, "If you have faith like a grain of mustard seed, you will say to this mountain, 'Move from here to there,' and it will move, and nothing will be impossible for you" (Matthew 17:20). How, Jesus, are You now unable to roll away the stone? He replies that it is not because He is unable to do this, but so that they may not suppose the miracle to be an illusion. He commanded the Jews themselves to roll away the stone with their own hands, leaving the greatest sign to himself, so that they may become witnesses.

—HIPPOLYTUS, "On Lazarus," in *Die griechischen christlichen Schriftsteller der ersten Jahrhunderte*, 1.2 (Berlin: Akademice-Verlag, 1897), 224–225.

Psalm 22:14–15:
I am poured out like water,
    and all my bones are out of joint;
my heart is like wax;
    it is melted within my breast;
my strength is dried up like a potsherd,
    and my tongue sticks to my jaws;
    you lay me in the dust of death.

When we refer to Christ as the Lord of Glory, we must understand the whole person of Christ, who being Lord of Glory was indeed crucified, but not in His glorious form. Similarly, when He is referred to as the Son of Man, the whole person of Christ must be meant, who being man upon earth, filled heaven with His glorious presence, but not in the same nature for which the title of man was given Him.

> —RICHARD HOOKER, *Of the Laws of Ecclesiastical Polity* (London: Will Stansby, 1611), 5.53.4.

It is the Son who possesses the glory of the Father, and it is in the glory of the Father that He will manifest himself, for the divinity of the Son and of the Father is One. Thus, if God says that He will not give His glory to another, and if the Son manifestly possesses the glory of the Father, it is evident that He is not another according to essence, but that He has the same nature as the Father.

> —THEODORET OF CYR, "Commentary on Isaiah 12.42.8–9," in *Isaiah 40–66*, *The Ancient Christian Commentary on Scripture*, ed. Mark W. Elliott (Downers Grove, IL: IVP, 2007), 38.

> **2 Corinthians 5:17:** Therefore, if anyone is in Christ, he is a new creation. The old has passed away; behold, the new has come.

We might imagine the following conversation:

The man to whom the Word of grace speaks thinks and says that he is not this new, peaceful, joyful man living in fellowship with God that Scripture attests. He asks permission to honestly admit that he does not know this man, at least not himself as this man.

The Word of grace replies: "All honor to your honesty, but My truth transcends it. Allow yourself, therefore, to be told in all truth and on the most solid grounds what you do not know, namely, that you are this man in spite of what you think."

Man: "You think that I can and should become this man in the course of time? But I do not have sufficient confidence in myself to believe this. Knowing myself, I shall never become this man."

The Word of grace: "You do well not to have confidence in yourself. But the point is not that you can and should become this man. What I am telling you is that, as I know you, you already are."

Man: "I understand that you mean this eschatologically. You are referring to the man I perhaps will be one day in some not clearly known transfiguration in a distant eternity. If only I had attained to this! And if only I could be certain that even then I should be this new man!"

The Word of grace: "You need to understand both yourself and Me better than you do. I am not inviting you to speculate about your being in eternity, but to receive and ponder the news that here and now you begin to be the new man and are already that which you will be eternally."

Man: "How can I accept this news? On what guarantee can I boldly take it seriously?"

The Word of grace: "I, Jesus Christ, am the One who speaks to you. You are what you are in Me, as I will to be in you. Hold fast to Me. I am your guarantee. My boldness is yours. With this boldness dare to be what you know you are."

—KARL BARTH, *Church Dogmatics*, vol. 4, pt. 1 (Edinburgh: T&T Clark, 1956), 250.

> **John 1:14:** And the Word became flesh and dwelt among us, and we have seen his glory, glory as of the only Son from the Father, full of grace and truth.

The glory of the Savior is His triumph over sin. Crucified as man, He is glorified as God. We say this not as though we believed that there were two individuals, one God and the other man, or that there are two persons in the Son of God, as some new heresy teaches. One and the same Son of God is also the Son of Man.

—JEROME, "Letter of Jerome to Pammachius and Oceanus" (AD 401), in *The Faith of the Early Fathers: A Sourcebook of Theological and Historical Passages from the Christian Writings of the Pre-Nicene and Nicene Eras*, vol. 2 (Collegeville: Liturgical Press, 1970), 186.

There is, therefore, one God the Father, and one Christ Jesus, who joined together all things unto himself. But in every respect, He is man, the formation of God.

He took man into himself, the invisible becoming visible, the incomprehensible being made comprehensible, the untouchable becoming capable of suffering. And the Word being made man, summed up all things in himself, celestial, spiritual, and invisible. The Word of God is supreme, taking the highest position, constituting the Head of the Church, so that He might draw the faithful to himself at the proper time.

—IRENAEUS, Against Heresies, in *Ante-Nicene Fathers*, vol. 1, ed. Alexander Roberts, James Donaldson, and A. Cleveland Coxe, trans. Alexander Roberts and William Rambaut (Buffalo, NY: Christian Literature Publishing Co., 1885), 442–443 (*Against Heresies*, 3.16.6).

Jesus Christ, true God, who is greater than all things in heaven and on earth, is also true man, pure and sinless, and who crushed death. Because death and the devil could not hold Him, He broke the grave's bonds in a manner more brilliant than the sun. We must never forget that Christ who is risen from the dead is true God and true man in one person.

—MARTIN LUTHER, *The Complete Sermons of Martin Luther*, vol. 6, ed. Eugene F. King and John Nicholas Lenker (Grand Rapids, MI: Baker Books, 2000), 13.

> **Ephesians 1:3–10:** Blessed be the God and Father of our Lord Jesus Christ, who has blessed us in Christ with every spiritual blessing in the heavenly places, even as he chose us in him before the foundation of the world, that we should be holy and blameless before him. In love he predestined us for adoption to himself as sons through Jesus Christ, according to the purpose of his will, to the praise of his glorious grace, with which he has blessed us in the Beloved. In him we have redemption through his blood, the forgiveness of our trespasses, according to the riches of his grace, which he lavished upon us, in all wisdom and insight making known to us the mystery of his will, according to his purpose, which he set forth in Christ as a plan for the fullness of time, to unite all things in him, things in heaven and things on earth.

The Church, though dispersed throughout the whole world, even to the ends of the earth, has received from the apostles and their disciples this faith: She believes in one God, the Father Almighty, Maker of heaven and earth and the sea, and all things that are in them.

And in one Christ Jesus, the Son of God, who became incarnate for our salvation; and in the Holy Spirit, who proclaimed through the prophets the movements and events of God, and the advents, and the birth from a virgin, and the passion, and the resurrection from the dead, and the ascension into heaven in the flesh of the beloved Christ Jesus, our Lord, and His future manifestation from heaven in the glory of the Father "to unite all things in him" (Ephesians 1:10) and to raise up anew all flesh of the whole human race, in order that to Christ Jesus, our Lord, and God, and Savior, and King, according to the will of the invisible Father, "every knee should bow, in heaven and on earth and under the earth, and every tongue confess that Jesus Christ is Lord, to the glory of God the Father" (Philippians 2:10–11).

—IRENAEUS, *Against Heresies*, in *Ante-Nicene Fathers*, vol. 1, ed. Alexander Roberts, James Donaldson, and A. Cleveland Coxe, trans. Alexander Roberts and William Rambaut (Buffalo, NY: Christian Literature Publishing Co., 1885), 330 (*Against Heresies*, 1.10.5).

Genesis 3:14–15:
  The LORD God said to the serpent,
"Because you have done this,
    cursed are you above all livestock
    and above all beasts of the field;
on your belly you shall go,
    and dust you shall eat
    all the days of your life.
I will put enmity between you and the woman,
    and between your offspring and her offspring;
he shall bruise your head,
    and you shall bruise his heel."

God will be our friend and the angels shall be our friends, and all things shall be at peace with us, and we shall enjoy a great and uninterrupted pleasure in their company. The wrath of God drove us out of paradise, but the grace of God invites us to return.

The Son of God in the name of His Father comes and calls to us to return from our banishment. He never stops calling us. He pleads with us to return. He came to reveal joyful tidings to us.

Christ calls us away from this cursed ground that produces briars and thorns to a better country. Our first parents were driven away, upset and unwilling to go, but we are invited back again.

—JONATHAN EDWARDS, "East of Eden," in *Sermons and Discourses, 1730–1733*, The Works of Jonathan Edwards, vol. 17, ed. Mark Valeri and Harry S. Stout (New Haven, CT; London: Yale University Press, 1999), 342–343.

Christ is much more powerful to save than Adam was to destroy. The sin of Adam has destroyed many. The righteousness of Christ will be no less efficacious to save many.

—JOHN CALVIN, *Commentaries on the Epistles of Paul the Apostle to the Romans*, trans. John Owen (Edinburgh: The Calvin Translation Society, 1849), 206.

1 Corinthians 1:22–25: For Jews demand signs and Greeks seek wisdom, but we preach Christ crucified, a stumbling block to Jews and folly to Gentiles, but to those who are called, both Jews and Greeks, Christ the power of God and the wisdom of God. For the foolishness of God is wiser than men, and the weakness of God is stronger than men.

We must be sanctified and made holy, and all the men and angels in the universe cannot do that. They do not have enough power to burn down the old image of Satan, nor skills enough to draw the image of God upon our souls.

This is a work of the almighty power and wisdom of God, which is Christ: "Christ the power of God and the wisdom of God" (1 Corinthians 1:24); "And what is the immeasurable greatness of his power toward us who believe, according to the working of his great might" (Ephesians 1:19).

There is no one else who can fill our hearts with grace. We must receive of His fullness and grace for grace.

It is He alone who has received the Spirit without measure: "For he whom God has sent utters the words of God, for he gives the Spirit without measure" (John 3:34).

No one else can give us spiritual wisdom, for no one else knows the things of the Spirit. And Christ alone can send into our hearts the Holy Spirit to dwell in us, to teach us of heavenly things.

There is no other vine that we can be ingrafted into who can provide vital spiritual nourishment, and at last eternal life, but Christ alone, by whom and for whom are all things, who is before all things, by whom all things consist. The almighty power of God gives us our natural life, and no less power will suffice to give us our spiritual life.

—JONATHAN EDWARDS, "Life Through Christ Alone," in *Sermons and Discourses, 1720–1723*, The Works of Jonathan Edwards, vol. 10, ed. Wilson H. Kimnach (New Haven, CT: Yale University Press, 2006), 524–525.

Psalm 104:1–2, 33–34:
Bless the LORD, O my soul!
    O LORD my God, you are very great!
You are clothed with splendor and majesty,
    covering yourself with light as with a garment,
    stretching out the heavens like a tent. . . .
I will sing to the LORD as long as I live;
    I will sing praise to my God while I have being.
May my meditation be pleasing to him,
    for I rejoice in the LORD.

Humility is the raiment of the Godhead. The Word who became man clothed himself in it, and therewith He spoke to us in our body. Every person who has been clothed with it has truly been made like Him, who came down from His own exaltedness, and hid the splendor of His majesty and concealed His glory with humility, lest creation should be utterly consumed by the contemplation of Him. Creation could not look upon Him unless He became part of creation and conversed with it, and neither could it hear the words of His mouth face-to-face.

—ISAAC OF NINEVEH, *The Ascetical Homilies of St. Isaac the Syrian*, trans. D. Miller (Boston: Holy Transfiguration, 1984), 381.

O Christ who is covered with light as though with a garment, who for my sake stood naked in front of Pilate, clothe me with that might which You caused to overshadow the saints, whereby they conquered this world of struggle. May Your divinity, Lord, take pleasure in me, and lead me above the world to be with You. O Christ, upon whom the many-eyed cherubim are unable to look because of the glory of Your appearance, yet out of Your love You received spit on Your face. Remove the shame from my face and grant me to have an unashamed face before you at the time of prayer. O Christ, because of our nature's sin You went out into the wilderness and vanquished the ruler of darkness, taking from him the victory after five thousand years; force to flee from me him who at all times forces the human race to sin.

—ISAAC OF NINEVEH, "The Second Part," in *Cistercian Studies*, vol. 175 (Kalamazoo, MI: Cistercian Publications, 1973), 59.

Colossians 2:9: For in him the whole fullness of deity dwells bodily.

Christ is finite and infinite; lacking knowledge and omniscient; less than God and equal with God; He existed from eternity and was born in time; He created all things and was a man of sorrows. It is on this principle that what is true of either nature is true of the person of Christ, that a multitude of passages of Scripture are to be explained. The forms of expression, therefore, long prevalent in the Church, "the blood of God," "God the mighty Maker died," etc., agree with Scripture. The person born of the Virgin Mary was a divine person. He was the Son of God. It is therefore correct to say that Mary was the mother of God.

—CHARLES HODGE, *Systematic Theology*, vol. 2 (Grand Rapids. MI: Wm. B. Eerdmans, 1946), 392–93.

To add up everything that has been said about this, there are only four things that complete the whole state of our Lord Jesus Christ: His deity, His manhood, the conjunction of both, and the distinction of the one from the other in the way they are joined. Four main heresies surrounding these states have arisen: Arians have bent themselves against the deity of Christ; Apollinarians by harming and misinterpreting that which belongs to His human nature; Nestorians by tearing Christ apart and dividing Him into two persons; the followers of Eutiches by combining in His person those natures which they should keep separate. Against these there have been four famous ancient general Councils: The Council of Nice to define against the Arians, against Apollinarians the Council of Constantinople, the Council of Ephesus against Nestorians, against Eutichians the Chalcedon Council. In four words Christ's nature has been defended: truly, perfectly, indivisibly, distinctly; the first applies to His being God, the second to His being man, the third to His being of both one, and the fourth to His continuing to be both.

—RICHARD HOOKER, *Of the Laws of Ecclesiastical Polity* (London: Will Stansby, 1611), 5.53.1.

> **1 Corinthians 6:19–20:** Or do you not know that your body is a temple of the Holy Spirit within you, whom you have from God? You are not your own, for you were bought with a price. So glorify God in your body.

I give praise to Your holy nature, Lord, for You have made my nature a sanctuary for Your hiddenness and a tabernacle for Your mysteries, a place where You can dwell and a holy temple for Your divinity, namely, for Him who holds the scepter of Your kingdom, who governs all You have brought into being, the glorious tabernacle of Your eternal being, the source of renewal for the ranks of fire that minister to You, the way to knowledge of You, the door to the vision of You, the summation of Your power and great wisdom, Jesus Christ, the Only Begotten from Your bosom and the remnant gathered in from Your creation, both visible and spiritual.

—ISAAC OF NINEVEH, "The Second Part," in *Cistercian Studies*, vol. 175 (Kalamazoo, MI: Cistercian Publications, 1973), 57.

In a mirror you will observe that every feature of the face is reflected—both the large and small features. Now our soul should be a mirror of Christ; we should reflect every feature; for every grace in Christ there should be a counterpart grace in us. The Lord give you this; then I can ask no more for you.

Your times are in his hand (Psalm 31). May you have the blessing of Asher: "As thy days, so shall thy strength be."

—ROBERT MURRAY M'CHEYNE, *Memoir and Remains of the Rev. Robert Murray M'Cheyne*, ed. Andrew A. Bonar (Edinburgh; London: Oliphant Anderson & Ferrier, 1894), 234–235.

> **Jude 1:20–23:** But you, beloved, building yourselves up in your most holy faith and praying in the Holy Spirit, keep yourselves in the love of God, waiting for the mercy of our Lord Jesus Christ that leads to eternal life. And have mercy on those who doubt; save others by snatching them out of the fire; to others show mercy with fear, hating even the garment stained by the flesh.

We plead the promises and predictions of God's Word that may encourage your hope and trust.

Be not afraid of the proud declarations of the prince of darkness, for they shall be made to serve the interest of Christ's kingdom.

Can there be a more delightful employment, this side of heaven, than to wrest souls from the jaws of death and hell, and to send the blessed news of salvation to a perishing world?

To promote the joy of the universe is the happiness of the redeemed in glory. And this spirit among Christians is heaven begun on earth.

If your hearts do not glow with holy affections toward perishing sinners, by which you are able to do something for their relief, then you have reason to fear and tremble that you have no inheritance among the saints in light.

—LEMUEL HAYNES, "Divine Decrees: An Encouragement to the Use of Means," in *Black Preacher to White America: The Collected Writings of Lemuel Haynes, 1774–1833,* ed. Richard Newman (Brooklyn, NY: Carlson Publishing, 1990), 99–100.

The Gospel of Christ contains joyful news to men of deliverance from evil. It is a proclamation of deliverance to the children of men from evils that are by far the greatest that humankind has ever been exposed to: evils that are truly infinitely dreadful, such as the guilt of sin, captivity and bondage to Satan, the wrath of God, and perfect and everlasting ruin and misery.

If we compare these things with things that are infinitely less in degree, it may serve to give us some idea of the joyfulness of these tidings.

—JONATHAN EDWARDS, "Of Those Who Walk in the Light of God's Countenance," in *Sermons and Discourses, 1743–1758,* The Works of Jonathan Edwards, vol. 25, ed. Wilson H. Kimnach and Harry S. Stout (New Haven, CT: Yale University Press, 2006), 702, 703–704.

> **John 20:30-31:** Now Jesus did many other signs in the presence of the disciples, which are not written in this book; but these are written so that you may believe that Jesus is the Christ, the Son of God, and that by believing you may have life in his name.

The authority of the Bible for Christology is found in its power to point to the One whom the people have met in the historical struggle of freedom. Through the reading of Scripture, the people hear other stories about Jesus that enable them to move beyond the privateness of their own story; through faith because of divine grace, they are taken from the present to the past and then thrust back into their contemporary history with divine power to transform the sociopolitical context. This event of transcendence enables the people to break the barriers of time and space as they walk and talk with Jesus in Palestine along with Peter, James, and John. They can hear His cry of pain and experience the suffering as He is nailed on the cross and pierced in the side.

—JAMES H. CONE, *God of the Oppressed* (Maryknoll, NY: Orbis, 1997), 102–103.

Strictly speaking, Christ himself is the scope of the Scriptures, so that it is only through focusing constantly upon Him, dwelling in His Word and assimilating His mind, that the interpreter can discern the real meaning of the Scriptures. What is required then is a theological interpretation of the Scriptures under the direction of their ostensive reference to God's self-revelation in Jesus Christ and within the general perspective of faith.

—THOMAS F. TORRANCE, *Reality and Evangelical Theology* (Louisville, KY: Westminster John Knox Press, 1981), 107.

Isaiah 53:3:
He was despised and rejected by men,
    a man of sorrows and acquainted with grief.

Is it not strange, the darkest hour
That ever dawned on sinful earth
Should touch the heart with softer power
For comfort than an angel's mirth?
That to the cross the mourner's eye should turn
Sooner than where the stars of Christmas burn?

Sooner than where the Easter sun
Shines glorious on yon open grave,
And to and fro the tidings run,
"Who died to heal, is risen to save?"
Sooner than where upon the Savior's friends
The very Comforter in light and love descends?

Yet so it is: for duly there
The bitter herbs of earth are set,
Till tempered by the Savior's prayer,
And with the Savior's life-blood wet,
They turn to sweetness, and drop holy balm,
Soft as imprisoned martyr's deathbed calm.

All turn to sweet—but most of all
That bitterest to the lip of pride,
When hopes presumptuous fade and fall,
Or Friendship scorns us, duly tried,
Or Love, the flower that closes up for fear
When rude and selfish spirits breathe too near.

Then like a long-forgotten strain
Comes sweeping o'er the heart forlorn
What sunshine hours had taught in vain
Of JESUS suffering shame and scorn,
As in all lowly hearts He suffers still,
While we triumphant ride and have the world at will. . . .

—JOHN KEBLE, "Good Friday," in *The Christian Year*
(New York: Stanford and Swords, 1853), 119–121.

Isaiah 53:3:
He was despised and rejected by men, a man of sorrows and
acquainted with grief.

. . . His pierced hands in vain would hide
His face from rude reproachful gaze,
His ears are open to abide
The wildest storm the tongue can raise,
He who with one rough word, some early day,
Their idol world and them shall sweep for aye away.

But we by Fancy may assuage
The festering sore by Fancy made,
Down in some lonely hermitage
Like wounded pilgrims safely laid,
Where gentlest breezes whisper souls distressed,
That Love yet lives, and Patience shall find rest.

O! shame beyond the bitterest thought
That evil spirit ever framed,
That sinners know what Jesus wrought,
Yet feel their haughty hearts untamed—
That souls in refuge, holding by the Cross,
Should wince and fret at this world's little loss.

Lord of my heart, by Thy last cry,
Let not Thy blood on earth be spent—
Lo, at Thy feet I fainting lie,
Mine eyes upon Thy wounds are bent,
Upon Thy streaming wounds my weary eyes
Wait like the parched earth on April skies.

Wash me, and dry these bitter tears,
O let my heart no further roam,
'Tis Thine by vows, and hopes, and fears.
Long since—O call Thy wanderer home;
To that dear home, safe in Thy wounded side,
Where only broken hearts their sin and shame may hide.

—JOHN KEBLE, "Good Friday," in *The Christian Year*
(New York: Stanford and Swords, 1853), 119–121.

John 9:10–12: So they said to him, "Then how were your eyes opened?" He answered, "The man called Jesus made mud and anointed my eyes and said to me, 'Go to Siloam and wash.' So I went and washed and received my sight." They said to him, "Where is he?" He said, "I do not know."

We can understand how His followers could believe Him divine, if He not only asserted himself to be divine but lived as a God would, taught like a divine instructor, revealed a perfection that was obviously not human in all His conduct in the world; and if dying, He rose from the dead. If He did none of these things, can their firm and passionate faith in His deity be explained?

—B. B. WARFIELD, *The Lord of Glory: A Study of the Designations of Our Lord in the New Testament with Especial Reference to His Deity* (New York: American Tract Society, 1907), 300.

If you wish to ponder the imponderable, first ask how He gave sight to the man born blind. All that He did was to anoint the blind man's eyes with mud. Yet mud blinds even those with sight and does not give sight to the blind. In the case of the blind man, those present were meant to learn that this is the one who took clay from the earth and fashioned Adam as the first human. And therefore, after such an impressive lesson, they would become vividly aware that this is the one who said through the prophet, "Open your mouth, and I will fill it."

—LEONTIUS OF BYZANTIUM, Pentecost Sermon I, in *Ancient Christian Doctrine: We Believe in the Crucified and Risen Lord* (Downers Grove, IL: IVP Academic, 2009), 33.

> **1 Corinthians 9:16:** For if I preach the gospel, that gives me no ground
> for boasting. For necessity is laid upon me. Woe to me if I do not preach
> the gospel!

There has been a long tradition that sees the mission of the Church primarily as obedience to a command. It has been customary to speak of "the missionary mandate." This way of putting the matter is certainly not without justification, and yet it seems to me that it misses the point. It tends to make mission a burden rather than a joy, to make it part of the law rather than part of the Gospel. If one looks at the New Testament evidence, one gets another impression. Mission begins with a kind of explosion of joy. The news that the rejected and crucified Jesus is alive is a truth that cannot possibly be suppressed. It must be told. Who could be silent about such a fact? The mission of the Church in the pages of the New Testament is more like the fallout from a vast explosion, a radioactive fallout that is not lethal but life-giving.

One searches in vain through the letters of Saint Paul to find any suggestion that he anywhere lays it on the conscience of his readers that they ought to be active in mission. For himself, it is inconceivable that he should keep silent. "Woe to me if I do not preach the gospel!" But nowhere do we find him telling his readers that they have a duty to do so. It is a striking fact, moreover, that almost all the proclamations of the Gospel that are described in Acts are in response to questions asked by those outside the Church.

—LESSLIE NEWBIGIN, *The Gospel in a Pluralist Society* (London: SPCK, 1989), 116.

Decisions must be made for or against Christ, for He is either the clue to history, or there is some other clue. The Gospel calls us back again and again to the real clue, the crucified and risen Jesus, so that we learn that the meaning of history is not existent within history itself, that history cannot find its meaning at the end of a process of development, but that history is given its meaning by what God has done through Jesus Christ and by what He has promised to do; and that the true horizon is not at the successful end of our projects but in His coming to reign.

—LESSLIE NEWBIGIN, *The Gospel in a Pluralist Society* (Grand Rapids, MI: Wm. B. Eerdmans Publishing, 1989), 125–126.

Psalm 85:7–13:
Show us your steadfast love, O Lord,
and grant us your salvation.
Let me hear what God the Lord will speak,
for he will speak peace to his people, to his saints;
but let them not turn back to folly.
Surely his salvation is near to those who fear him,
that glory may dwell in our land.
Steadfast love and faithfulness meet;
righteousness and peace kiss each other.
Faithfulness springs up from the ground,
and righteousness looks down from the sky.
Yes, the Lord will give what is good,
and our land will yield its increase.
Righteousness will go before him
and make his footsteps a way.

In some cases, though a believer may lose his sense of peace, yet the grounds of his peace remain firm and sure; in sad or dark conditions his soul is day and night in pursuit of peace, and he will never leave the chase till he has recovered it, knowing that God will first and last speak peace to his soul. He has that abiding seed of grace in his soul that will in time recover his peace (Psalm 85:8).

Do your enemies threaten to take away this or that from you? They can never take that peace from you that Christ has given as a legacy. When there are great storms within or without, yet even then a believer may find peace in the Prince of Peace (Isaiah 9:6).

When one's imperfections are many, a perfect Savior can keep him in perfect peace in the midst of them (Isaiah 26:3–4). Though one's sacrifices are imperfect, yet Christ, the perfect priest, can speak peace to his soul. Peace is that never-fading garland that Christ will so settle upon the heads of the upright, that none shall be able to remove it.

—THOMAS BROOKS, "A Word in Season," in *The Complete Works of Thomas Brooks*, vol. 5, ed. Alexander Balloch Grosart (Edinburgh; London; Dublin: James Nichol; James Nisbet and Co.; G. Herbert, 1867), 510–512.

Matthew 24:14: And this gospel of the kingdom will be proclaimed throughout the whole world as a testimony to all nations, and then the end will come.

Here is the motive of our mission: the final victory awaits the completion of our task. "And then the end will come." There is no other verse in the Word of God that says, "And then the end will come."

When is Christ coming again? When the Church has finished its task. When will this age end? When the world has been evangelized.

"What will be the sign of your coming and of the end of the age?" (Matthew 24:3). "This gospel of the kingdom will be proclaimed throughout the whole world as a testimony to all nations; and then the end will come."

Again, when the Church has fulfilled its divinely appointed mission, the end will come. Do you love the thought of the Lord's appearing? Then you will make every effort to take the Gospel into all the world.

It troubles me in the light of the clear teaching of God's Word, in the light of our Lord's explicit definition of our task in the Great Commission, that we take it so lightly. "All authority in heaven and on earth has been given to me" (Matthew 28:18). This is the good news of the kingdom.

His is the kingdom; He reigns in heaven, and He manifests His reign on earth in and through His Church. When we have accomplished our mission, He will return and establish His kingdom in glory.

To us it is given not only to wait for, but also to hasten, the coming of the day of God. This is the mission of the Gospel of the kingdom, and this is our mission.

—GEORGE E. LADD, *The Gospel of the Kingdom* (Grand Rapids, MI: Wm. B. Eerdmans Publishing, 1959), 139–140.

John 8:50–59: "Yet I do not seek my own glory; there is One who seeks it, and he is the judge. Truly, truly, I say to you, if anyone keeps my word, he will never see death." The Jews said to him, "Now we know that you have a demon! Abraham died, as did the prophets, yet you say, 'If anyone keeps my word, he will never taste death.' Are you greater than our father Abraham, who died? And the prophets died! Who do you make yourself out to be?" Jesus answered, "If I glorify myself, my glory is nothing. It is my Father who glorifies me, of whom you say, 'He is our God.' But you have not known him. I know him. If I were to say that I do not know him, I would be a liar like you, but I do know him and I keep his word. Your father Abraham rejoiced that he would see my day. He saw it and was glad." So the Jews said to him, "You are not yet fifty years old, and have you seen Abraham?" Jesus said to them, "Truly, truly, I say to you, before Abraham was, I am." So they picked up stones to throw at him, but Jesus hid himself and went out of the temple.

I am trying here to prevent anyone saying the really foolish thing that people often say about Him: "I'm ready to accept Jesus as a great moral teacher, but I don't accept His claim to be God." That is the one thing we must not say. A man who was merely a man and said the sort of things Jesus said would not be a great moral teacher. He would either be a lunatic—on the level with the man who says he is a poached egg—or else he would be the Devil of Hell. You must make your choice. Either this man was, and is, the Son of God, or else a madman or something worse. You can shut Him up for a fool, you can spit at Him and kill Him as a demon, or you can fall at His feet and call Him Lord and God, but let us not come with any patronizing nonsense about His being a great human teacher. He has not left that open to us. He did not intend to. Now, it seems to me obvious that He was neither a lunatic nor a fiend: and consequently, however strange or terrifying or unlikely it may seem, I have to accept the view that He was and is God.

—C. S. LEWIS, *Mere Christianity* (London: Collins, 1952), 54–56.

John 14:6: Jesus said to him, "I am the way, and the truth, and the life. No one comes to the Father except through me."

Jesus says in effect, "If you are ashamed of Me, if, when you hear this call, you turn the other way, I also will look the other way when I come again as God, without disguise. If anything whatever is keeping you from God and from Me, whatever it is, throw it away. If it is your eye, pull it out. If it is your hand, cut it off. If you put yourself first, you will be last. Come to Me, everyone who is carrying a heavy load; I will set that right. Your sins, all of them, are wiped out; I can do that. I am rebirth, I am Life. Eat Me, drink Me, I am your food. And finally, do not be afraid, I have overcome the world." That is the issue. Look for yourself, and you will find in the long-run only hatred, loneliness, despair, rage, ruin, and decay. But look for Christ, and you will find Him, and with Him everything else thrown in.

—C. S. LEWIS, *Mere Christianity* (New York: Harper Collins, 2001), 226–227.

After all, Christ must be everything: the beginning, the middle, and the end of our salvation. We must lay Him down as the first or foundation stone; rest the others and intermediate ones on Him, and also attach the rafters or the roof to Him.

He is the first, the middle, and the last rung in the ladder to heaven. Through Him we must begin, must continue, and must complete our progress to life.

—MARTIN LUTHER, *What Luther Says: An Anthology*, comp. Ewald M. Plass (St. Louis, MO: Concordia Publishing House, 1959), entry no. 545, 187.

Revelation 16:15: "Behold, I am coming like a thief! Blessed is the one who stays awake, keeping his garments on, that he may not go about naked and be seen exposed!"

Having blessed them and gone a little ahead of them, He was carried even to heaven, that He might share the Father's throne even with the flesh that was united to Him. And this new pathway the Word made for us when He appeared in human form. When the time is right, He will come again in the glory of His Father with the angels and will take us up to be with Him. Therefore, let us glorify Him who, being God the Word, became man for our sakes; who suffered willingly in the flesh, and rose from the dead and abolished corruption; who was taken up, and hereafter shall come with great glory to judge the living and the dead and will give to each according to their deeds; by whom and with whom to God the Father be glory and power with the Spirit, to ages of ages. Amen.

—CYRIL OF ALEXANDRIA, *Commentary on the Gospel of St. Luke*, trans. R. Payne Smith (Long Island: Studion Publisher, 1983), 620.

The doctrine of the second coming teaches us that we do not and cannot know when the world drama will end. The curtain may be rung down at any moment: say, before you have finished reading this paragraph. This seems to some people intolerably frustrating. So many things would be interrupted. Perhaps you were going to get married next month, perhaps you were going to get a raise next week; you may be on the verge of a great scientific discovery; you may be maturing great social and political reforms.

Surely, no good and wise God would be so very unreasonable as to cut all this short. Not now, of all moments! But we think this way because we keep assuming that we know the play. We do not know the play. We do not even know whether we are in Act I or Act V. We do not know who are the major and who the minor characters. Only the Author knows.

—C. S. LEWIS, "The World's Last Night," in *The World's Last Night and Other Essays* (New York: Harvest, 1952), 105.

Jeremiah 23:5–6: "Behold, the days are coming, declares the Lᴏʀᴅ, when I will raise up for David a righteous Branch, and he shall reign as king and deal wisely, and shall execute justice and righteousness in the land. In his days Judah will be saved, and Israel will dwell securely. And this is the name by which he will be called: 'The Lᴏʀᴅ is our righteousness.'"

I once was a stranger to grace and to God,
    I knew not my danger, and felt not my load;
    Though friends spoke in rapture of Christ on the tree,
    Jehovah Tsidkenu was nothing to me.
I oft read with pleasure, to sooth or engage,
    Isaiah's wild measure and John's simple page;
    But e'en when they pictured the blood-sprinkled tree
    Jehovah Tsidkenu seem'd nothing to me.
Like tears from the daughters of Zion that roll,
    I wept when the waters went over His soul;
    Yet thought not that my sins had nail'd to the tree
    Jehovah Tsidkenu—'twas nothing to me.
When free grace awoke me, by light from on high,
    Then legal fears shook me, I trembled to die;
    No refuge, no safety in self could I see—
    Jehovah Tsidkenu [Righteousness] my Savior must be.
My terrors all vanished before the sweet name;
    My guilty fears banished, with boldness I came
    To drink at the fountain, life-giving and free—
    Jehovah Tsidkenu is all things to me.
Jehovah Tsidkenu! my treasure and boast,
    Jehovah Tsidkenu! I ne'er can be lost;
    In Thee I shall conquer by flood and by field—
    My cable, my anchor, my breastplate and shield!
Even treading the valley, the shadow of death,
    This watchword shall rally my faltering breath,
    For while from life's fever my God sets me free,
    Jehovah Tsidkenu my death-song shall be.
—ROBERT MURRAY M'CHEYNE, *Memoir and Remains of the Rev. Robert Murray M'Cheyne*, ed. Andrew A. Bonar (Edinburgh; London: Oliphant Anderson & Ferrier, 1894), 574.

> **Hebrews 4:8–11, 16:** For if Joshua had given them rest, God would not have spoken of another day later on. So then, there remains a Sabbath rest for the people of God, for whoever has entered God's rest has also rested from his works as God did from his. Let us therefore strive to enter that rest, so that no one may fall by the same sort of disobedience. . . . Let us then with confidence draw near to the throne of grace, that we may receive mercy and find grace to help in time of need.

He is our strong, mighty, and powerful King who has preceded us in death and every misery and has overcome them all for us. Whoever does anything to us does it to Christ himself. He has made us rulers together with Him over all creation, so that nothing in heaven and earth can harm us. Death and the devil can do nothing to us because He has conquered both through His death. After all, He died for us. For himself He did not need to die, but He died in order to defeat death for us and now He rules over both of those enemies, as indicated by the prophet Hosea: "O death, I will be your death; I have become a vanquisher and a victor" (see 1 Corinthians 15:54–55; Hosea 13:14).

Through His wonderful resurrection, therefore, we have become sovereigns and conquerors of hell and sin. He has promised this to us, and for our sake went down into the depths in order to preserve us from this cruel and horrible descent into hell. Through His joyous resurrection He has also become a great high priest for us, who has obtained direct access to the Father and has reconciled us to the Father through His suffering and dying. By His merits and good works, He has earned for us a welcome access to the Father and abolished our eternal death; in its place He has given us through His rising eternal resurrection and endless life.

—CASPAR HUBERINUS, "A Comforting Sermon on the Resurrection of Christ, Useful for Those Weak in Faith to Read, 1525," in *Early Protestant Spirituality*, The Classics of Western Spirituality, ed. Scott H. Hendrix and Bernard McGinn, trans. Scott H. Hendrix (New York; Mahwah, NJ: Paulist Press, 2009), 113–114.

Luke 23:27–28: And there followed him a great multitude of the people and of women who were mourning and lamenting for him. But turning to them Jesus said, "Daughters of Jerusalem, do not weep for me, but weep for yourselves and for your children."

The death of the Lord Jesus Christ on the cross of Calvary was not an accident; it was God's work. It was God who sent Him there. How often is the whole glory of the cross missed when men sentimentalize it away and say, "He was too good for the world, He was too pure. His teaching was too wonderful; and cruel men crucified Him!" The result is that we begin to feel sorry for Him, forgetting that He himself turned on those "daughters of Jerusalem" who were beginning to feel sorry for Him, and said, "Do not weep for me, but weep for yourselves and for your children."

If our view of the cross is one that makes us feel sorry for the Lord Jesus Christ, it just means that we have never truly seen it. It was God who sent Him there. It was not an accident, but something deliberate. It was a great public act of God. God has done something here in public on the stage of world history, in order that it might be seen, and looked at, and recorded once and forever—the most public action that has ever taken place.

—D. MARTYN LLOYD-JONES, *The Cross: The Vindication of God* (Carlisle, PA: Banner of Truth, 1976/1999), 4.

1 John 4:19: We love because he first loved us.

God so loved us as to be willing to pay the price of His only, dearest Child. Him He sent into our misery, hell, and death, and allowed Him to drain these to the dregs. This is the way to be saved.

—MARTIN LUTHER, *What Luther Says: An Anthology*, comp. Ewald M. Plass (St. Louis, MO: Concordia Publishing House, 1959), entry no. 550, 189.

How does one come to love? The heart of humanity is so base that it cannot love unless it has first seen the benefit of loving. God took His Son and sent Him into our mire, sin, and misery, and poured forth the entire store of His mercy that we might boast of all His goodness as though it were our own.

He made himself a beloved Father and He gave us His Son, poured out His great treasure most generously, and drowned all our sins and filth in the vast sea of His great goodness. This so that the heart cannot but let this great love and blessing draw it to love in return. And then be prepared willingly to fulfill the divine commandments.

Otherwise, the heart cannot love. It must find that it has been loved first. One cannot love first.

Therefore, God comes, takes hold of the heart, and says: "Learn to know me." "Why, who are you?" "I am Christ. I have plunged into your wretchedness. I have drowned your sins in my righteousness."

This knowledge softens your heart. Therefore, you cannot but turn to Him. In this way—when one learns who Christ is—love is taught.

—MARTIN LUTHER, *What Luther Says: An Anthology*, comp. Ewald M. Plass (St. Louis, MO: Concordia Publishing House, 1959), entry no. 2564, 825.

> **Ephesians 2:19–22:** So then you are no longer strangers and aliens, but you are fellow citizens with the saints and members of the household of God, built on the foundation of the apostles and prophets, Christ Jesus himself being the cornerstone, in whom the whole structure, being joined together, grows into a holy temple in the Lord. In him you also are being built together into a dwelling place for God by the Spirit.

God has been pleased to provide His Son to take away our guilt and disgrace, to be the glory among us, and to put great honor upon us, even a covering for our nakedness.

And not only so, but to clothe us and make us glorious, to be to us wisdom and to bring us out of our shameful ignorance and darkness. He is our righteousness, for the removal of our guilt and to provide acceptance with God. He is our sanctification, to change us from sinful to holy and to be our full redemption, to deliver us from all trouble and danger that we might be happy and blessed forever. He makes us as gold tried in the fire, and that although poor we might become rich; that He might lift us from the dunghill and set us among princes.

It is a great reason to praise God, that He would give us who were under bondage to sin and Satan such a glorious victory over our adversaries and cause us to triumph over those who held us captive. God gives us all the privileges of the children of a King.

—JONATHAN EDWARDS, "Glorying in the Savior," in *Sermons and Discourses,
1723–1729*, The Works of Jonathan Edwards, vol. 14, ed. Harry S. Stout and Kenneth P. Minkema (New Haven, CT: Yale University Press, 1997), 468.

> **Exodus 15:25–26:** And he cried to the Lord, and the Lord showed him a log, and he threw it into the water, and the water became sweet. There the Lord made for them a statute and a rule, and there he tested them, saying, "If you will diligently listen to the voice of the Lord your God, and do that which is right in his eyes, and give ear to his commandments and keep all his statutes, I will put none of the diseases on you that I put on the Egyptians, for I am the Lord, your healer."

Are you not amazed sometimes that you should have so much as a hope, that poor and needy as you are, the Lord thinks of you? But let not all that you feel discourage you. For if our Physician is almighty, our disease cannot be desperate, and if He casts none out that come to Him, why should you fear? Our sins are many, but His mercies are more; our sins are great, but His righteousness is greater; we are weak, but He is powerful. Most of our complaints are owing to unbelief, and the remainder to a legal spirit.

—JOHN NEWTON, *Cardiphonia*, in *The Works of John Newton*, vol. 1 (New York: Robert Carter, 1847), 343.

You will not look after the Physician of your souls, you will not prize the Physician of souls, you will not desire the Physician of souls. You will not fall in love, in league with the Physician of souls, you will not resign yourselves to the Physician of souls, until you come to see your wounds, until you come to feel your diseases, until you see the tokens, the sores of divine wrath and displeasure upon you.

—THOMAS BROOKS, *The Complete Works of Thomas Brooks*, vol.1, ed. Alexander Balloch Grosart (Edinburgh; London; Dublin: James Nichol; James Nisbet and Co.; G. Herbert, 1866), 238.

John 13:1, 12–15; 15:12–13: Now before the Feast of the Passover, when Jesus knew that his hour had come to depart out of this world to the Father, having loved his own who were in the world, he loved them to the end. . . . When he had washed their feet and put on his outer garments and resumed his place, he said to them, "Do you understand what I have done to you? You call me Teacher and Lord, and you are right, for so I am. If I then, your Lord and Teacher, have washed your feet, you also ought to wash one another's feet. For I have given you an example, that you also should do just as I have done to you. . . . This is my commandment, that you love one another as I have loved you. Greater love has no one than this, that someone lay down his life for his friends."

Christ is love covered over in flesh.

—THOMAS GOODWIN, *The Heart of Christ* (Edinburgh: Banner of Truth, 2011), 61.

Christ died to prove that God's love is an ocean without shores or bottom.

—JONATHAN EDWARDS, "That God Is the Father of Lights," in *The Blessing of God: Previously Unpublished Sermons of Jonathan Edwards*, ed. Michael McMullen (Nashville, TN: Broadman, 2003), 350.

He will love to the end of their lives, to the end of their sins, to the end of their temptations, to the end of their fears.

—JOHN BUNYAN, *The Work of Jesus Christ as an Advocate*, in *The Works of John Bunyan*, vol. 1, ed. George Offor (Edinburgh: Banner of Truth, 1991), 201.

He loves life into us.

—JOHN OWEN, *On Communion with God*, in *The Works of John Owen*, vol. 2, ed. W. H. Goold (Edinburgh: Banner of Truth, 1965), 63.

Luke 2:11–12: "For unto you is born this day in the city of David a Savior, who is Christ the Lord. And this will be a sign for you: you will find a baby wrapped in swaddling cloths and lying in a manger."

I believe that Jesus Christ, true God, begotten of the Father from eternity, and also true man, born of the Virgin Mary, is my Lord!

—MARTIN LUTHER, *Luther's Small Catechism* (St. Louis, MO: Concordia, 1986), 13.

Are you afraid? Then come to Him, lying in the lap of the fairest and sweetest maid. You will see how great is the divine goodness that seeks above all else that you should not despair. Trust Him! Trust Him! Here is the Child in whom is salvation. To me there is no greater consolation given to humankind than this, that Christ became man, a child, a babe, playing in the lap of His most gracious mother. Who is there whom this sight would not comfort? Now is overcome the power of sin, death, hell, conscience, and guilt, if you come to judge this Babe and believe that He is come, not to judge you, but to save.

—MARTIN LUTHER, *Martin Luther's Christmas Book*, ed. Roland H. Bainton (Minneapolis: Augsburg, 1948), loc. 275 of 593, Kindle.

DAY
216

> **John 6:37–40:** "All that the Father gives me will come to me, and whoever comes to me I will never cast out. For I have come down from heaven, not to do my own will but the will of him who sent me. And this is the will of him who sent me, that I should lose nothing of all that he has given me, but raise it up on the last day. For this is the will of my Father, that everyone who looks on the Son and believes in him should have eternal life, and I will raise him up on the last day."

If any reader of this paper desires salvation, and wants to know what to do, I advise him to go this very day before the Lord Jesus Christ, in a private place, and entreat Him in prayer to save his soul.

Tell Him that you have heard that He receives sinners, and has said, "Whoever comes to me I will never cast out" (John 6:37).

Tell Him that you are a poor sinner, and that you come to Him on the faith of His own invitation.

Tell Him you put yourself wholly and entirely in His hands—that you feel helpless and hopeless in yourself—and that except He saves you, you have no hope to be saved.

Beseech Him to deliver you from the guilt, the power, and the consequences of sin.

Do not doubt His willingness to save you because you are a sinner. It is Christ's office to save sinners. He says himself, "I have not come to call the righteous but sinners to repentance" (Luke 5:32).

Wait not, because you feel unworthy. Wait for nothing. Wait for no one. Waiting comes from the devil.

Just as you are, go to Christ. The worse you are, the more need you have to go to Him. You will never save yourself by staying away.

—J. C. RYLE, *Practical Religion: Being Plain Papers on the Daily Duties, Experience, Dangers, and Privileges of Professing Christians* (London: Charles Murray, 1900), 85–86.

> **1 Corinthians 1:30–31:** And because of him you are in Christ Jesus, who became to us wisdom from God, righteousness and sanctification and redemption, so that, as it is written, "Let the one who boasts, boast in the Lord."

The life and character of Jesus Christ is truly the Holy of Holies in the history of the world. Two thousand years have passed away since He appeared, in the fullness of time, on this earth to redeem a fallen race from sin and death, and to open a never-ceasing fountain of righteousness and life. The ages before Him anxiously awaited His coming, as the fulfillment of the desire of all nations; the ages after Him proclaim His glory, and ever extend His dominion. He is the author of the new creation; the Way, the Truth, and the Life; the Prophet, Priest, and King of regenerate humanity. He is Immanuel, God with us; the eternal Word become flesh; very God and very man in one person, the Savior of the world.

—PHILIP SCHAFF, *The Person of Christ: The Miracle of History*, Michigan Historical Reprint Series (New York: Charles Scribner, 1866), 3–4.

In short, I am a riddle to myself, a heap of inconsistency. But it is said, "We have an Advocate with the Father." Here hope revives; though wretched in myself, I am complete in Him. He is made of God, wisdom, righteousness, sanctification, and redemption. On this rock I build. I trust it shall be well with me at last, and that I shall by and by praise, love, and serve Him without these limitations.

—JOHN NEWTON, *The Works of John Newton*, vol. 6 (Carlisle, PA: Banner of Truth, 2015), 98.

> **Romans 8:31–34:** What then shall we say to these things? If God is for us, who can be against us? He who did not spare his own Son but gave him up for us all, how will he not also with him graciously give us all things? Who shall bring any charge against God's elect? It is God who justifies. Who is to condemn? Christ Jesus is the one who died—more than that, who was raised—who is at the right hand of God, who indeed is interceding for us.

Because we have such a powerful king who has preceded us in death and has conquered all for us, who will harm us? Hence neither death nor the devil, heights nor depths, neither present nor future can turn us away from this Christ (see Romans 8:38–39). He has taken on our weakness and was tempted from every side but, in contrast to us, without sin (see Hebrews 4:15), so that He could bestow faith on our weakness, come to our aid, and represent us to the Father as often as we need it.

We receive this genuine benefit from His resurrection when we believe that He has done everything for our sake and has become our own. Because we could not in ourselves cover our sin, we have One who is our surety and has paid everything for us. If death tries to destroy us with eternal death, He has conquered death, and suffered it for our sake so that for us it is no more. If hell opens its jaws and tries to devour us, Christ has already been there for us, closed its jaws, and worn down its might. If the multitude of our sins tries to make us lose heart and give up hope, we have One who was given for us and has given us all things with himself: all righteousness, godliness, and all that accompanies them. He is our spouse who has taken us to himself in marriage. Whatever belongs to us—death, sin, unrighteousness—is now covered by Him. Everything that He has— righteousness, eternal life, peace—is now ours. We can now say to Him with great joy: "You are mine, and I am Yours." As it is written: "He who touches you touches the apple of his eye" (Zechariah 2:8).

—CASPAR HUBERINUS, "A Comforting Sermon on the Resurrection of Christ, Useful for Those Weak in Faith to Read, 1525," in *Early Protestant Spirituality*, The Classics of Western Spirituality, ed. Scott H. Hendrix and Bernard McGinn, trans. Scott H. Hendrix (New York; Mahwah, NJ: Paulist Press, 2009), 116–117.

Revelation 1:17–18: When I saw him, I fell at his feet as though dead. But he laid his right hand on me, saying, "Fear not, I am the first and the last, and the living one. I died, and behold I am alive forevermore, and I have the keys of Death and Hades."

Throughout the year we hear how our Lord Jesus Christ by His triumph overwhelmed and defeated death and the devil; the devil He strangled in His own body; death He drowned in His own blood; sin He erased with His martyrdom and suffering. All this He personally accomplished, but not for himself. For as the true, eternal God and Lord over all things, He did not require such a victory for himself; even less did He need to become man, and still less to suffer under Pontius Pilate. However, because He did accomplish this for you, me, and everyone else, we all benefit. That is the power and the fruit of Christ's suffering and resurrection.

—MARTIN LUTHER, *The Complete Sermons of Martin Luther*, vol. 6, ed. Eugene F. King and John Nicholas Lenker (Grand Rapids, MI: Baker Books, 2000), 13.

By His resurrection, Christ won the victory over sin, the law, the flesh, the world, the devil, death, hell, and every evil. And this, His victory, He accomplished for us. These tyrants and enemies of ours may accuse and frighten us, but they dare not condemn us, for Christ, whom God the Father raised from the dead, is our righteousness and our victory.

—MARTIN LUTHER, *Commentary on St. Paul's Epistle to the Galatians*, trans. Theodore Conrad Graebner (Grand Rapids, MI: Zondervan, 1939), 11–12.

> **Romans 8:27–28:** And he who searches hearts knows what is the mind of the Spirit, because the Spirit intercedes for the saints according to the will of God. And we know that for those who love God all things work together for good, for those who are called according to his purpose.

Who, therefore, will charge us with sin when we have this high priest, who for our sake offered the unique sacrifice that is more precious than heaven and earth? He intercedes for us, protects us, so that nothing can harm us no matter how versatile and powerful sin and the devil may be. Christ has risen from the dead in order to help us in every situation, listen to us, and be available to us. Before He died, He could not be with everyone everywhere at once. Since He is risen, however, He can give to all aid and counsel when needed; He also fortifies the weak and confirms those who are strong. He has entered the kingdom of the Father so that He can always be near to help us (see Matthew 28:20) and to protect us from violence. For He sits at the right hand of the Father with all power and authority, and every force in heaven and on earth must be subject to Him (see Philippians 2:9–11).

He cannot and will not allow any of His faithful ones to be harmed. He may look on for a while, watching us; He may let us swim for a while without drowning. For a time, He lets us suffer onslaughts and vexations so that our faith and confidence in Him become stronger, and we learn to trust Him boldly in the face of all opposition. In a way, He is testing His own grace that He has poured into us so that it takes root and grows strong, but He remains near us and takes care of us. We are exceedingly dear to Him, for we cost Him dearly. He paid a high price for us; namely, His own blood. He will not let us go to ruin or allow His own blood to count for nought.

—CASPAR HUBERINUS, "A Comforting Sermon on the Resurrection of Christ, Useful for Those Weak in Faith to Read, 1525," in *Early Protestant Spirituality*, The Classics of Western Spirituality, ed. Scott H. Hendrix and Bernard McGinn, trans. Scott H. Hendrix (New York; Mahwah, NJ: Paulist Press, 2009), 116–117.

> **John 14:1, 27; 16:33:** "Let not your hearts be troubled. Believe in God; believe also in me." . . . "Peace I leave with you; my peace I give to you. Not as the world gives do I give to you. Let not your hearts be troubled, neither let them be afraid." . . . "I have said these things to you, that in me you may have peace. In the world you will have tribulation. But take heart; I have overcome the world."

The peace that Christ gives He calls "My peace." It is especially His own to give, because He bought it by His own blood, purchased it by His own substitution, and is appointed by the Father to dispense it to a perishing world.

Who can be surprised that a legacy like this should be backed up by the renewed emphatic charge, "Let not your hearts be troubled, neither let them be afraid"? There is nothing lacking on Christ's part for our comfort, if we will only come to Him, believe, and receive.

The chief of sinners has no cause to be afraid. If we will only look to the one true Savior, there is remedy for every trouble of the heart. Half our doubts and fears arise from a dim perception of the real nature of Christ's Gospel.

—J. C. RYLE, *Expository Thoughts on John*, vol. 3 (New York: Robert Carter & Brothers, 1880), 87–88.

> **John 6:68–69:** Simon Peter answered him, "Lord, to whom shall we go? You have the words of eternal life, and we have believed, and have come to know, that you are the Holy One of God."

"Where will you go?" You who will not receive Christ, where do you propose to go?

Where do you think to find anyone else who has the words of eternal life?

To whom will you flee for help?

Where do poor lost souls think to find another Savior?

Is there another God who can deliver you from the wrath of this God, who is Jehovah?

Is there another Savior whom you think can compare to Christ?

Is there another captain you intend to enlist under by whose power you can be delivered from all evil? Who can conquer all your enemies and bestow upon you an eternal crown and kingdom?

Do you expect to find another Savior, who will indulge you and allow you to go on in sin as you please?

Where is this other Savior? Who is he?

In what part of the world does he dwell? Let us know.

This "other Savior" will be found to be only that old serpent, the devil! It will come to this at last.

What do you expect of the devil? Is he able to save you?

Is he able to fight against God and overcome Him?

Will he ever bestow eternal life upon you?

Has he the words of eternal life?

Certainly, you expect eternal life, or something as good, from some being or other. Who is it?

Consider and see who it is.

Come, therefore, and trust in Him, and yield yourself to Him, sweetly reposing yourself on Him, the only Lord and Savior. For He alone has the words of eternal life.

—JONATHAN EDWARDS, "Life Through Christ Alone," in *Sermons and Discourses, 1720–1723*, The Works of Jonathan Edwards, vol. 10, ed. Wilson H. Kimnach (New Haven, CT: Yale University Press, 2006), 528–530.

2 Corinthians 1:3-5: Blessed be the God and Father of our Lord Jesus Christ, the Father of mercies and God of all comfort, who comforts us in all our affliction, so that we may be able to comfort those who are in any affliction, with the comfort with which we ourselves are comforted by God. For as we share abundantly in Christ's sufferings, so through Christ we share abundantly in comfort too.

Your earthly friends can console your loss but cannot make it up to you. We must all admit that we are miserable comforters.

But you may go and share your loss with Jesus, and you will have both support and healing. His love and His presence are far beyond that of the nearest and most affectionate earthly friend.

Though you are bereaved of your earthly loved one, you may go to your spiritual Husband, and seek His compassion and His company.

He is the fountain of all the wisdom and care, the tender affection and faithfulness that you enjoyed in your departed loved one. In Him is an infinite source of all these things and of all good.

In Him you may have light in your darkness, comfort in your sorrow, and fullness of joy in anticipation of the glory of another world, an everlasting union with your dear one, in the glorious presence of the Redeemer, in whose presence is fullness of joy, and at whose right hand are pleasures for evermore.

—JONATHAN EDWARDS, "The Sorrows of the Bereaved Spread Before Jesus," in *The Works of Jonathan Edwards*, vol. 2, ed. Edward Hickman (Carlisle, PA: Banner of Truth, 1834/1998), 968.

Proverbs 8:27–31:
"When he established the heavens, I was there;
  when he drew a circle on the face of the deep,
when he made firm the skies above,
  when he established the fountains of the deep,
when he assigned to the sea its limit,
  so that the waters might not transgress his command,
when he marked out the foundations of the earth,
  then I was beside him, like a master workman,
and I was daily his delight,
  rejoicing before him always,
rejoicing in his inhabited world
  and delighting in the children of man."

Christ is so lovely that the angels in heaven adore Him. Their hearts overflow with love for Him, and they are continually, day and night without ceasing, praising Him and giving Him glory. He is so lovely that God the Father infinitely delights in Him.

Christ is His beloved Son, the brightness of His glory, whose beauty the Father continually sees with infinite delight, without ever being weary of beholding Him. And if the angels and God himself love Christ so much more than anyone or anything else, surely all children on earth ought to love Him above all things in this world.

Everything that is lovely in God the Father is in Jesus Christ, and everything that is lovely in any man is in Him, for He is man as well as God, and He is the holiest, most humble, and in every way the most excellent man that ever was. He is the true delight of heaven.

There is nothing in heaven, that glorious place, that is brighter or more lovely than Christ. By becoming man, He was as a flower springing up out of the earth, lovelier than any seen in all this world.

There is more goodness to be enjoyed in Christ than in anything or anyone in all the world. He is not only loving, but all-sufficient for any need of humankind. There is enough provision in His person to supply all our wants and satisfy all our desires.

—JONATHAN EDWARDS, "Children Ought to Love the Lord Jesus Christ Above All," in *Sermons and Discourses: 1739–1742*, The Works of Jonathan Edwards, vol. 22, ed. Harry S. Stout (New Haven, CT: Yale University Press, 2003), 171–172.

> **Colossians 1:21–23:** And you, who once were alienated and hostile in mind, doing evil deeds, he has now reconciled in his body of flesh by his death, in order to present you holy and blameless and above reproach before him, if indeed you continue in the faith, stable and steadfast, not shifting from the hope of the gospel that you heard, which has been proclaimed in all creation under heaven, and of which I, Paul, became a minister.

The chief article and foundation of the Gospel is that before you take Christ as an example, you accept Him as a gift that God has given you and that is your own. When you hear or read of Christ doing or suffering something, do not doubt that Christ himself belongs to you. On this you may depend.

This is what it means to have a proper grasp of the Gospel, of the overwhelming goodness of God, which neither prophet, apostle, nor angel was able to fully express, and which no heart could adequately fathom. The Gospel is the expression of the great love of God for us, whereby the heart and conscience become joyous, secure, and content. This is what preaching the Christian faith means and why the apostles were called the twelve messengers.

Faith in God's provision of a Savior redeems you from sin, death, and hell and enables you to overcome temptation. When you have Christ as the foundation of your salvation, then you take Him as your example, your mentor, giving yourself in service to others just as Christ has given himself for you.

Good works do not make you a Christian, rather they come forth from you because you are a Christian. As widely as a gift differs from an example, so widely does faith differ from works, for faith possesses nothing of its own, only the deeds and life of Christ. So you see that the Gospel is not a book of laws and commandments, but a book of divine promises in which God gives us all His possessions and benefits in Christ.

—MARTIN LUTHER, "A Brief Instruction on What to Look for and Expect in the Gospels (1521)," in *The Annotated Luther: Word and Faith*, ed. Kirsi I. Stjerna, Hans J. Hillerbrand, and Timothy J. Wengert, vol. 2 (Minneapolis: Fortress Press, 2015), 30.

> **Matthew 11:29:** Take my yoke upon you, and learn from me, for I am gentle and lowly in heart, and you will find rest for your souls.

Jesus is the great teacher of lowliness of heart. We need to learn daily from Him. See the Master taking a towel and washing His disciples' feet. Follower of Christ, will you not humble yourself? See Him as the Servant of all, and surely you cannot be proud!

Is not this sentence the summary of His biography: "He humbled himself"? (see Philippians 2:8). Was He not on earth always stripping off first one robe of honor and then another, until, naked, He was nailed to the cross? And there, did He not empty himself, pouring out His lifeblood, giving up all for us, until they laid Him penniless in a borrowed grave?

How low was our dear Redeemer brought! How then can we be proud? Stand at the foot of the cross and count the drops of blood by which you have been cleansed. See the crown of thorns. Mark His scourged back, still gushing with crimson stripes.

See His hands and feet given up to the piercing irons, His whole being to mockery and scorn. See the throes of inward grief, visible in His outward frame. Hear the groaning cry, "My God, my God, why have you forsaken me?" (Psalm 22:1).

And if you do not lie prostrate on the ground before that cross, you have never seen it; if you are not humbled in the presence of Jesus, then you do not know Him. You were so lost that nothing could save you but the sacrifice of God's Only Begotten Son.

—CHARLES H. SPURGEON, "June 3—Evening," in *Morning and Evening* (Geanies House, Fearn, Scotland: Christian Focus, 1994), 329.

Psalm 79:9: Help us, O God of our salvation, for the glory of your name; deliver us, and atone for our sins, for your name's sake!

Christ our Priest makes God our Father and himself our Lord. He sits in heaven above as our Mercy Seat, and there intercedes for us before the Father without ceasing, pleading on our behalf.

This is the greatest comfort that can come to a human being, and no sweeter sermon can be preached to the human heart. This He has proved in the Gospel by everything He says and does. In addition, in order to atone for us, He gave himself at the cost of His very life and blood, in spite of the wrath, which we have deserved. Is it possible to preach anything more comforting than this to the troubled conscience?

—MARTIN LUTHER, *What Luther Says: An Anthology*, comp. Ewald M. Plass (St. Louis, MO: Concordia Publishing House, 1959), entry 552, 190–191.

I find deep comfort in this thought, that Jesus is perfect Man, no less than perfect God. He in whom I am told by Scripture to trust is not only a great High Priest, but a feeling High Priest. He is not only a powerful Savior, but an empathizing Savior. He is not only the Son of God, mighty to save, but the Son of man, able to feel.

God knows all this well. He knows the very secrets of man's heart. He knows the ways by which that heart is most easily approached, and the springs by which that heart is most readily moved. He has wisely made it so that the Savior should be feeling as well as mighty.

He has given us One who has not only a strong hand to pluck us as wood from the fire but also an empathizing heart on which those who labor and are heavy laden may find rest.

—J. C. RYLE, *Holiness: Its Nature, Hindrances, Difficulties and Roots* (Moscow, ID: Charles Nolan Publishers, 1877/2001), 238–239.

Ephesians 1:4–6: Even as he chose us in him before the foundation of the world, that we should be holy and blameless before him. In love he predestined us for adoption to himself as sons through Jesus Christ, according to the purpose of his will, to the praise of his glorious grace, with which he has blessed us in the Beloved.

Christ is the true high priest, our real bishop, who has taken away from us the Father's anger and, together with our sin, placed it on himself and thereby reconciled us to God. In place of God's robust justice and potent anger, Christ obtained for us the abundant gift of the Father's mercy. For God's righteousness is such that it cannot leave any sin unpunished, especially since, through Adam's fall, we became subject to the judgment of God and became the children of wrath and of eternal damnation, even though from the beginning of the world we were ordained to become children of God and destined for eternal life.

In order that God's justice may remain intact and to provide a way to punish sin as God's justice demands, Christ, while we were still enemies of God and could merit nothing through our works, loved us so much that He freely gave himself for us amid this misery, and took upon himself the wrath of His Father, removing it from us. In this way, the justice of God, which cannot allow any sin to go unpunished, is satisfied.

—CASPAR HUBERINUS, "A Comforting Sermon on the Resurrection of Christ, Useful for Those Weak in Faith to Read, 1525," in *Early Protestant Spirituality*, The Classics of Western Spirituality, ed. Scott H. Hendrix and Bernard McGinn, trans. Scott H. Hendrix (New York; Mahwah, NJ: Paulist Press, 2009), 114.

Matthew 7:7–11: "Ask, and it will be given to you; seek, and you will find; knock, and it will be opened to you. For everyone who asks receives, and the one who seeks finds, and to the one who knocks, it will be opened. Or which one of you, if your son asks for bread, will give him a stone? Or if he asks for a fish, will give him a serpent? If you then, who are evil, know how to give good gifts to your children, how much more will your Father who is in heaven give good things to those who ask him!"

O my dear Lord Jesus Christ, you have said, "Ask, and it will be given to you; seek, and you will find; knock, and it will be opened to you" (Matthew 7:7). In keeping with this promise, give to me, Lord, not gold or silver, but a strong and firm faith. While I search, let me find not the pleasures of the world, but comfort and refreshment through Your blessed and healing Word.

Open to me when I knock. I desire nothing that this world cherishes, for by it I would not be uplifted. Grant me Your Holy Spirit, who enlightens my heart, and comforts and strengthens me. He secures my faith and trust in Your grace to the very end. Amen.

—MARTIN LUTHER, *Luther's Prayers*, ed. Herbert Brokering (Minneapolis: Augsburg, 1994), no. 171, 102.

Romans 7:18-25: For I know that nothing good dwells in me, that is, in my flesh. For I have the desire to do what is right, but not the ability to carry it out. For I do not do the good I want, but the evil I do not want is what I keep on doing. Now if I do what I do not want, it is no longer I who do it, but sin that dwells within me. So I find it to be a law that when I want to do right, evil lies close at hand. For I delight in the law of God, in my inner being, but I see in my members another law waging war against the law of my mind and making me captive to the law of sin that dwells in my members. Wretched man that I am! Who will deliver me from this body of death? Thanks be to God through Jesus Christ our Lord!

What can we do when sin causes anxiety of conscience? Remember that God's Son came from heaven and became a man to take upon himself your sin and the sin of the world. Because He died willingly on the cross, doing penance for our sin, He made satisfaction for it, and in our stead became the one who paid for it. This priceless death and bloodshed of Jesus Christ are your own, if you believe that Christ died as much for you as for Peter and Paul. You have been baptized into the death of Christ (Romans 6:3); do not underestimate its consolation. The death of Christ is comfort and help for you, because through His death you have died to sin, may receive with certainty the forgiveness of sins, and will see resurrection of the body and eternal life. Christian baptism is a covenant and testimony that through faith you have a good conscience by virtue of the forgiveness of sins through the death and resurrection of Christ. You are also assured of this through the Lord's Supper, when He says that His blood is shed for the forgiveness of sins (Matthew 26:28). If you have led a sinful life, hasten to call upon the name of the Lord and you will find help (Romans 10:13).

—URBANUS RHEGIUS, "Apothecary of the Soul for the Healthy and the Sick in These Dangerous Times, 1529," in *Early Protestant Spirituality*, The Classics of Western Spirituality, ed. Scott H. Hendrix and Bernard McGinn, trans. Scott H. Hendrix (New York; Mahwah, NJ: Paulist Press, 2009), 122.

Romans 12:19–20: Beloved, never avenge yourselves, but leave it to the wrath of God, for it is written, "Vengeance is mine, I will repay, says the Lord." To the contrary, "if your enemy is hungry, feed him; if he is thirsty, give him something to drink; for by so doing you will heap burning coals on his head."

We long to go back into the tangle of our life and make right the things that are wrong—at least to suffer where we have caused others to suffer.

And something like that Christ did for us when He died instead of us on the cross; He atoned for all our sins.

The sorrow for sins committed against one's fellowmen does indeed remain in the Christian's heart. And he will seek by every means that is within his power to repair the damage that he has done.

But atonement at least has been made—made as truly as if the sinner himself had suffered with and for those whom he has wronged. And the sinner himself, by the mystery of grace, becomes right with God.

All sin at its root is sin against God. "Against thee, thee only have I sinned" is the cry of a true penitent.

How terrible is the sin against God! Who can recall the wasted moments and years? Gone they are, never to return; gone our allotted span of life; gone the day in which a man can work. Who can measure the irrevocable guilt of a wasted life?

Yet even for such guilt God has provided a fountain of cleansing in the precious blood of Christ. God has clothed us with Christ's righteousness as with a garment; in Christ we stand spotless before the judgment seat of God.

—J. GRESHAM MACHEN, *Christianity and Liberalism*, new edition (Grand Rapids, MI; Cambridge, U.K.: Wm. B. Eerdmans Publishing, 2009), 109–110.

> **Isaiah 53:4–5:**
> Surely he has borne our griefs
>   and carried our sorrows;
> yet we esteemed him stricken,
>   smitten by God, and afflicted.
> But he was pierced for our transgressions;
>   he was crushed for our iniquities;
> upon him was the chastisement that brought us peace,
>   and with his wounds we are healed.

Let us consider how God has provided comfort for all our afflictions in giving us a Redeemer of such glory and such love, especially when we consider the results of that great display of His beauty and love in His death.

He suffered that we might be delivered.

His soul was overwhelmingly sorrowful even unto death, to take away the sting of sorrow and that we might have everlasting comfort.

He was oppressed and afflicted that we might be supported.

He was overwhelmed in the darkness of death and of hell, that we might have the light of life.

He was cast into the furnace of God's wrath, that we might swim in the rivers of pleasure.

His heart was overwhelmed in a flood of sorrow and anguish, that our hearts might be filled and overwhelmed with a flood of eternal joy.

And now let consider: our Redeemer was dead but is alive, and He lives forevermore.

If we are united to Him, our souls will be like a tree, planted by a river, that never dies. It is said that He will be their light in darkness and their morning star that is as bright as the coming day.

And in a little while, He will arise as the sun in full glory. And our sun shall no more set, and there shall be no cloud, no veil upon His face or upon our hearts, but the Lord shall be our everlasting Light and our Redeemer.

—JONATHAN EDWARDS, "To Lady Mary Pepperrell," in *Letters and Personal Writings*, The Works of Jonathan Edwards, vol. 16, ed. George S. Claghorn (New Haven, CT: Yale University Press, 1998), 418–419. Written by Edwards, November 28, 1751, to comfort a grieving mother on the loss of her son.

> **Numbers 21:8–9:** And the Lᴏʀᴅ said to Moses, "Make a fiery serpent and set it on a pole, and everyone who is bitten, when he sees it, shall live." So Moses made a bronze serpent and set it on a pole. And if a serpent bit anyone, he would look at the bronze serpent and live.

Look to Jesus and live! Look at this opening Scripture and you will see your disease and your remedy. You have been bitten by the great serpent. The poison of sin is through and through your whole heart, but Christ was raised up on the cross that you may look and live.

Now, do not look so long and so harassingly at your own heart and feelings. What will you find there but the bite of the serpent? You were shaped in sin, and the whole of your natural life has been spent in sin.

The more God opens your eyes, the more you will feel that you are *lost in yourself.* This is your disease.

Now for the remedy: look to Christ; for the glorious Son of God so loved lost souls, that He took on Him a body and died for us—bore our curse and obeyed the law in our place. Look to Him and live.

Look now at Romans 5:19. By the disobedience of Adam, many were made sinners. We had no hand in Adam's sin, and yet the guilt of it comes upon us. Though we did not eat the forbidden fruit, the sin and misery have been laid at our door.

In the same way, by the obedience of Christ, many are made righteous. Christ is the glorious One who stood for many. His perfect life is sufficient to cover you.

You had no hand in His obedience. You were not alive when He came into the world and lived and died; and yet, through His perfect obedience, you may stand before God robed in righteousness.

—ROBERT MURRAY M'CHEYNE, *Memoir and Remains of the Rev. Robert Murray M'Cheyne,* ed. Andrew A. Bonar (Edinburgh: Banner of Truth, 1844/1966), 278–280.

Psalm 103:1–5; 8, 11–12:
Bless the LORD, O my soul,
  and all that is within me,
  bless his holy name!
Bless the LORD, O my soul,
  and forget not all his benefits,
who forgives all your iniquity,
  who heals all your diseases,
who redeems your life from the pit,
  who crowns you with steadfast love and mercy,
who satisfies you with good
  so that your youth is renewed like the eagle's. . . .
The LORD is merciful and gracious,
  slow to anger and abounding in steadfast love. . . .
For as high as the heavens are above the earth,
  so great is his steadfast love toward those who fear him;
as far as the east is from the west,
  so far does he remove our transgressions from us.

Persevere, therefore, and be joyful in the Lord. You are preserved in the faithful hands of the Almighty God, your Father. Christ covers your sin with His innocence. No one can snatch you out of the hand of your heavenly Father (John 10:28). You are dealing with a momentary distress, in which Christ has already preceded you (Hebrews 4:15). You are to be made like Him, dying to sin, leaving behind the sinful life (Romans 6:10–11), and living with Christ, your Lord, forever. Your sins are already gone and paid for. Satan has been conquered, and God is waiting for you together with all His saints. You cannot be condemned any more than Christ can be condemned. Cling to Him in true faith. If sin, death, and hell cannot hurt Christ, neither can they harm you, because you are in Christ. He has paid for your guilt and sets you free when you believe this Gospel.

—URBANUS RHEGIUS, "Apothecary of the Soul for the Healthy and the Sick in These Dangerous Times, 1529," in *Early Protestant Spirituality*, The Classics of Western Spirituality, ed. Scott H. Hendrix and Bernard McGinn, trans. Scott H. Hendrix (New York; Mahwah, NJ: Paulist Press, 2009), 125.

Psalm 35:1–2:
Contend, O Lord, with those who contend with me;
fight against those who fight against me!
Take hold of shield and buckler
and rise for my help!

When a Christian is weak and can hardly pray for himself, Jesus Christ is praying for him. What a comfort is this: when Satan is tempting, Christ is praying!

—THOMAS WATSON, *All Things for Good, or A Divine Cordial* (Carlisle, PA: Banner of Truth, 1663/2001), 23.

I ought to study Christ as a living Savior more—as a Shepherd, carrying the sheep—as a King, reigning in and over the souls He has redeemed—as a Captain, fighting with those who fight with me, as One who has engaged to bring me through all temptations and trials, however impossible to flesh and blood.

I am often tempted to ask, "How can this Man save us? How can Christ in heaven deliver me from temptations raging within me, and nets enclosing me?" This is the father of lies again! Because I know He is able to save to the uttermost.

I ought to study Christ as an Intercessor. He prayed most for Peter, who was to be most tempted. He will pray for me.

If I could hear Christ praying for me in the next room, I would not fear a million enemies. Yet the distance should make no difference; He is praying for me!

—ROBERT MURRAY M'CHEYNE, *Memoir and Remains of the Rev. Robert Murray M'Cheyne*, ed. Andrew A. Bonar (Edinburgh; London: Oliphant Anderson & Ferrier, 1894), 158.

John 2:1–10: On the third day there was a wedding at Cana in Galilee, and the mother of Jesus was there. Jesus also was invited to the wedding with his disciples. When the wine ran out, the mother of Jesus said to him, "They have no wine." And Jesus said to her, "Woman, what does this have to do with me? My hour has not yet come." His mother said to the servants, "Do whatever he tells you." Now there were six stone water jars there for the Jewish rites of purification, each holding twenty or thirty gallons. Jesus said to the servants, "Fill the jars with water." And they filled them up to the brim. And he said to them, "Now draw some out and take it to the master of the feast." So they took it. When the master of the feast tasted the water now become wine, and did not know where it came from (though the servants who had drawn the water knew), the master of the feast called the bridegroom and said to him, "Everyone serves the good wine first, and when people have drunk freely, then the poor wine. But you have kept the good wine until now."

We learn from these verses *the Almighty power of our Lord Jesus Christ*. We are told of a miracle that Jesus did at a marriage feast when the wine ran out. By a mere act of will He changed water into wine, and so supplied the need of all the guests.

The manner in which the miracle took place deserves special notice. We are not told of any outward visible action that preceded or accompanied it. It is not said that He touched the waterpots. It is not said that He commanded the water to change its quality, or that He prayed to His Father about it. He simply willed the change, and it took place. We read of no prophet or apostle in the Bible who did a miracle in this way. He who could do such a work, in such a manner, was no one less but God.

It is a comforting thought that the same power of will that our Lord here displayed is still exercised on behalf of His believing people. They have no reason to be held back because they cannot see Him interceding for them.

If He wills their salvation and the supply of all their spiritual needs, they are as safe and well provided for as if they saw Him standing by them.

—J. C. RYLE, *Expository Thoughts on John*, vol. 1 (Carlisle, PA: Banner of Truth, 1869/2012), 65–66.

> **Romans 8:14–17:** For all who are led by the Spirit of God are sons of God. For you did not receive the spirit of slavery to fall back into fear, but you have received the Spirit of adoption as sons, by whom we cry, "Abba! Father!" The Spirit himself bears witness with our spirit that we are children of God, and if children, then heirs—heirs of God and fellow heirs with Christ, provided we suffer with him in order that we may also be glorified with him.

It is only through the union of the witness of revelation and the inward witness of the Spirit in our hearts that we are able to scale this pinnacle of faith and say with the confidence and love of a son or daughter, "Abba Father!"

It is the same Person who is the Father of the Lord Jesus Christ in the inexpressible mystery of the Trinity who is the Father of believers in the mystery of His adoptive grace.

God the Father is not only the one who adopts us; He also considers those who believe in Jesus' name His own children.

—JOHN MURRAY, *Redemption: Accomplished and Applied* (Grand Rapids, MI: Wm. B. Eerdmans Publishing, 1955), 132, 134, 140.

Once I was a slave but now I am a son; once I was dead but now I am alive; once I was darkness but now I am light in the Lord; once I was a child of wrath, an heir of hell, but now I am an heir of heaven; once I was Satan's bond-servant but now I am God's freeman; once I was under the spirit of bondage but now I am under the Spirit of adoption that seals up to me the remission of my sins, the justification of my person, and the salvation of my soul.

—THOMAS BROOKS, *Heaven on Earth*, in *The Complete Works of Thomas Brooks*, vol. 2, ed. Alexander Balloch Grosart (Edinburgh: James Nichol, 1866), 345.

1 Peter 2:24–25: He himself bore our sins in his body on the tree, that we might die to sin and live to righteousness. By his wounds you have been healed. For you were straying like sheep, but have now returned to the Shepherd and Overseer of your souls.

Christ is a Savior. He did not come on earth to be a conqueror, or a philosopher, or a mere teacher of morality. He came to save sinners. He came to do what man could never do for himself—to do what money and learning can never obtain—to do what is essential to man's real happiness—He came to take away sin.

Christ is a complete Savior. He takes away sin. He did not merely make vague proclamations of pardon, mercy, and forgiveness. He took our sins upon himself and carried them away. He allowed them to be laid upon himself and bore them in His own body on the tree. The sins of everyone who believes on Jesus are made as though they never existed. The Lamb of God has taken them away.

—J. C. RYLE, *Expository Thoughts on John*, vol. 1 (Carlisle, PA: Banner of Truth, 1869/2012), 40–41.

Romans 8:1–4, 9–11: There is therefore now no condemnation for those who are in Christ Jesus. For the law of the Spirit of life has set you free in Christ Jesus from the law of sin and death. For God has done what the law, weakened by the flesh, could not do. By sending his own Son in the likeness of sinful flesh and for sin, he condemned sin in the flesh, in order that the righteous requirement of the law might be fulfilled in us, who walk not according to the flesh but according to the Spirit. . . . You, however, are not in the flesh but in the Spirit, if in fact the Spirit of God dwells in you. Anyone who does not have the Spirit of Christ does not belong to him. But if Christ is in you, although the body is dead because of sin, the Spirit is life because of righteousness. If the Spirit of him who raised Jesus from the dead dwells in you, he who raised Christ Jesus from the dead will also give life to your mortal bodies through his Spirit who dwells in you.

Even if you had committed all the sins in the world, more than enough grace is still available. God has blessed you in Christ, and this same grace has been secured and applied. The matter of your salvation is certain, for the same Christ is God's Son by nature in the divine being, Truth itself. As a man, He has our flesh and blood. Who can be a more reliable giver of the promise of grace than the One who is the truth of the promise? It is impossible, therefore, that you believe in Christ but are not blessed by God, freed from sin, and made an heir of God and co-heir with Christ. For heaven and earth will pass away, but the Word of God remains forever. Believe firmly and do not doubt. The Almighty has become a man who was born, died on the cross, rose from the dead, ascended to heaven, and has delivered to us all that which was promised. Expect from God through Christ nothing but grace and mercy. Outside of Christ there is no consolation or help; in Him salvation is abundantly greater, higher, and richer that anyone can imagine!

—URBANUS RHEGIUS, "Apothecary of the Soul for the Healthy and the Sick in These Dangerous Times, 1529," in *Early Protestant Spirituality*, The Classics of Western Spirituality, ed. Scott H. Hendrix and Bernard McGinn, trans. Scott H. Hendrix (New York; Mahwah, NJ: Paulist Press, 2009), 125–126.

Hebrews 4:9–10: So then, there remains a Sabbath rest for the people of God, for whoever has entered God's rest has also rested from his works as God did from his.

As much as the Lord may be pleased to indulge us with comforts and mercies here, still this is not, and cannot be, our Sabbath rest.

Indwelling sin, the temptations of Satan, changing dispensations, and the vanity that is inseparably linked with everything we cling to on earth, will in some way disturb our peace.

But there is a brighter world, where sin and sorrow can never enter. Every moment brings us nearer to it.

Then every imperfection shall cease, and our dearest desires shall be satisfied beyond our present comprehension.

Then we shall see Him whom, having not seen, we love. We shall see Him in all His glory, not as now, through the medium of the sacraments, but face to face, without a veil.

We shall see Him and be completely transformed into His perfect image. Then, likewise, we shall see all those whom He has redeemed, and join with the immeasurable multitude of all nations, people, and languages, in singing the triumphant song of Moses and the Lamb forever!

Then we shall look back with wonder on all the way the Lord has led us through this wilderness, and shall say, "He has done all things well."

May this blessed hope comfort our hearts, strengthen our hands, and not allow us to consider anything too costly or too hard, so that we may finish our course with joy.

—JOHN NEWTON, *The Works of John Newton*, vol. 6 (London: Hamilton, Adams & Co., 1824), 47–48.

Luke 4:16–19: And he came to Nazareth, where he had been brought up. And as was his custom, he went to the synagogue on the Sabbath day, and he stood up to read. And the scroll of the prophet Isaiah was given to him. He unrolled the scroll and found the place where it was written,

> "The Spirit of the Lord is upon me,
>   because he has anointed me
>   to proclaim good news to the poor.
> He has sent me to proclaim liberty to the captives
>   and recovering of sight to the blind,
>   to set at liberty those who are oppressed,
> to proclaim the year of the Lord's favor."

When Jesus expels demons and heals the sick, He is driving out of creation the powers of destruction and is healing and restoring created beings who are injured or sick. The lordship of Christ, to which the healings witness, restores creation to health. Jesus' healings are not supernatural miracles in a natural world. They are the only truly natural thing in a world that is unnatural, demonized, and wounded. Finally, with the resurrection of Christ, the new creation begins, *pars pro toto*, with the crucified one.

—JURGEN MOLTMANN, *The Way of Jesus Christ: Christology in Messianic Dimensions*, trans. M. Kohl (Minneapolis: Fortress, 1993), 98–99.

The Lord did not come to make a display of His powers, but rather to heal and teach those who were suffering. A person aiming at display would simply appear, seeking to impress his beholders; but Christ came to heal and to teach the Way, not simply to sojourn here, but to give himself to the aid of those in need, and so He appeared in a fashion that they could bear and understand, that He may not, by exceeding the requirements of the sufferers, trouble the very persons that needed Him, rendering God's appearance useless.

—ATHANASIUS, *On the Incarnation*, trans. Archibald Robertson (London: D. Nutt, 1891), 74.

> **Psalm 41:1-2:**
> Blessed is the one who considers the poor!
>   In the day of trouble the LORD delivers him;
> the LORD protects him and keeps him alive;
>   he is called blessed in the land;
>   you do not give him up to the will of his enemies.

I suggest you take a lodging as near to Gethsemane as you can and walk daily to Mount Golgotha; and borrow that telescope that gives you a view of the unseen world. A view of what is passing within the veil has a marvelous effect on composing our spirits in regard to the little things that are daily passing here.

Praise the Lord, who has enabled you to fix your supreme affection upon Him who is alone the proper and suitable object of it, and from whom you cannot meet a denial or fear of change.

He loved you first, and He will love you forever.

And if He is pleased to arise and smile upon you, you no more need to beg for happiness from the prettiest creature upon earth than you would need the light of a candle on a midsummer noon.

Basically, I pray and hope the Lord will sweeten your cross, and either in kind or in kindness make up for what you have lost.

Wait, pray, and believe, and all shall be well. A cross we must have somewhere; and they who are favored with health, plenty, peace, and a conscience sprinkled with the blood of Jesus must have more reasons for thankfulness than grief.

Look around you and take notice of the severe sufferings that many of the Lord's own people are experiencing, and your trials will appear comparatively light.

—JOHN NEWTON, *Wise Counsel: John Newton's Letters to John Ryland Jr.*, ed. Grant Gordon (Carlisle, PA: Banner of Truth, 2009), 100.

Exodus 33:18-23: Moses said, "Please show me your glory." And he said, "I will make all my goodness pass before you and will proclaim before you my name 'The LORD.' And I will be gracious to whom I will be gracious, and will show mercy on whom I will show mercy. But," he said, "you cannot see my face, for man shall not see me and live." And the LORD said, "Behold, there is a place by me where you shall stand on the rock, and while my glory passes by I will put you in a cleft of the rock, and I will cover you with my hand until I have passed by. Then I will take away my hand, and you shall see my back, but my face shall not be seen."

O how infinitely great is the privilege and happiness of those who go to be with Christ in His glory, such as this passage of Scripture describes!

The privilege of the twelve disciples was great, in being so constantly with Christ as His family, in His state of humiliation.

And great was the privilege of Moses, when he was with Christ on Mount Sinai, and asked Him to show him His glory, and he saw His back, as He passed by, and proclaimed His name.

But will it not be it an infinitely greater privilege to be with Christ in heaven, where He sits on the right hand of God, in the glory of the King and God of angels, and of the whole universe, shining forth as the great Light, the bright sun of that world of glory? There we will be living in the full, constant, and everlasting view of His beauty and brightness, free to talk with Him and fully enjoy His love. There to fellowship with Him in the pleasure and joy He has with His Father, there to sit with Him on His throne, and reign with Him in the possession of all things. There to partake with Him in the joy and glory of His victory over His enemies and the advancement of His cause in the world. To join with Him in joyful songs of praise, to His Father and our Father, to His God and our God, forever and ever. Is not such a privilege worth seeking after?

—JONATHAN EDWARDS, "True Saints, When Absent from the Body, Are Present with the Lord," in *Sermons and Discourses, 1743–1758*, The Works of Jonathan Edwards, vol. 25, ed. Wilson H. Kimnach and Harry S. Stout (New Haven, CT: Yale University Press, 2006), 243–244.

Matthew 27:27-31, 37-38: Then the soldiers of the governor took Jesus into the governor's headquarters, and they gathered the whole battalion before him. And they stripped him and put a scarlet robe on him, and twisting together a crown of thorns, they put it on his head and put a reed in his right hand. And kneeling before him, they mocked him, saying, "Hail, King of the Jews!" And they spit on him and took the reed and struck him on the head. And when they had mocked him, they stripped him of the robe and put his own clothes on him and led him away to crucify him. . . . And over his head they put the charge against him, which read, "This is Jesus, the King of the Jews." Then two robbers were crucified with him, one on the right and one on the left.

As Christ's enemies were allowed to freely persecute and afflict Him, and Christ, as it were, yielded himself wholly into their hands to be mocked and spit upon, that they might be as bold as they wished in deriding Him, executing their worst hatred and cruelty before His friends, then doubtless His friends will be allowed to freely enjoy Him in this life and in the life to come.

He will give himself up to His friends to enjoy Him, as He did to be abused by His enemies, since that was why He allowed himself to be abused in the first place. Christ will surely give himself as much to His saints as He has already given himself for them through His death. He whose arms were spread to suffer, to be nailed to the cross, will doubtless be opened as wide to embrace those for whom He suffered. He whose side was opened to the spear of His enemies, to give access to their malice and cruelty, and to shed His blood, will doubtless be opened to welcome the love of His saints.

—JONATHAN EDWARDS, *The "Miscellanies": Entries Nos. 501–832*, The Works of Jonathan Edwards, vol. 18, ed. Ava Chamberlain (New Haven, CT: Yale University Press, 2000), 370.

Isaiah 25:6–9:
On this mountain the LORD of hosts will make for all peoples
   a feast of rich food, a feast of well-aged wine,
   of rich food full of marrow, of aged wine well refined.
And he will swallow up on this mountain
   the covering that is cast over all peoples,
   the veil that is spread over all nations.
   He will swallow up death forever;
and the Lord GOD will wipe away tears from all faces,
   and the reproach of his people he will take away
   from all the earth, for the LORD has spoken.
It will be said on that day,
   "Behold, this is our God; we have waited for him, that he might
      save us.
   This is the LORD; we have waited for him;
   let us be glad and rejoice in his salvation."

What do we do when death terrifies? If Christ himself were not there, death would be an unbearable ordeal. Through Christ, however, death has already been abolished and conquered. The soul does not suffer eternal death; it goes to Christ, just as the thief on the cross in his distress heard Christ say, "Truly, I say to you, today you will be with me in paradise" (Luke 23:43). The body rests in the certain hope of blessed, immortal life, and on the last day it must rise with honor and glory, so that body and soul will be eternally with Christ and all the elect.

Remember, therefore, and do not doubt that the body of Christ lay in the grave and rose again on the third day into a new, eternal life and will never die again. The bodies of all Christians will also, once they have fallen asleep, rest a while in the grave in the certain hope of a joyful resurrection, and they must rise again into eternal life at the last day, when there will be no more sin or death, but only life, joy, and blessedness forever and ever.

—URBANUS RHEGIUS, "Apothecary of the Soul for the Healthy and the Sick in These Dangerous Times, 1529," in *Early Protestant Spirituality*, The Classics of Western Spirituality, ed. Scott H. Hendrix and Bernard McGinn, trans. Scott H. Hendrix (New York; Mahwah, NJ: Paulist Press, 2009), 127–128.

Psalm 23:1: The LORD is my shepherd; I shall not want.

In Him I have an offering, an altar, a temple, a priest, a sun, a shield, a Savior, a Shepherd, a hiding place, a resting place, food, medicine, riches, honor, wisdom, righteousness, holiness, in short, everything.

No document could contain an inventory of the unsearchable, inexhaustible blessings and treasures that are hidden in Him, and communicated by Him to poor sinners who believe in His name.

But though I am, I trust, an heir, I am still a minor, and in my actual experience, I am too often more like a servant than a son.

But there is a time appointed of the Father. I hope one day to be of age, and to come to the full enjoyment of my boundless inheritance.

—JOHN NEWTON, *One Hundred and Twenty-Nine Letters from the Rev. John Newton to Josiah Bull*, ed. William Bull (London: Hamilton, Adams, and Co., 1847), 191–192.

Blessed be God, though we are regularly ashamed and humiliated because of what we are in ourselves, we have reason to rejoice continually in Christ Jesus.

He is revealed unto us under the various names, characters, relations, and offices, which He bears in Scripture, and He holds out to our faith a cure for every wound, a cordial for every discouragement, and a sufficient answer to every objection that sin or Satan can suggest against our peace.

If we are guilty, He is our Righteousness. If we are sick, He is our Physician. If we are weak, helpless, and defenseless, He is the compassionate and faithful Shepherd who has taken charge of us. And He will not allow anything to disappoint our hopes or to separate us from His love.

He knows what we are made of, He remembers that we are but dust, and He has engaged to guide us by His counsel, support us by His power, and at length, to receive us into His glory, that we may be with Him forever.

—JOHN NEWTON, "Letter III," in *The Works of John Newton*, vol. 1, ed. Richard Cecil (London: Hamilton, Adams & Co., 1824), 439.

1 Timothy 2:5–6: For there is one God, and there is one mediator between God and men, the man Christ Jesus, who gave himself as a ransom for all, which is the testimony given at the proper time.

All things must be dipped in the blood of Christ and brought back unto the Father by the mediation of the Son himself; just as the Father does everything through the Son, so must the flowing back match the flowing out.

—MEISTER ECKHART, "Sermon 56," in Bernard McGinn, *The Mystical Thought of Meister Eckhart* (New York: The Crossroad Publishing Co., 2001), 126.

We need not be afraid to look at sin, and study its nature, origin, power, extent, and vileness, if we only look at the same time at the Almighty medicine provided for us in the salvation that is in Jesus Christ.

Though sin has abounded, grace has much more abounded. In the everlasting covenant of redemption, to which Father, Son, and Holy Spirit are parties, through the Mediator of that covenant, Jesus Christ the righteous, perfect God and perfect Man in one Person, and in the work that He did on the cross by dying for our sins and rising again for our justification, through the offices He fills as our Priest, Substitute, Physician, Shepherd, and Advocate, the precious blood that cleanses from all sin, the everlasting righteousness He brought to the fore in the perpetual intercession that He carries on as our Representative at God's right hand, even His power to save to the uttermost the chief of sinners, and His willingness to receive and pardon the most vile, His readiness to bear with the weakest by the grace of the Holy Spirit, which He plants in the hearts of all His people, renewing, sanctifying, and causing old things to pass away and all things to become new—in all this (what a brief sketch it is!)—in all this, I say, there is a full, perfect, and complete remedy for the horrific disease of sin.

Awful and tremendous as the right view of sin undoubtedly is, no one need faint or despair if we will take a right view of Jesus Christ at the same time.

—J. C. RYLE, *Holiness: Its Nature, Hindrances, Difficulties and Roots* (Chicago: Moody Publishers, 2010), 33–34.

Psalm 56:1–4, 8–13:
Be gracious to me, O God, for man tramples on me;
    all day long an attacker oppresses me;
my enemies trample on me all day long,
    for many attack me proudly.
When I am afraid,
    I put my trust in you.
In God, whose word I praise,
    in God I trust; I shall not be afraid.
    What can flesh do to me? . . .
You have kept count of my tossings;
    put my tears in your bottle.
    Are they not in your book?
Then my enemies will turn back
    in the day when I call.
    This I know, that God is for me.
In God, whose word I praise,
    in the Lord, whose word I praise,
in God I trust; I shall not be afraid.
    What can man do to me?
I must perform my vows to you, O God;
    I will render thank offerings to you.
For you have delivered my soul from death,
    yes, my feet from falling,
that I may walk before God
    in the light of life.

Set this love and the safety that is in it before your eyes; and behold it while these things make their assaults upon you. These words, "God loves me," will support you when dangers may assail you.

And this is what is meant when we are exhorted to rejoice in the Lord, to make our boast in the Lord, to triumph in Christ, and to set the Lord always before our face. For he that can do this steadfastly cannot be overcome.

For in God there is more than what is in the world, either to help or to hinder; wherefore, if God is my helper, if God loves me, if Christ is my redeemer, and has bestowed His love that passes knowledge upon me, who can be against me? And if they be against me, what disadvantage do I reap, since even all this works for my good? This is improving the love of God and of Christ to my advantage.

—JOHN BUNYAN, *All Love's Excelling: The Saint's Knowledge of Christ's Love* (Carlisle, PA: Banner of Truth, 1692/1998), 119–120.

Ephesians 1:3–6: Blessed be the God and Father of our Lord Jesus Christ, who has blessed us in Christ with every spiritual blessing in the heavenly places, even as he chose us in him before the foundation of the world, that we should be holy and blameless before him. In love he predestined us for adoption to himself as sons through Jesus Christ, according to the purpose of his will, to the praise of his glorious grace, with which he has blessed us in the Beloved.

When we assert that our Lord Jesus Christ, the Son of God, the Creator, came to us as with a physical body, we do not want anyone to think that we are agreeing with those heretics who claim that He is only a man, and therefore want to prove that He could not be or do anything more than a man. Rather, we maintain that the Word was divine even while taking on a physical body, and that He was also God, according to the Scriptures.

—NOVATIAN, *A Treatise Concerning the Trinity*, in *Ante-Nicene Fathers*, vol. 5, ed. Alexander Roberts, James Donaldson, and A. Cleveland Coxe (Buffalo, NY: Christian Literature Publishing Co., 1886), 20.

If Christ was only man, how does He say, "And now glorify me with the glory which I had with You before the world existed"? If, before the world existed, He had glory with God, and maintained His glory with the Father, He existed before the world. He would not have had the glory unless He himself had existed before. For no one could possess anything unless he himself should first exist to keep it. But man could not have glory before the foundation of the world, since he was created after the world; but Christ had glory before the world. Therefore, He was not only a man, but also God, because He existed before the world.

—NOVATIAN, *A Treatise Concerning the Trinity*, in *Ante-Nicene Fathers*, vol. 5, ed. Alexander Roberts, James Donaldson, and A. Cleveland Coxe (Buffalo, NY: Christian Literature Publishing Co., 1886), 626.

> **Mark 4:37–41:** And a great windstorm arose, and the waves were break-ing into the boat, so that the boat was already filling. But he was in the stern, asleep on the cushion. And they woke him and said to him, "Teacher, do you not care that we are perishing?" And he awoke and rebuked the wind and said to the sea, "Peace! Be still!" And the wind ceased, and there was a great calm. He said to them, "Why are you so afraid? Have you still no faith?" And they were filled with great fear and said to one another, "Who then is this, that even the wind and the sea obey him?"

A Christian can never lose his inward peace, either totally or finally. It is true that by sin, Satan, and the world a Christian's peace may be somewhat interrupted, but it can never be finally lost.

The greatest storms in this world that beat upon a believer will in time blow over, and the Sun of Righteousness, the Prince of Peace, will shine as gloriously upon him as ever. Under the word *shalom* the Jews comprehend peace, prosperity, and success.

When the worst of men have done their worst against the people of God, yet the issue shall be peace, prosperity, and success. "My peace I give unto you," that is, peace with God and peace with conscience purchased with His blood.

And what power or policy is there that can deprive us of this legacy? Surely none. The peace that Christ gives is based upon His blood, upon His righteousness, upon His justice, upon His intercession, and upon a cov-enant of peace, and therefore it must be a lasting peace, an abiding peace.

—THOMAS BROOKS, "A Word in Season," in *The Complete Works of Thomas Brooks*, vol. 5, ed. Alexander Balloch Grosart (Edinburgh; London; Dublin: James Nichol; James Nisbet and Co.; G. Herbert, 1867), 510–512.

Psalm 94:19: When the cares of my heart are many, your consolations cheer my soul.

Why should you be such an enemy to your own peace? Why read over the evidence of God's love to your soul, as a person does a book they intend to prove wrong? Why do you study evasions, and turn off those comforts that are due you?

—JOHN FLAVEL, *Keeping the Heart: How to Maintain Your Love for God* (Fearn, Scotland: Christian Focus, 2012), 94.

The Gospel possesses something distinctive, namely, the coming of the Savior, our Lord Jesus Christ, His suffering and His resurrection. For the beloved prophets preached in anticipation of Him, but the Gospel is the imperishable finished work. All these things together are good if you believe with love.

—IGNATIUS OF ANTIOCH, "To the Philadelphians 9.1–2," in Michael W. Holmes, *Apostolic Fathers* (Grand Rapids, MI: Baker Academic, 2007), 245.

> **Hebrews 10:19–25:** Therefore, brothers, since we have confidence to enter the holy places by the blood of Jesus, by the new and living way that he opened for us through the curtain, that is, through his flesh, and since we have a great priest over the house of God, let us draw near with a true heart in full assurance of faith, with our hearts sprinkled clean from an evil conscience and our bodies washed with pure water. Let us hold fast the confession of our hope without wavering, for he who promised is faithful. And let us consider how to stir up one another to love and good works, not neglecting to meet together, as is the habit of some, but encouraging one another, and all the more as you see the Day drawing near.

When, however, you see that the nations enter into faith, that churches are raised, that altars are not sprinkled with the blood of beasts but purified by the precious blood of Christ; when you see the priests and the Levites not dispensing the blood of goats and bulls but the Word of God through the Holy Spirit, then say that Jesus has succeeded to Moses and become greater than him—not Jesus the son of David but Jesus the Son of God. When you see that Christ our Passover has been sacrificed for us and we eat the unleavened bread in sincerity and in truth; when you see in the church the fruits of the good soil bearing thirtyfold, sixtyfold, and a hundredfold, that is, widows, virgins, and martyrs; when you see that the seed of Israel is increased from those who are born not of blood nor of human will but of the will of God; and when you see the children of God, who had been dispersed, forming one congregation; when you see the people of God keeping the Sabbath not by resting from their common business but by resting from the business of sin, then you must agree that Jesus is greater than Moses.

—ORIGEN, *Homilies on Joshua* 2.1, in *Sources Chrétiennes,* vol. 438, ed. H. de Lubac, J. Daniélou and C. Mondésert (Paris: Editions du Cerf, 1941, 1998), 71:116–118.

1 Thessalonians 4:16–17: For the Lord himself will descend from heaven with a cry of command, with the voice of an archangel, and with the sound of the trumpet of God. And the dead in Christ will rise first. Then we who are alive, who are left, will be caught up together with them in the clouds to meet the Lord in the air, and so we will always be with the Lord.

The only one who can dispel all the clouds and darkness that sin raises between us and the throne of God; the only one who can remove the fire, storms, and tempests that the law kindles and stirs up around Him; the only one who can unveil His glorious face, and reveal His holy heart, and show us those infinite treasures and storehouses of goodness, mercy, love, and kindness, which have lived in Him from all eternity; the only one who can help us discover these eternal springs of patience and forgiveness—is Christ.

—JOHN OWEN, *Temptation and Sin*, in *The Works of John Owen*, vol. 6, ed. William Goold (Edinburgh: Johnson & Hunter; 1850–1855; reprint by Banner of Truth, 1966), 401.

This I know, that as soon as we behold the person of Christ, we shall see a glory in Him a thousand times greater than we can conceive now. The greatness of infinite wisdom, love, and power within Him will be continually before us.

And all the glories of the person of Christ that we have before weakly and faintly inquired into will be visible to us forever. Therefore, the ground and cause of our blessedness is that we shall ever be with the Lord, as He himself prayed, "That they . . . may be with me where I am, to see my glory" (John 17:24).

We cannot perfectly behold Him until we are with Him where He is. Our sight of Him will be direct, intuitive, and constant. There is a glory that will also be in us when we behold the glory of Christ, that right now we cannot understand.

—JOHN OWEN, "Meditations and Discourses on the Glory of Christ," in *The Works of John Owen*, vol. 1, ed. William Goold (Edinburgh: Johnson & Hunter; 1850–1855; reprint by Banner of Truth, 1965), 379.

> **1 John 3:2:** Beloved, we are God's children now, and what we will be has not yet appeared; but we know that when he appears we shall be like him, because we shall see him as he is.

Look at His life, the standing wonder of all ages. Those who have not worshiped Him have admired Him. His life is incomparable, unique; there is nothing like it in all the history of humankind. Our imagination has never been able to create anything approximating the perfect beauty of His life.

Think of His death. There have been may heroic and martyr's deaths, but there is not one that can be set side by side with Christ's death. He did not pay the debt of natures as others have; and yet He paid our nature's debt. He did not die because He must; He died because He would. The only "must" that came upon Him was the necessity of all-conquering love. The cross of Christ is the greatest wonder of fact or fiction. Fiction invents many marvelous things, but nothing that can be compared with the cross of Christ.

Think of our Lord's resurrection. If this is one of the things that is shown you by the Holy Spirit, it will fill you with holy delight. Instead of the grave being a dungeon into which all men seem to go, but could never come out, Christ, by His resurrection, has made a tunnel right through the grave. Jesus, by dying, has conquered death for all believers.

Now think of His ascension. But why should I take you over all these scenes with which you are familiar? What a wondrous fact that, when the cloud received Him out of the disciples' sight, the angels lifted Him to His heavenly home!

Think of Him now, at His Father's right hand, adored of all the heavenly host; and then let your mind fly forward to the glory of His second coming, the final judgment with its terrors, the millennium with its indescribable bliss, and the heaven of heavens, with its endless and unparalleled splendor. If these things are shown to you by the Holy Spirit, the vision will indeed glorify Christ, and you will sit down, and sing with the blessed Virgin, "My soul magnifies the Lord, and my spirit rejoices in God my Savior" (Luke 1:46–47).

—CHARLES SPURGEON, "The Chief Office of the Holy Spirit," in *Spurgeon on the Holy Spirit* (New Kensington, PA: Whitaker House, 2000), 61.

Galatians 6:14: But far be it from me to boast except in the cross of our Lord Jesus Christ, by which the world has been crucified to me, and I to the world.

The saints' delight is in Christ: He is their joy, crown, rejoicing; their life, food, health, strength, desire. He is their righteousness, salvation, blessedness. Without Him they have nothing; in Him they have all things. May I never boast in anything but the cross of our Lord Jesus Christ. He has, from the foundation of the world, been the hope, expectation, and delight of all believers.

—JOHN OWEN, *Communion with the Triune God*, ed. Kelly Kapic and Justin Taylor (Wheaton, IL: Crossway, 1657/2007), 236.

If Christ is the Sun of Righteousness, we should, when we are cold and needy, flee to Him as the One having sufficient resources to supply all our needs.

Are we in the dark? He is Light. Are we ill? He is our Healer. Are we dying? He is our Life. Are we alone and without comfort? He is the fullness of Love.

He is the Son of God, and we should seek Him alone; He is all we need for time and eternity: our Prophet, our Priest, our King, who atones for all our sins and enables us to overcome all shortcomings and failures and makes us more than conquerors.

—RICHARD SIBBES, "The Sun of Righteousness," in *The Works of Richard Sibbes*, vol. 7, ed. Alexander Balloch Grosart (reprint, Edinburgh: Banner of Truth, 2001), 171.

> **John 17:15–23:** "I do not ask that you take them out of the world, but that you keep them from the evil one. They are not of the world, just as I am not of the world. Sanctify them in the truth; your word is truth. As you sent me into the world, so I have sent them into the world. And for their sake I consecrate myself, that they also may be sanctified in truth. I do not ask for these only, but also for those who will believe in me through their word, that they may all be one, just as you, Father, are in me, and I in you, that they also may be in us, so that the world may believe that you have sent me. The glory that you have given me I have given to them, that they may be one even as we are one, I in them and you in me, that they may become perfectly one, so that the world may know that you sent me and loved them even as you loved me."

The work of redemption that the Gospel declares unto us above all else leads us to love. For that work was the most glorious and wonderful work of love ever seen. Love is the most important thing the Gospel reveals about God the Father and His Son Jesus Christ.

The Gospel brings to light the love between the Father and the Son and declares how that love has been shown in mercy, and how Christ is God's beloved Son in whom He is well pleased.

The Gospel reveals the love Christ has for His Father and the wonderful fruits of that love—in particular, His doing such great things as well as His suffering such great things in obedience to the Father, at the same time honoring the Father's justice, authority, and law.

There is also revealed how the Father and the Son are one in love, that we might become one with them as well, and with one another, agreeable to Christ's prayer in John 17.

—JONATHAN EDWARDS, *Charity and Its Fruits*, in *Ethical Writings*, The Works of Jonathan Edwards, vol. 8, ed. Paul Ramsey (New Haven, CT: Yale University Press, 1749/1989), 143–145.

> **1 John 1:1–3:** That which was from the beginning, which we have heard, which we have seen with our eyes, which we looked upon and have touched with our hands, concerning the word of life—the life was made manifest, and we have seen it, and testify to it and proclaim to you the eternal life, which was with the Father and was made manifest to us— that which we have seen and heard we proclaim also to you, so that you too may have fellowship with us; and indeed our fellowship is with the Father and with his Son Jesus Christ.

It is in Christ alone that we may have a clear, distinct view of the glory of God and His excellence.

> —JOHN OWEN, "Meditations and Discourses Concerning the Glory of Christ," in *The Works of John Owen*, vol. 1, ed. William Goold (Edinburgh: Banner of Truth, 1965), 299.

We are unable to know You, or feel the effects of Your love toward us, except through Christ, who is the brightness of Your glory, the express image of Your Person, God the Father, the Son of Man with us.

> —THEODORE BEZA, Maister Beza's *Household Prayers for the Consolation and Perfection of a Christian Life*, trans. J. Barnes (London: Nicholas Okes, 1608), C4.

This is the original glory of Christ, given to Him by His Father, and which by faith we may behold. He, and He alone, declares, represents, and makes known, unto angels and humans, the essential glory of the invisible God, His attributes and His will—without which, a perpetual comparative darkness would have been on all of creation, especially here on earth.

> —JOHN OWEN, "Meditations and Discourses Concerning the Glory of Christ," in *The Works of John Owen*, vol. 1, ed. William Goold (Edinburgh: Banner of Truth, 1965), 294–295.

2 John 1:3: Grace, mercy, and peace will be with us, from God the Father and from Jesus Christ the Father's Son, in truth and love.

I grant the best of humankind have no perfection of peace; and this because they have no perfection of grace. If perfect grace is present in the life, there might be perfect peace; but the perfection of both is reserved for another world. Sometimes a believer may long for the sense of peace, sweet peace, even though the grounds of his peace are fixed, certain, and constant.

The grounds of a Christian's peace are these: We are in Christ, reconciled with God, justified, forgiven, adopted, given the covenant of grace and peace.

Though these are sure and everlasting, the sense of peace may ebb and flow, rise and fall, in a believer's heart, especially if he is fighting sin or strong temptation, or is under a cloud of sadness, or when unbelief has gained the throne. If the heart is quarrelsome or troublesome, or when the believer has fallen from their first love, or when they have brought great guilt upon their soul, or especially if they are no longer communing with God, peace will certainly be lacking.

And what power is there that can deprive us of this legacy? The peace that Christ gives is rooted in His shed blood, His righteousness, His intercession, and His covenant of peace, which is a lasting peace, an abiding peace.

—THOMAS BROOKS, "A Word in Season," in *The Complete Works of Thomas Brooks*, vol. 5, ed. Alexander Balloch Grosart (Edinburgh; London; Dublin: James Nichol; James Nisbet and Co.; G. Herbert, 1867), 510–512.

DAY
259

1 Corinthians 15:42–49: So is it with the resurrection of the dead. What is sown is perishable; what is raised is imperishable. It is sown in dishonor; it is raised in glory. It is sown in weakness; it is raised in power. It is sown a natural body; it is raised a spiritual body. If there is a natural body, there is also a spiritual body. Thus it is written, "The first man Adam became a living being"; the last Adam became a life-giving spirit. But it is not the spiritual that is first but the natural, and then the spiritual. The first man was from the earth, a man of dust; the second man is from heaven. As was the man of dust, so also are those who are of the dust, and as is the man of heaven, so also are those who are of heaven. Just as we have borne the image of the man of dust, we shall also bear the image of the man of heaven.

The real difficulty, the supreme mystery with which the Gospel confronts us, does not lie in the Good Friday message of atonement, nor in the Easter message of resurrection, but in the Christmas message of incarnation. The really staggering Christian claim is that Jesus of Nazareth was God made man—that the second person of the Godhead became the "second man," determining human destiny, the second representative head of the race, and that He took humanity without loss of deity, so that Jesus of Nazareth was as truly and fully divine as He was human. Here are two mysteries for the price of one—the plurality of persons within the unity of God, and the union of Godhead and manhood in the person of Jesus. It is here, in the thing that happened at the first Christmas, that the profoundest and most unfathomable depths of the Christian revelation lie.

—J. I. PACKER, *Knowing God* (Downers Grove, IL: IVP, 1973), 53.

Lamentations 3:31–33:
For the Lord will not
    cast off forever,
but, though he cause grief, he will have compassion
    according to the abundance of his steadfast love;
for he does not afflict from his heart
    or grieve the children of men.

My brethren, though God is just, yet His mercy may be said to be more natural to Him than all His acts of justice; that is, vindictive justice. In these acts of justice, there is a satisfaction to a behavior, in that He meets and is level with sinners. Yet there is something in it that is contrary to Him: "He does not retain his anger forever, because he delights in steadfast love" (Micah 7:18). When He exercises acts of justice, it is for a higher end, not simply for the thing itself. There is always something in His heart against it.

But when He shows mercy, manifesting His nature and disposition, He does it with His whole heart. There is nothing in Him that is against it. The act itself pleases Him. There is no reluctance in Him.

Therefore, in Lamentations, when it speaks of punishing, it says, "He does not afflict from his heart or grieve the children of men." But when it comes to showing mercy, He says, "I will rejoice in doing them good . . . with all my heart and all my soul" (Jeremiah 32:41). And so acts of justice might be called his "strange deed" or "alien work" (Isaiah 28:21).

—THOMAS GOODWIN, *The Works of Thomas Goodwin*, vol. 2, (Grand Rapids, MI: Reformation Heritage, 2006), 179–80.

> **Revelation 12:10–11:** And I heard a loud voice in heaven, saying, "Now the salvation and the power and the kingdom of our God and the authority of his Christ have come, for the accuser of our brothers has been thrown down, who accuses them day and night before our God. And they have conquered him by the blood of the Lamb and by the word of their testimony, for they loved not their lives even unto death."

I understand by the expression "by the blood of the Lamb" that our Lord's death effectively took away sin.

When John the Baptist first pointed to Jesus, he said, "Behold, the Lamb of God, who takes away the sin of the world!" (John 1:29). Our Lord Jesus took away our sin by His death.

Beloved, we can be sure that He offered an acceptable and effective propitiation, because He said, "It is finished" (John 19:30). Either He put away sin, or He did not. If He did not, how will it ever be put away?

If He did, then believers are clear. Altogether apart from anything that we do or are, our glorious Substitute took away our sin, just like the scapegoat carried the sin of Israel into the wilderness.

In the case of all those for whom our Lord offered himself as a substitutionary sacrifice, the justice of God is not in any way kept from operation; it is consistent with justice that God should forgive the redeemed.

Two thousand years ago, Jesus paid the dreadful debt of all His elect, and made a full atonement for the whole mass of iniquities of those who shall believe in Him, thereby removing the tremendous load and casting it by one lift of His pierced hand into the depths of the sea.

—CHARLES H. SPURGEON, "The Blood of the Lamb, the Conquering Weapon," in *The Metropolitan Tabernacle Pulpit Sermons*, vol. 34 (London: Passmore & Alabaster, 1888), 508–509.

> **John 12:31–32:** "Now is the judgment of this world; now will the ruler of this world be cast out. And I, when I am lifted up from the earth, will draw all people to myself."

He stretched out His hands on the cross, that He might encompass the ends of the world; for this Golgotha is the very center of the earth.

—CYRIL OF JERUSALEM, "The Catechetical Lectures of S. Cyril, Archbishop of Jerusalem," in *S. Cyril of Jerusalem, S. Gregory Nazianzen,* A Select Library of the Nicene and Post-Nicene Fathers of the Christian Church, 2nd ser., vol. 7, ed. Philip Schaff and Henry Wace, trans. Edwin Hamilton Gifford (Buffalo, NY: Christian Literature Co., 1894), 267.

If any Christian wants to know why Jesus Christ suffered death on the cross and not in some other way, let them be told that no other way than this was supremely good for us, and that it was well that the Lord suffered this for our sakes. For if He came himself to bear the curse laid upon us, how else could He have "become a curse," unless He received the death set for a curse? And that death is the cross, for it is written: "cursed is everyone who is hanged on a tree" (Galatians 3:13). Again, the Lord's death is the ransom of all, and by His death "the dividing wall of hostility" (Ephesians 2:14) is broken down and the call of the Gentiles comes about. How could He have called us if He had not been crucified? For it is only on the cross that a man dies with arms outstretched. Here, again, we see the fitness of His death and of those outstretched arms: it was that He might draw His ancient people with the one and the Gentiles with the other, and join and unite both together in himself. Even so, He foretold the manner of His redeeming death, "I, when I am lifted up from the earth, will draw all people to myself" (John 12:32). Again, the air is the sphere of the devil, the enemy of our race who, having fallen from heaven, endeavors with the other evil spirits who shared in his disobedience both to keep souls from the truth and to hinder the progress of those who are trying to follow it.

—ATHANASIUS, *On the Incarnation of the Word,* A Select Library of the Nicene and Post-Nicene Fathers of the Christian Church, 2nd ser., vol. 4, ed. and trans. Philip Schaff and Henry Wace (Buffalo, NY: Christian Literature Publishing Co., 1892), 291 (*On the Incarnation,* 4.25).

1 Corinthians 2:14–16: The natural person does not accept the things of the Spirit of God, for they are folly to him, and he is not able to understand them because they are spiritually discerned. The spiritual person judges all things, but is himself to be judged by no one. "For who has understood the mind of the Lord so as to instruct him?" But we have the mind of Christ.

I counsel you to think highly of Christ, and of free grace, more than you did before; for I know that Christ is not known among us. I think that I see more of Christ than I ever saw; and yet I see but little of what may be seen.

Oh, that He would draw back the curtains, and that the King would come out of His hall and His palace, that I might see Him! Christ's love is glory and it is heaven; it would soften hell's pain to be filled with it.

What would I refuse to suffer, if I could get but a drink of love to my heart's desire! Oh, what price could be given for Him? Angels cannot tell us.

His weight, His worth, His sweetness, His overpassing beauty! If men and angels would come and look to that great and princely One, their emptiness could never take up His depth, their narrowness could never comprehend His breadth, height, and length.

If ten thousand worlds of angels were created, they might all tire themselves in wondering at His beauty and begin again to wonder anew.

Oh, that I could come near Him, to kiss His feet, to hear His voice, to feel the fragrance of His ointments! But alas! I have little of Him and I long for more.

—SAMUEL RUTHERFORD, "Letter 175," in *Letters of Samuel Rutherford* (Carlisle, PA: Banner of Truth, 1664/2012), 331.

> **Luke 24:25–27, 44–45:** And he said to them, "O foolish ones, and slow of heart to believe all that the prophets have spoken! Was it not necessary that the Christ should suffer these things and enter into his glory?" And beginning with Moses and all the Prophets, he interpreted to them in all the Scriptures the things concerning himself. . . . Then he said to them, "These are my words that I spoke to you while I was still with you, that everything written about me in the Law of Moses and the Prophets and the Psalms must be fulfilled." Then he opened their minds to understand the Scriptures.

If we would grow in grace and in the knowledge of our Lord and Savior Jesus Christ, we cannot do better than to study what the Old Testament types tell us of His person and work. We sometimes forget that the writers of the New Testament were students of the Old Testament, that it was their Bible, and that they would naturally allude again and again to the types and shadows, expecting their readers also to be familiar with them. If we fail to see these allusions, we lose much of the beauty of the passage, and cannot rightly understand it. In the gospel of John, there are constant references to the types. In the first chapter, our attention is drawn to the Lamb of God, and our thoughts go back to all the lambs that had been sacrificed, from Abel's lamb in Genesis 3, to the last offered in the temple. In the closing verse of the chapter, there is evident reference to Jacob's ladder. In verse 14, Christ is shown to be the Antitype of the Tabernacle, for it tells us how "the Word was made flesh and dwelt among us," while in chapter 2, He compares himself to the temple, for He says, "Destroy this temple and in three days I will raise it up." In chapter 3, we see Him in the brazen serpent; in chapter 4, He compares himself to Jacob's well; in chapter 6, we are reminded of the smitten rock, for He himself was the rock out of which would flow the rivers of living water. In chapters 8 and 9, He is the light of the world; in chapter 10, the Antitype of all the shepherds of the Old Testament; in chapter 12, He is the corn of wheat that brought forth the sheaf of the first fruits; and in chapter 15, the True Vine in contrast with the vine that He brought out of Egypt. In almost every chapter an Old Testament type is set before us.

—ADA R. HABERSHON, *Study of the Types* (Grand Rapids, MI: Kregel Publications, 1957), 19–20.

Philippians 3:7–11: But whatever gain I had, I counted as loss for the sake of Christ. Indeed, I count everything as loss because of the surpassing worth of knowing Christ Jesus my Lord. For his sake I have suffered the loss of all things and count them as rubbish, in order that I may gain Christ and be found in him, not having a righteousness of my own that comes from the law, but that which comes through faith in Christ, the righteousness from God that depends on faith—that I may know him and the power of his resurrection, and may share his sufferings, becoming like him in his death, that by any means possible I may attain the resurrection from the dead.

The plain truth is that without Christ there is no happiness in this world. He alone can give the Comforter who abides forever.

He is the sun; without Him men never feel warm.

He is the light; without Him men are always in the dark.

He is the bread; without Him men are always starving.

He is the living water; without Him men are always thirsty.

Give them what you like—place them where you please—surround them with all the comforts you can imagine—it makes no difference. Separate from Christ, the Prince of Peace, a man cannot be truly happy.

—J. C. RYLE, *Practical Religion: Being Plain Papers on the Daily Duties, Experience, Dangers, and Privileges of Professing Christians* (Carlisle, PA: Banner of Truth, 1878/2013), 236.

> **John 14:16–20:** "And I will ask the Father, and he will give you another Helper, to be with you forever, even the Spirit of truth, whom the world cannot receive, because it neither sees him nor knows him. You know him, for he dwells with you and will be in you. I will not leave you as orphans; I will come to you. Yet a little while and the world will see me no more, but you will see me. Because I live, you also will live. In that day you will know that I am in my Father, and you in me, and I in you."

The place that Jesus occupies in our soul He will never vacate, for in us is His home of homes, and it is the greatest delight for Him to dwell there.

In this endless love, we are led and protected by God, and we never shall be lost. This beloved soul was preciously knitted to Him in its making, by a knot so subtle and so mighty that it is united in God. In this uniting it is made endlessly holy. All the souls that will be saved in heaven without end are knit in this knot, and united in this union, and made holy in this holiness.

Greatly ought we to rejoice that God dwells in our soul; and more greatly ought we to rejoice that our soul dwells in God. Our soul is created to be God's dwelling place, and the dwelling of our soul is God, who is uncreated. Our soul sits in God in true rest, our soul stands in God in sure strength, and our soul is rooted in God in endless love. Therefore, if we want to have knowledge of our soul, communion and discourse with it, we must seek it in our Lord God in whom it is enclosed.

—JULIAN OF NORWICH, "Showings," in *The Classics of Western Spirituality* (Mahwah, NJ: Paulist Press, 1978), 164, 284–285.

Luke 19:5–10: And when Jesus came to the place, he looked up and said to him, "Zacchaeus, hurry and come down, for I must stay at your house today." So he hurried and came down and received him joyfully. And when they saw it, they all grumbled, "He has gone in to be the guest of a man who is a sinner." And Zacchaeus stood and said to the Lord, "Behold, Lord, the half of my goods I give to the poor. And if I have defrauded anyone of anything, I restore it fourfold." And Jesus said to him, "Today salvation has come to this house, since he also is a son of Abraham. For the Son of Man came to seek and to save the lost."

The love of Christ to sinners is the very essence and marrow of the Gospel. That He should love us at all, and care for our souls—that He should love us before we love Him, or even know anything about Him—that He should love us so much as to come into the world to save us, take our nature upon Him, bear our sins, and die for us on the cross—all this is too wonderful indeed!

But the love of Christ to saints is no less wonderful, in its way, than His love to sinners, though far less considered.

That He should bear with all their countless infirmities from grace to glory—that He should never be tired of their endless inconsistencies and petty provocations—that He should go on forgiving and forgetting incessantly, and never be provoked to cast them off and give them up—all of this is marvelous indeed!

This loving Savior is One who delights to receive sinners. Let no man be afraid to continue with Christ after he has once come to Him and believed.

Let him not fancy that Christ will cast him off because of his failures and dismiss him to his former hopelessness on account of his infirmities. Such thoughts are entirely unwarranted by anything in the Scriptures. Jesus will never reject any servant because of feeble service or weak performance.

Those whom Jesus receives He keeps. Those whom He loves first He loves last. His promise shall never be broken, and it is for saints as well as for sinners: "Whoever comes to me I will never cast out" (John 6:37).

—J. C. RYLE, *Expository Thoughts on John*, vol. 3 (Carlisle, PA: Banner of Truth, 1880/2012), 1–3.

> **Colossians 2:13–14:** And you, who were dead in your trespasses and the uncircumcision of your flesh, God made alive together with him, having forgiven us all our trespasses, by canceling the record of debt that stood against us with its legal demands. This he set aside, nailing it to the cross.

There is help provided for poor lost sinners in Jesus Christ. When we were helpless, the Only Begotten Son of God helped us. When He saw our miserable case, He pitied us. He was able to help when no one else was able.

He was wise enough, strong enough, worthy enough. He came into the world and took on the nature of man. He laid down His life, shed His own precious blood, and thereby made full satisfaction for our sins.

He paid a sufficient price to pay all the debt we owed to God. He paid a sufficient price to purchase heaven. He ascended into heaven and is appointed by God to rule over the whole world.

He gives full salvation to sinners that He has purchased by His obedience and sufferings. He overcame the devil and all the enemies of our souls.

God opens our eyes and gives us new hearts. He brings all His people that trust in Him to heaven. God makes them perfectly holy and fit for heaven. He will raise up their bodies at the end of the world and make both soul and body new and glorious for all eternity.

—JONATHAN EDWARDS, "Preaching the Gospel Brings Poor Sinners to Christ," in *The Salvation of Souls: Nine Previously Unpublished Sermons on the Call of Ministry and the Gospel*, ed. Richard Bailey and Gregory Wills (Wheaton, IL: Crossway, 2002), 152.

Romans 1:1–6: Paul, a servant of Christ Jesus, called to be an apostle, set apart for the gospel of God, which he promised beforehand through his prophets in the holy Scriptures, concerning his Son, who was descended from David according to the flesh and was declared to be the Son of God in power according to the Spirit of holiness by his resurrection from the dead, Jesus Christ our Lord, through whom we have received grace and apostleship to bring about the obedience of faith for the sake of his name among all the nations, including you who are called to belong to Jesus Christ.

We Christians should know that if God is not on one side of the scale to give it weight, we, on our side, sink to the ground. In other words: if it cannot be said that God died for us, but only a man, we are lost; but if God's death and a dead God lie in the balance, His side goes down and ours goes up like a light and empty scale. Yet He can also readily go up again or leap out of the scale! But He could not sit on the scale unless He became a man like us, so that it could be called God's dying, God's martyrdom, God's blood, and God's death. For God in His own nature cannot die; but now that God and man are united in one person, it is called God's death when the man dies who is one substance or one person with God.

—MARTIN LUTHER, *On the Councils and the Church*, quoted in the *Formula of Concord: Solid Declaration* VIII:44, *Concordia: The Lutheran Confessions*, ed. McCain et al. (St. Louis, MO: Concordia, 2005, 2006) 588–589.

(Christ) remained unbrokenly "in the form of God." It cannot be denied that this is what lies beneath this whole way of understanding the idea of the two natures of Christ, on the basis of which alone can this dual method of speaking of Him be defended or even understood to our Lord's first followers as a whole, and to himself as well, He was nothing other than God manifest in the flesh.

—B. B. WARFIELD, *The Lord of Glory: A Study of the Designations of Our Lord in the New Testament with Especial Reference to His Deity* (American Tract Society, 1907), 225, 248.

> **John 12:31–32:** "Now is the judgment of this world; now will the ruler of this world be cast out. And I, when I am lifted up from the earth, will draw all people to myself."

For Christ came into this world, and took man's nature upon himself, that He might be made a sacrifice for the sins of the whole world, and so reconcile us to God the Father; that He alone might declare unto us how this was done through the good pleasure of the Father, that we, by fixing our eyes upon Christ, might be drawn and carried straight to the Father.

For we must not think, as before we have warned you, that by the curious searching of the majesty of God, anything can be known about our salvation, but only by taking hold of Christ, who, according to the will of the Father, hath given himself to death for our sins. When you acknowledge this to be the will of God through Christ, then wrath ceases, fear and trembling vanish away; neither does God appear any other than merciful, who by His determinate counsel would that His Son should die for us, that we might live through Him.

—MARTIN LUTHER, *Commentary on Galatians* (London: James Duncan, 1830), 29.

John 14:18-20: "I will not leave you as orphans; I will come to you. Yet a little while and the world will see me no more, but you will see me. Because I live, you also will live. In that day you will know that I am in my Father, and you in me, and I in you."

Other joys do not so fill the heart. But to know the Lord Jesus as our guarantee satisfies the soul and brings it into rest under the eye of our pardoning God. I had a thought the other day that has filled my heart often since. It explains that wonderful verse "I will not leave you as orphans; I will come to you."

Jesus, at the right hand of the Father, is still present with all His brothers and sisters in this valley of weeping. His human nature is at the right hand of God upon the throne—the lamb who was slain. But His divine nature is unlimited and is present in every dwelling of every disciple in this world.

Dear friend, do you feel that Jesus is your Elder Brother? Then remember that, by reason of His divinity, He is now by your side, afflicted in all your afflictions, touched with your weaknesses, and able to save you completely. He is as much beside you as He was beside Mary when she sat at His feet.

Tell Him all your sorrows, all your doubts and anxieties. He has a listening ear. Oh, what a friend is Jesus, your friend and mine! What an open heart He has for all the wants, doubts, and difficulties of His people! He has special care for His sick, weak, and dying disciples.

—ROBERT MURRAY M'CHEYNE, "To Miss A. S. L.: August 16, 1840," in *Memoir and Remains of the Rev. Robert Murray M'Cheyne*, ed. Andrew A. Bonar (Edinburgh; London: Oliphant Anderson & Ferrier, 1894), 245–247.

1 John 2:1: My little children, I am writing these things to you so that you may not sin. But if anyone does sin, we have an advocate with the Father, Jesus Christ the righteous.

To view the heavenly empathy of our Lord from the aspect of our existential need, it is necessary for our comfort and perseverance in faith to know that in all the temptations of this life we have an Empathizer, and Helper, and Comforter in the person of Him from whom we must hide nothing, who feels with us in every weakness and temptation, and knows exactly what our physical, psychological, moral, and spiritual situation is.

And this He knows because He himself was tempted, just as we are, without sin. He who has this feeling of temptation with us appears in the presence of God for us and is our Advocate with the Father, and He invests His empathy and help with an effectiveness that is nothing less than omnipotent compassion.

—JOHN MURRAY, *The Heavenly Priestly Activity of Christ* (London: Westminster Chapel, 1958), 8.

O the comfort! We are not under the law, but under grace! The Gospel is a plan for sinners, and we have an Advocate with the Father. There is the unshaken ground of hope.

A reconciled Father, a prevailing Advocate, a powerful Shepherd, a compassionate Friend, a Savior who is able and willing to save to the uttermost. He knows what we are made of; He remembers that we are but dust.

And has opened for us a new and blood-sprinkled way of access to the throne of grace, that we may obtain mercy and find grace to help in every time of need.

—JOHN NEWTON, "Letter 7, September 1772," in *The Works of John Newton*, vol. 1 (London: Hamilton, Adams & Co., 1824), 455–458.

John 15:15: No longer do I call you servants, for the servant does not know what his master is doing; but I have called you friends, for all that I have heard from my Father I have made known to you.

If we need a powerful friend, Jesus is almighty: our help is in Him who made heaven and earth, who raises the dead, and who hushes the tempest and raging waves into a calm with a word.

If we need a present friend, a help at hand in the hour of trouble, Jesus is always near, beside our path by day, and our bed by night; nearer than the light by which we see, or the air we breathe; nearer than we are to ourselves; so that not a thought, a sigh, or a tear, escapes His notice.

Since His love and His wisdom are infinite, and He has already done so much for us, shall we not trust Him to the end?

His mercies are countless as the sands, and hereafter we shall see cause to count our trials among our chief mercies.

—JOHN NEWTON, "Letter LXXIII," in *The Aged Pilgrim's Thoughts Over Sin and the Grave, Illustrated in a Series of Letters to Walter Taylor* (London: Baker and Fletcher, 2nd ed., 1825), 169–170.

Wouldn't you choose a friend who is both far better than you in certain ways but is also your equal in others? While people want a near and dear friend of superior dignity, there is also a desire in them to have a friend who shares their circumstances. This is Christ.

Though He is the great God, yet He has brought himself down to be on the same level as you so as to become a man as you are, that He might not only be your Lord, but your brother, and that He might be more able to be a companion for such as you are.

This is one result of Christ's taking upon Him man's nature, that His people might gain a more personal relationship with Him than the infinite distance of the divine nature would allow.

—JONATHAN EDWARDS, "The Excellency of Christ," in *The Works of Jonathan Edwards*, vol. 1, ed. Edward Hickman (Carlisle, PA: Banner of Truth, 1834/1998), 688.

John 13:3–9, 12–17: Jesus, knowing that the Father had given all things into his hands, and that he had come from God and was going back to God, rose from supper. He laid aside his outer garments, and taking a towel, tied it around his waist. Then he poured water into a basin and began to wash the disciples' feet and to wipe them with the towel that was wrapped around him. He came to Simon Peter, who said to him, "Lord, do you wash my feet?" Jesus answered him, "What I am doing you do not understand now, but afterward you will understand." Peter said to him, "You shall never wash my feet." Jesus answered him, "If I do not wash you, you have no share with me." Simon Peter said to him, "Lord, not my feet only but also my hands and my head!" . . . When he had washed their feet and put on his outer garments and resumed his place, he said to them, "Do you understand what I have done to you? You call me Teacher and Lord, and you are right, for so I am. If I then, your Lord and Teacher, have washed your feet, you also ought to wash one another's feet. For I have given you an example, that you also should do just as I have done to you. Truly, truly, I say to you, a servant is not greater than his master, nor is a messenger greater than the one who sent him. If you know these things, blessed are you if you do them."

If a lesser creature is slightly exalted above another, by having more food, or a bigger shelter, how highly he thinks of himself! He separates himself from those that are below him! And he expects others to be impressed if he expresses even the smallest humility.

Meanwhile, Christ humbles himself to wash our feet; but how would great men (or greater creatures) account themselves ashamed by their acts of far less humility!

—JONATHAN EDWARDS, "The Excellency of Christ," in *The Works of Jonathan Edwards*, vol. 1, ed. Edward Hickman (Carlisle, PA: Banner of Truth, 1834/1998), 680–681.

1 Corinthians 15:14–20: If Christ has not been raised, then our preaching is in vain and your faith is in vain. We are even found to be misrepresenting God, because we testified about God that he raised Christ, whom he did not raise if it is true that the dead are not raised. For if the dead are not raised, not even Christ has been raised. And if Christ has not been raised, your faith is futile and you are still in your sins. Then those also who have fallen asleep in Christ have perished. If in Christ we have hope in this life only, we are of all people most to be pitied. But in fact Christ has been raised from the dead, the firstfruits of those who have fallen asleep.

The souls of those who believe in Jesus Christ, the Son of God, and in His great and selfless sacrifice, are resurrected by God in this present life; and a sign of this resurrection is the grace of the Holy Spirit, which He gives to the soul of every Christian, as though a new soul.

—ST. SYMEON THE NEW THEOLOGIAN, *The First Created Man* (Platina: St. Herman of Alaska Brotherhood, 1994), 48.

Christ is the first fruits of those who rise again. We rise again because He was raised from the dead. Christ first ascended, so we shall ascend in Christ. Christ is first loved; we are loved in the Beloved.

Christ is first blessed; we are blessed with all spiritual blessings in Jesus Christ. So, whatever is in Christ, we have as we believe in Him. We have the Spirit in us, who was first in Christ. God put the Spirit in Christ, as the second Adam, so that we should receive the Spirit as well. He is first in all things; He must have the preeminence.

Christ has the preeminence before time, in time, and after time. All is first in Christ, and then in us. He is the elder Brother. We give Christ His due honor and respect, knowing all we have is because of Him.

—RICHARD SIBBES, "A Description of Christ," in *The Complete Works of Richard Sibbes*, vol. 1, ed. Alexander Balloch Grosart (Edinburgh; London; Dublin: James Nichol; James Nisbet and Co.; W. Robertson, 1862), 18.

1 John 4:4: Little children, you are from God and have overcome them, for he who is in you is greater than he who is in the world.

Luke 1:30–33: And the angel said to her, "Do not be afraid, Mary, for you have found favor with God. And behold, you will conceive in your womb and bear a son, and you shall call his name Jesus. He will be great and will be called the Son of the Most High. And the Lord God will give to him the throne of his father David, and he will reign over the house of Jacob forever, and of his kingdom there will be no end."

Now, when a Christian comprehends the greatness of the person, he will recognize the greatness of the fruit. How meager are sin, death, and the devil in contrast to Christ. Since Christ is greater than heaven and earth, mightier than sin, death, and the devil, it therefore stands to reason that everything, all He suffers and does, is of paramount importance. Mighty was His suffering; mighty, too, was His resurrection from the dead.

—MARTIN LUTHER, *The Complete Sermons of Martin Luther*, vol. 6, ed. Eugene F. King and John Nicholas Lenker (Grand Rapids, MI: Baker Books, 2000), 11.

Though something of Christ be revealed in one age, and something more in another, yet eternity itself cannot fully reveal Him.

"I see something," said Luther, "which blessed Augustine did not see; and those that come after me will see that which I do not see."

Studying Christ is like discovering a new country. At first, men sit down by the seaside, upon the borders of the land. And there they dwell, but then they eventually search farther and farther into the heart of the country.

The best of us are still only upon the borders of this vast continent!

—JOHN FLAVEL, *The Works of John Flavel*, vol. 1 (Carlisle, PA: Banner of Truth, 1820/1997), 36.

> **Philippians 2:5–8:** Have this mind among yourselves, which is yours in Christ Jesus, who, though he was in the form of God, did not count equality with God a thing to be grasped, but emptied himself, by taking the form of a servant, being born in the likeness of men. And being found in human form, he humbled himself by becoming obedient to the point of death, even death on a cross.

A true incarnation of the Logos [Word], or of the second person in the Godhead. The motive is the unfathomable love of God; the end, the redemption of the fallen race, and its reconciliation with God. This incarnation is neither a conversion of God into a man, nor a conversion of a man into God; neither a humanizing of the divine, nor a deification of the human; nor on the other hand is it a mere outward, transitory connection of the two factors, but an actual and abiding union of the two in one personal life.

It is primarily and preeminently a condescension and self-humiliation of the divine Logos to human nature, and at the same time a consequent assumption and exaltation of the human nature to inseparable and eternal communion with the divine Word. The Logos assumes the body, soul, and spirit of man, and enters into all the circumstances and infirmities of human life on earth, with the single exception of sin, which indeed is not an essential or necessary element of humanity, but accidental to it. The Lord of the universe took the form of a servant; the immutable God became a suffering man; the immortal One submitted himself to the dominion of death; Majesty assumed into itself lowliness; strength, weakness; eternity, mortality. The same, who is true God, is also true Man, without either element being altered or annihilated by the other or being degraded to a mere accident.

—PHILIP SCHAFF, *History of the Christian Church*, vol. 3 (Grand Rapids, MI: Wm. B. Eerdmans Publishing, 1910), 142.

Colossians 2:11–14: In him also you were circumcised with a circumcision made without hands, by putting off the body of the flesh, by the circumcision of Christ, having been buried with him in baptism, in which you were also raised with him through faith in the powerful working of God, who raised him from the dead. And you, who were dead in your trespasses and the uncircumcision of your flesh, God made alive together with him, having forgiven us all our trespasses, by canceling the record of debt that stood against us with its legal demands. This he set aside, nailing it to the cross.

One Person of the Holy Trinity, namely the Son and Word of God, having become incarnate, offered himself in the flesh as a sacrifice to the divinity of the Father, and of the Son himself, and of the Holy Spirit, in order that the first transgression of Adam might be forgiven. For the sake of this great and selfless gift there might be performed another new birth and re-creation of man through holy baptism, in which we are cleansed by water and the power of the Holy Spirit. From the time of baptism, in the name of the Father, Son, and Holy Spirit, through faith in the death, burial, and resurrection of our Lord, believers are dead to this evil world, and alive again, as though resurrected from the dead; that is, their souls are brought to life again and receive the grace of the Holy Spirit as Adam knew it before his transgression. They know the anointing of the Holy Spirit and the presence of Jesus Christ, having become associates with God. They also remember His sacrifice through the sacrament of Communion, partaking of the bread and wine, becoming the body and blood of Christ, who being incarnate offered himself freely as a sacrifice.

—ST. SYMEON THE NEW THEOLOGIAN, *The First Created Man* (Platina: St. Herman of Alaska Brotherhood, 1994), 46–47.

> **John 15:4–5:** Abide in me, and I in you. As the branch cannot bear fruit by itself, unless it abides in the vine, neither can you, unless you abide in me. I am the vine; you are the branches. Whoever abides in me and I in him, he it is that bears much fruit, for apart from me you can do nothing.

The work given to us, "abide in me," will prepare us for the work undertaken by Him: "I in you." The two parts of the injunction have their unity in that central, deep-meaning word *in*. There is no deeper word in Scripture. God is *in* all. God dwells in Christ. Christ lives in God. We are in Christ. Christ is in us: our life taken up into His; His life received into ours; in a divine reality that words cannot express, we are in Him and He in us. And the words "abide in me, and I in you" tell us to believe this divine mystery, and to count upon our God the husbandman, and Christ the vine, to make it divinely true. No thinking or teaching or praying can grasp it; it is a divine mystery of love. Just as little as we can affect the union can we understand it. Let us just look at this infinite, divine, omnipotent Vine loving us, holding us, working in us. Let us through faith in His working abide and rest in Him, ever turning our hearts and hope to Him alone. And let us count upon Him to fulfill in us the mystery: You in me, and I in You.

Blessed Lord, You call me to abide in You. How can I, Lord, except You show Yourself to me, waiting to receive and welcome and keep me? I pray You show me how You as the Vine undertake to do all that You do. To be occupied with You is to abide in You. Here I am, Lord, a branch, cleansed and abiding—resting in You, and awaiting the inflow of Your life and grace.

—ANDREW MURRAY, "Abide," in *The True Vine* (Chicago: Moody Publishers, 2007), 28.

Psalm 87:1–3, 7:
On the holy mount stands the city he founded;
  the Lᴏʀᴅ loves the gates of Zion
  more than all the dwelling places of Jacob.
Glorious things of you are spoken,
  O city of God. . . .
Singers and dancers alike say,
  "All my springs are in you."

Christ has both the will and skill, power and authority, to give us everlasting life, for the Father sent Him forth, and sealed Him to that purpose.
All the springs of our joy are in Him. Our privilege is to accept Christ's
invitation to us. What will we do for Him if we will not feast with Him?

> —RICHARD SIBBES, "A Discovery of the Near and Dear Love, Union, and Com-
> munion Between Christ and the Church," in *The Works of Richard Sibbes*, vol. 2, ed.
> Alexander Balloch Grosart (Carlisle, PA: Banner of Truth, 1639/2001), 34.

God in Christ allows such poor creatures as you and me to come to Him,
to love communion with Him, and to maintain a communication of love
with Him. You may go to God and tell Him how you love Him and open
your heart and He will accept it. He is come down from heaven and has
taken upon himself the human nature, that he might be near to you and
might be, as it were, your companion.

> —JONATHAN EDWARDS, "The Spirit of the True Saints Is a Spirit of Divine Love,"
> in *The Glory and Honor of God*, The Previously Unpublished Sermons of Jonathan
> Edwards, vol. 2, ed. Michael McMullen (Nashville, TN: Broadman, 2004), 339.

1 Corinthians 12:3: Therefore I want you to understand that no one speaking in the Spirit of God ever says "Jesus is accursed!" and no one can say "Jesus is Lord" except in the Holy Spirit.

Endeavor to know the *Father*. Approach Him in deep repentance and confess that you are not worthy to be called His son; receive the kiss of His love; let the ring that is the token of His eternal faithfulness be on your finger; sit at His table and let your heart rejoice in His grace.

Then press forward and seek to know the *Son of God*, who, although He is the brightness of His Father's glory, humbled himself and became a man for our sakes. Know Him in the singular complexity of His nature: eternal God, and yet suffering, finite man; follow Him as He walks the waters with the tread of deity, and as He sits down at the well, tired in the weariness of humanity. Do not be satisfied unless you know Jesus Christ as your Friend, your Brother, your Husband, your all.

—CHARLES H. SPURGEON, "May 8—Evening," in *Morning and Evening* (Geanies House, Fearn, Scotland: Christian Focus, 1994), 275.

> **Matthew 16:21–26:** From that time Jesus began to show his disciples that he must go to Jerusalem and suffer many things from the elders and chief priests and scribes, and be killed, and on the third day be raised. And Peter took him aside and began to rebuke him, saying, "Far be it from you, Lord! This shall never happen to you." But he turned and said to Peter, "Get behind me, Satan! You are a hindrance to me. For you are not setting your mind on the things of God, but on the things of man." Then Jesus told his disciples, "If anyone would come after me, let him deny himself and take up his cross and follow me. For whoever would save his life will lose it, but whoever loses his life for my sake will find it. For what will it profit a man if he gains the whole world and forfeits his soul? Or what shall a man give in return for his soul?"

Jesus Christ of Nazareth suffered on the cross and satisfied the justice of God for us in no other way than that we should believe on Him, stand in His footsteps, and walk in the way that He has opened, obeying the commands of the Father, even as the Son did. They who speak, think, or believe otherwise of Christ, each in His own way makes Christ an idol.

—H. ZWINGLI, "The Seven Articles, VI," in *Selected Works*, trans. Lawrence A. McLouth, Henry Preble, and George W. Gilmore (Philadelphia: University of Pennsylvania, 1901), 148.

> **John 16:5–7:** "But now I am going to him who sent me, and none of you asks me, 'Where are you going?' But because I have said these things to you, sorrow has filled your heart. Nevertheless, I tell you the truth: it is to your advantage that I go away, for if I do not go away, the Helper will not come to you. But if I go, I will send him to you."

My Father and I have but one friend who lies in our bosom and proceeds from us both, the Holy Spirit. I will go away but I will send Him to you. He will be a better Comforter for you than I could be in My bodily presence. He will tell you, if you will listen to Him, and not grieve Him, nothing but stories of My love. All His words in your heart will be to glorify Me, and to increase the expression of My love to you.

So that you will have My heart as surely and as speedily as if I were with you, He will continually break your heart with My love for you or your love for Me. He will tell you, while I am in heaven, that there is as true a connection between Me and you, and as true a dearness of affection in Me toward you, as is between my Father and Me, and that it is as impossible to break this bond as to break the bond between My Father and Me.

—THOMAS GOODWIN, *The Heart of Christ* (Edinburgh: Banner of Truth, 2011), 19–20.

O God, the king of glory, who has exalted Your only Son, Jesus Christ, with great triumph unto Your kingdom in heaven, we beseech You, leave us not comfortless, but send to us Your Holy Spirit to comfort us, and exalt us unto the same place where our Savior has gone before; who lives and reigns with You and the Holy Spirit, now and forever. Amen.

—THOMAS CRANMER, from The Book of Common Prayer, 1549, in *Early Protestant Spirituality*, The Classics of Western Spirituality, ed. Scott H. Hendrix and Bernard McGinn, trans. Scott H. Hendrix, (New York; Mahwah, NJ: Paulist Press, 2009), 225.

> **Colossians 1:18-20:** And he is the head of the body, the church. He is the beginning, the firstborn from the dead, that in everything he might be preeminent. For in him all the fullness of God was pleased to dwell, and through him to reconcile to himself all things, whether on earth or in heaven, making peace by the blood of his cross.

Christ is our pattern. He is first the Son of God by nature. We are the sons of God by adoption. He is the predestinated Son of God to save us, to be our Head. We are predestined to be parts of His body. He is the Son of God's love. We are beloved in Him.

Therefore, let us look to Him and be thankful to God for Him. When we thank God for ourselves, let us thank God first for giving us Christ, who is the pattern to whom we to be are conformed. Let us give thanks for Him, as Peter said, "Blessed be the God and Father of our Lord Jesus Christ!" (1 Peter 1:3).

When we begin to think of anything in ourselves, let us go to our Head, to Christ, in whom we have all we have and all we hope to have. Of His fullness we receive, not only grace for grace, but glory for glory.

—RICHARD SIBBES, "The Redemption of Our Bodies," in *The Works of Richard Sibbes*, vol. 5, ed. Alexander Balloch Grosart (Edinburgh; London; Dublin: James Nichol; James Nisbet and Co.; W. Robertson, 1863), 166.

Lamentations 3:19–24:
Remember my affliction and my wanderings,
the wormwood and the gall!
My soul continually remembers it
and is bowed down within me.
But this I call to mind,
and therefore I have hope:
The steadfast love of the LORD never ceases;
his mercies never come to an end;
they are new every morning;
great is your faithfulness.
"The LORD is my portion," says my soul,
"therefore I will hope in him."

God has a multitude of mercies. As our hearts are the source of a variety of sins, so God is the father of variety of mercies. There is no sin or misery, but that God has a mercy for it. He has a multitude of mercies of every kind.

There are likewise a variety of miseries, which we are subject to, so He has a treasury of mercies, divided into several promises in the Scriptures, like so many boxes of treasures.

If your heart is hard, His mercies are tender.

If your heart is dead, He has mercy to revive it.

If you are sick, He has mercy to heal you.

If you are sinful, He has mercies to sanctify and cleanse you.

As great and as varied as are our wants, so great and varied are His provisions. So, we may come boldly to find grace and mercy to help us in our time of need. All the mercies that are in His heart He has transplanted into the promises of Scripture, where they grow, and He has an abundance of them, suited to all the many diseases of the soul.

—THOMAS GOODWIN, *The Works of Thomas Goodwin*, vol. 2 (Grand Rapids, MI: Reformation Heritage, 2006), 187–188.

> **1 John 1:6–10:** If we say we have fellowship with him while we walk in darkness, we lie and do not practice the truth. But if we walk in the light, as he is in the light, we have fellowship with one another, and the blood of Jesus his Son cleanses us from all sin. If we say we have no sin, we deceive ourselves, and the truth is not in us. If we confess our sins, he is faithful and just to forgive us our sins and to cleanse us from all unrighteousness. If we say we have not sinned, we make him a liar, and his word is not in us.

If God says that He saves by God, still God does not save except by Christ. Why, then, should people hesitate to call Christ God, when they observe that He is declared to be God by the Father according to the Scriptures? Yes, if God the Father does not save except by God, no one can be saved by the Father unless he has confessed Christ to be God, in whom and by whom the Father promises that He will give him salvation. Reasonably, whoever acknowledges Him to be God, may find salvation in Christ.

> — NOVATIAN, *A Treatise Concerning the Trinity*, in *Ante-Nicene Fathers*, vol. 5, ed. Alexander Roberts, James Donaldson, and A. Cleveland Coxe (Buffalo, NY: Christian Literature Publishing Co., 1886), 621.

If we do not preach about sin and God's judgment on it, we cannot present Christ as Savior from sin and the wrath of God. And if we are silent about these things and preach a Christ who saves only from self and the sorrows of this world, we are not preaching the Christ of the Bible.

We are, in effect, bearing false witness and preaching a false Christ. Our message is "another Gospel, which is not another." Such preaching may soothe some, but it will help no one; for a Christ who is not seen and sought as a Savior from sin will not be found to save from self or from anything else.

An imaginary Christ will not bring a real salvation; and a half-truth presented as the whole truth is a complete untruth.

> —J. I. PACKER, "The Puritan View of Preaching the Gospel," in *A Quest for Godliness: The Puritan Vision of the Christian Life* (Wheaton, IL: Crossway, 1990), 164–165.

> **Jude 1:24–25:** Now to him who is able to keep you from stumbling and to present you blameless before the presence of his glory with great joy, to the only God, our Savior, through Jesus Christ our Lord, be glory, majesty, dominion, and authority, before all time and now and forever. Amen.

Christ will not leave us until He has made us like himself, all glorious within and without, and presented us blameless before His Father. What a comfort this is to the conflicts of our unruly hearts, that it shall not always be this way!

Let us endure a little while, and we shall be happy forever. Let us think when we are troubled with our sins that Christ has this command from His Father, that "a bruised reed he will not break, and a faintly burning wick he will not quench" (Isaiah 42:3), until He has subdued all.

This puts a shield into our hands to beat back "all the flaming darts of the evil one" (Ephesians 6:16). Satan will object, "You are a great sinner." We may answer, "Christ is a strong Savior." Satan will object, "You have no faith, no love." We may reply, "Yes, a spark of faith and love."

Satan says: "But it is so little and weak that it will vanish and come to nothing." We reply: "But Christ will honor it, until He has brought judgment to victory."

—RICHARD SIBBES, *The Bruised Reed* (Carlisle, PA: Banner of Truth, 1630/1998), 123.

Satan had the first word, but Christ the last. Satan must be speechless after a plea of our Advocate.

—JOHN BUNYAN, *The Work of Jesus Christ as an Advocate*, in *The Works of John Bunyan*, vol. 1, ed. G. Offor (Edinburgh: Banner of Truth, 1991), 194.

Ephesians 1:3–6: Blessed be the God and Father of our Lord Jesus Christ, who has blessed us in Christ with every spiritual blessing in the heavenly places, even as he chose us in him before the foundation of the world, that we should be holy and blameless before him. In love he predestined us for adoption to himself as sons through Jesus Christ, according to the purpose of his will, to the praise of his glorious grace, with which he has blessed us in the Beloved.

It was "from everlasting" that He signed the contract with His Father, that He would pay blood for blood, suffering for suffering, agony for agony, and death for death, on behalf of His people; it was "from everlasting" that He gave himself up without a word of complaint.

And this that from the crown of His head to the sole of His foot He might sweat great drops of blood, that He might be spit upon, pierced, mocked, rent asunder, and crushed beneath the pains of death. He had always, even before time began, been the payment for us. Pause, my soul, and wonder!

You have been in the person of Jesus "from everlasting." Not only when you were born into the world did Christ love you, but His delight was with the sons of men before there were any sons of men. Often did He think of them; from everlasting to everlasting He had set His affection upon them.

—CHARLES H. SPURGEON, "February 27—Evening," in *Morning and Evening* (Geanies House, Fearn, Scotland: Christian Focus, 1994), 127.

Jeremiah 31:15, 18–19:
Thus says the Lord:
"A voice is heard in Ramah,
 lamentation and bitter weeping.
Rachel is weeping for her children;
 she refuses to be comforted for her children,
 because they are no more." . . .
"I have heard Ephraim grieving,
'You have disciplined me, and I was disciplined,
 like an untrained calf;
bring me back that I may be restored,
 for you are the Lord my God.
For after I had turned away, I relented,
 and after I was instructed, I struck my thigh;
I was ashamed, and I was confounded,
 because I bore the disgrace of my youth.'"

There is comfort concerning such suffering, in that your very sins move Him to pity more than to anger. Christ takes part with you, and is far from being provoked against you, as all His anger is against your sin to ruin it; yea, His pity is increased the more toward you, even as the heart of a father is to a child that has some loathsome disease, or as one is to a member of his body that has leprosy; he hates not the member, for it is his own flesh, but the disease, and that provokes him to pity the part affected all the more. What shall He not do for us, when our sins, which are both against Christ and us, are turned as motives to Him to pity us the more?

And He, loving your person and hating the sin, allows His hatred to fall only upon the sin, in order to free you from it, but His mercy shall be the more extended to you, and this as much when you fall under sin as under any other affliction. Therefore, fear not.

—THOMAS GOODWIN, *The Heart of Christ* (Edinburgh: Banner of Truth, 2011), 155–156.

> **Luke 15:4–7:** "What man of you, having a hundred sheep, if he has lost one of them, does not leave the ninety-nine in the open country, and go after the one that is lost, until he finds it? And when he has found it, he lays it on his shoulders, rejoicing. And when he comes home, he calls together his friends and his neighbors, saying to them, 'Rejoice with me, for I have found my sheep that was lost.' Just so, I tell you, there will be more joy in heaven over one sinner who repents than over ninety-nine righteous persons who need no repentance."

Jesus loves to rescue sinners from going down into the pit.

He comes to us full of tenderness, with tears in His eyes, with mercy in His hands, and with love in His heart.

Believe Him to be a great Savior of great sinners.

—CHARLES H. SPURGEON, "The Believing Thief," in *Majesty in Misery*, Calvary's Mournful Mountain, vol. 3 (Carlisle, PA: Banner of Truth, 2005), 263.

The Son of Man has on earth the power to forgive sins, not by virtue of the human nature, but by virtue of the divine nature, for in the divine nature resides the power to authoritatively forgive sins, whereas in the human nature resides the power to instrumentally and ministerially forgive sins.

—THOMAS AQUINAS, *"Summa Theologica" of St. Thomas Aquinas*, trans. Reginaldus de Piperno (London: R. & T. Washbourne, 1922), Book III, Question 16, Article 11.

Matthew 2:10-11: When they saw the star, they rejoiced exceedingly with great joy. And going into the house, they saw the child with Mary his mother, and they fell down and worshiped him. Then, opening their treasures, they offered him gifts, gold and frankincense and myrrh.

"The Word became flesh" (John 1:14); God became man; the divine Son became a Jew; the Almighty appeared on earth as a helpless human baby, unable to do more than lie and stare and wriggle and make noises, needing to be fed and changed and taught to talk like any other child.

And there was no illusion or deception in this: the babyhood of the Son of God was a reality. The more you think about it, the more staggering it gets. Nothing in fiction is so fantastic as is this truth of the incarnation.

—J. I. PACKER, *Knowing God* (Downers Grove, IL: IVP, 1973), 53.

Think of His incarnation, His birth in Bethlehem. There was greater glory among the oxen in the stall than ever was seen where those born in marble halls were wrapped in purple and fine linen. Was there ever another infant like Christ? Never. I am not surprised that the wise men *fell down* to worship Him.

—CHARLES H. SPURGEON, "The Chief Office of the Holy Spirit," in *Spurgeon on the Holy Spirit* (New Kensington, PA: Whitaker House, 2000), 61.

John 6:51: "I am the living bread that came down from heaven. If anyone eats of this bread, he will live forever. And the bread that I will give for the life of the world is my flesh."

The glory of the Incarnation is that it presents to our adoring gaze not a humanized God or a deified man, but a true God-man—one who is all that God is and at the same time all that man is: on whose mighty arm we can rest, and to whose human sympathy we can appeal. We cannot afford to lose either the God in the man or the man in God; our hearts cry out for the complete God-man, whom the Scriptures offer us.

—B. B. WARFIELD, *Selected Shorter Writings of Benjamin B. Warfield*, vol. 1, ed. John E Meeter (Phillipsburg: P&R Publishing, 2001), 166.

He took a human nature into personal union with himself. Accordingly, assumption is the theological term to describe the act; and it would be truer to speak of the human nature of Christ as existing in God than of God as existing in it. Jesus Christ is primarily not a man in whom God dwells, but God who has assumed into personal union with himself a human nature as an organ through which He acts.

—B. B. WARFIELD, *The Works of Benjamin B. Warfield*, vol. 10 (New York: Oxford University Press, 1927–1932. Reprint, Grand Rapids, MI: Baker, 1981), 259–260, 264–265.

In every way, therefore, we may perceive that the Word of God, even when He was man, nevertheless continued to be one Son. For He performs those works that belong to deity, possessing the majesty and glory of the Godhead inseparable from Him. If we believe, He will crown us with His grace: by whom and with whom to God the Father be glory and dominion with the Holy Spirit, to ages of ages. Amen.

—CYRIL OF ALEXANDRIA, "Homilies on the Gospel of Luke 10," in *We Believe in One Lord Jesus Christ*, ed. John Anthony McGuckin (Downers Grove, IL: IVP, 2009), 67.

> **2 Corinthians 5:21:** For our sake he made him to be sin who knew no sin, so that in him we might become the righteousness of God.

This is the Gospel, which we preach to you every time we stand before you, namely, that Christ Jesus, the Lamb of God, was offered to God as a substitute for ungodly, unclean, unacceptable man.

So that we might not die, Christ died.

So that we might not be cursed, Jesus was cursed and nailed to the cross.

So that we might be received, He was rejected.

So that we might be approved, He was despised.

So that we might live forever, He bowed His head and gave up His spirit.

If any man wants to understand theology, he had better begin here. This is the first and main point.

Those for whom Christ died as a Substitute can no more be damned than Christ himself can be. It is not possible that hell can enclose them, or where would be the justice and the integrity of God?

Does He demand of the man, and then take a Substitute, and then take the man again? Does He demand the payment of our debt, and receive that payment at the hand of Christ, and then arrest us a second time for the same debt?

Then, at the great judgment seat of Christ in heaven, where is justice? The honor of God, the faithfulness of God, the integrity of God are certain promises to every soul who believes that if Christ died for him, he will not die, but will be exempt from the curse of the law.

—CHARLES H. SPURGEON, "Redeeming the Unclean," in *The Metropolitan Tabernacle Pulpit Sermons*, vol. 61 (London: Passmore & Alabaster, 1915), 221–223.

DAY

294

> **Revelation 21:1–3:** Then I saw a new heaven and a new earth, for the first heaven and the first earth had passed away, and the sea was no more. And I saw the holy city, new Jerusalem, coming down out of heaven from God, prepared as a bride adorned for her husband. And I heard a loud voice from the throne saying, "Behold, the dwelling place of God is with man. He will dwell with them, and they will be his people, and God himself will be with them as their God."

In that resurrection morning, when the Sun of Righteousness shall appear in the heavens, shining in all His brightness and glory, He will come forth as a bridegroom; He shall come in the glory of His Father, with all His holy angels.

That will indeed be a joyful meeting of the glorious bridegroom and His bride. He will appear in all His glory without any veil: and then the saints shall shine forth as the sun in the kingdom of their Father, and at the right hand of their Redeemer.

Then will come the time when Christ will invite His Church to enter with Him into the palace of His glory, which He has prepared from the foundation of the world, and lead her in with Him, and in all their finery, ascend together into the heaven of heavens; the whole multitude of glorious angels waiting upon them, and present themselves together before the Father, when Christ shall say, "Here am I, and the children whom You have given me." And they shall, in that union, together receive the Father's blessing, and shall thenceforth rejoice together, in uninterrupted and everlasting glory, in the love and embrace of one another, and eternal enjoyment of the love of the Father.

—JONATHAN EDWARDS, "The Church's Marriage to Her Sons, and to Her God," in *Sermons and Discourses, 1743–1758*, The Works of Jonathan Edwards, vol. 25, ed. Wilson H. Kimnach and Harry S. Stout (New Haven, CT: Yale University Press, 2006), 183–184.

Revelation 22:17: The Spirit and the Bride say, "Come." And let the one who hears say, "Come." And let the one who is thirsty come; let the one who desires take the water of life without price.

Only a step to Jesus!
Then why not take it now?
Come, and thy sin confessing,
To Him, thy Savior bow.

Only a step, only a step!
Come, He waits for thee.
Come, and thy sin confessing,
Thou shalt receive a blessing,
Do not reject the mercy He freely offers thee!

Only a step to Jesus!
Believe, and thou shalt live.
Lovingly now He is waiting,
And ready to forgive.

Only a step to Jesus!
A step from sin to grace.
What has thy heart decided?
The moments fly apace.

Only a step to Jesus!
Oh, why not come and say,
Gladly to thee, my Savior,
I give myself away!

—FANNY CROSBY, *Bells at Evening and Other Verses*
(New York: The Biglow & Main Co., 1905), 171.

> **Matthew 5:17–18:** "Do not think that I have come to abolish the Law or the Prophets; I have not come to abolish them but to fulfill them. For truly, I say to you, until heaven and earth pass away, not an iota, not a dot, will pass from the Law until all is accomplished."

Brethren, what a wonderful thing it is that a mass of promises, and prophecies and types, apparently so different from one another, should all be accomplished in one Person! Take away Christ for one moment, and I could give the Old Testament to any wise man and say to him: "Go home and construct in your imagination an ideal character who would exactly fit everything foreshadowed in the Old Testament. Remember, he must be a prophet like Moses, and yet a champion like Joshua; he must be an Aaron and a Melchizedek; he must be both David and Solomon, Noah and Jonah, Judah and Joseph. Nay, he must not only be the lamb that was slain and the scapegoat that was not slain, the turtle dove that was dipped in blood and the priest who slew the bird; but he must be the altar, the tabernacle, the mercy-seat, and the shewbread."

To puzzle this wise man further, we remind him of prophecies so apparently contradictory that one would think they never could meet in one man. Such as these: "All kings shall fall down before Him, and all nations shall serve Him" and yet, "He is despised and rejected of men."

Blessed Savior! In You we see everything fulfilled that God spoke of long ago through the prophets. In You we discover everything carried out in substance, which God set forth in the mist of sacrificial smoke.

Glory be to Your name! "It is finished." All is summed up in You.

—CHARLES H. SPURGEON, "It Is Finished," in *Majesty in Misery*, Calvary's Mournful Mountain, vol. 3 (Carlisle, PA: Banner of Truth, 2005), 218–220.

> **1 Corinthians 15:20–24:** But in fact Christ has been raised from the dead, the firstfruits of those who have fallen asleep. For as by a man came death, by a man has come also the resurrection of the dead. For as in Adam all die, so also in Christ shall all be made alive. But each in his own order: Christ the firstfruits, then at his coming those who belong to Christ. Then comes the end, when he delivers the kingdom to God the Father after destroying every rule and every authority and power.

It was no common man who suffered, but God in man's nature. Adam by the tree fell; you by the Tree are brought to Paradise. Fear not the serpent; he shall not cast you out; for he is fallen out of heaven. And I say not unto you, "This day you shall depart, but this day you shall be with me." Be of good courage; you shall not be cast out. Fear not the fiery sword; it shrinks from its Lord.

—CYRIL OF JERUSALEM, "The Catechetical Lectures of S. Cyril, Archbishop of Jerusalem," in *S. Cyril of Jerusalem, S. Gregory Nazianzen*, A Select Library of the Nicene and Post-Nicene Fathers of the Christian Church, 2nd ser., vol. 7, ed. Philip Schaff and Henry Wace, trans. Edwin Hamilton Gifford (Buffalo, NY: Christian Literature Co., 1894), 255, 269.

The cross of Christ is the Tree of Life and the Tree of Knowledge combined. Blessed be God!

There is neither prohibition nor flaming sword to keep us back; but it stands like a tree by the side of the highway, which gives its shade to every passenger without distinction.

Watch and pray. We live in a sifting time: error gains ground every day. May the name and love of our Savior Jesus keep us and all His people!

—JOHN NEWTON, "Letter IV—January 10, 1760," in *The Works of John Newton*, vol. 2, ed. Richard Cecil (London: Hamilton, Adams & Co., 1824), 67–68.

Matthew 11:29-30: "Take my yoke upon you, and learn from me, for I am gentle and lowly in heart, and you will find rest for your souls. For my yoke is easy, and my burden is light."

"Learn from me, for I am gentle and lowly in heart." Yes, Christ was meek. If He had not been, He would not have been the one He claimed to be. But if He had not been meek, He would not have suffered so much either. The world would have shuddered at the wrong it did Him, but His meekness concealed the world's guilt. He did not assert His rights; He did not plead His innocence. He did not talk about the fact that they were sinning against Him; He did not point out their guilt with a single word. Even in His last moment, He asked His Father to forgive them, because they did not know what they were doing.

—SOREN KIERKEGAARD, *Upbuilding Discourses in Various Spirits*, Kierkegaard's Writings, vol. 15, ed. and trans. Howard V. Hong and Edna H. Hong (Princeton, NJ: Princeton University Press, 1993), 244.

Men are apt to have contrary conceptions of Christ, but He tells them His disposition here, and by preventing such hard thoughts of Him, to allure them unto Him the more. We are apt to think that He, being holy, is therefore of a severe disposition against sinners, and not able to bear them. But He says He is gentle and lowly in heart, meek by nature and temper.

—THOMAS GOODWIN, *The Heart of Christ* (Edinburgh: Banner of Truth, 2011), 63.

Isaiah 53:7–9:
He was oppressed, and he was afflicted,
    yet he opened not his mouth;
like a lamb that is led to the slaughter,
    and like a sheep that before its shearers is silent,
    so he opened not his mouth.
By oppression and judgment he was taken away;
    and as for his generation, who considered
that he was cut off out of the land of the living,
    stricken for the transgression of my people?
And they made his grave with the wicked
    and with a rich man in his death,
although he had done no violence,
    and there was no deceit in his mouth.

In dying, He did not merely surrender himself to that alienation from God which, as seen in the Old Testament, is the climax of what man suffers as one whose life is over. In a sense, He did this too, as attested by His word on the cross: "My God, my God, why have you forsaken me?" It is no accident that this saying has come down to us in Aramaic and is a direct quotation of Psalm 22:1. His vicarious bearing of the sin of all Israel, and indeed the whole world, points beyond the comfortless, intolerable situation of the righteous man of the Old Testament alienated from God in Sheol.

> —KARL BARTH, *Church Dogmatics*, vol. 3, pt. 2, ed. G. W. Bromiley and T. F. Torrance, trans. T. H. L. Parker (London: T&T Clark, 2004), 603.

Christ raised that cry from the cross without sin; we could hardly do so without imperfection and fault. He was truly obedient then with all His heart and all His soul. He declared His eagerness to obey by the fact that He was led like a sheep to its slaughter; He did not cry out or fight back, in fact, the head official wondered at His silence.

> —PETER VERMIGLI, *On the Death of Christ, from Philippians,* in *Life, Letters, and Sermons,* The Peter Martyr Library, vol. 5, ed. and trans. John Patrick Donnelly (Kirksville, MO: Thomas Jefferson University Press, 1999), 242.

DAY

300

Luke 7:36–39, 44–47: One of the Pharisees asked him to eat with him, and he went. . . . A woman of the city, who was a sinner, when she learned that he was . . . in the Pharisee's house, brought an alabaster flask of ointment . . . she began to wet his feet with her tears and wiped them with [her] hair . . . and kissed his feet and anointed them with the ointment. . . . When the Pharisee . . . saw this, he said to himself, "If this man were a prophet, he would have known who and what sort of woman this is who is touching him, for she is a sinner." . . . Turning toward the woman [Jesus] said to Simon, "Do you see this woman? I entered your house; you gave me no water for my feet, but she has wet my feet with her tears and wiped them with her hair. You gave me no kiss, but from the time I came in she has not ceased to kiss my feet. You did not anoint my head with oil, but she has anointed my feet with ointment. Therefore I tell you, her sins, which are many, are forgiven—for she loved much. But he who is forgiven little, loves little."

As once the Savior took His seat—
Attracted by His fame,
And lowly bending at His feet
A humble suppliant came.

Ashamed to lift her streaming eyes
His holy glance to meet,
She poured her costly sacrifice
Upon the Savior's feet.

Oppressed with sin and sorrow's weight
And sinking in despair,
With tears she washed His sacred feet
And wiped them with her hair.

"Depart in peace," the Savior said,
"Thy sins are all forgiven."
The trembling sinner raised her head
In peaceful hope of heaven.

—PHOEBE H. BROWN, "Hymn #95," *The Christian Hymnbook for the Sanctuary and Home* (Dayton, OH: Christian Publishing Association, 1872), 585.

> **John 17:22–23:** The glory that you have given me I have given to them, that they may be one even as we are one, I in them and you in me, that they may become perfectly one, so that the world may know that you sent me and loved them even as you loved me.

Behold the generosity of the Lord Jesus Christ: though a tenth of His wealth would have made the heavenly host rich beyond measure, He was not content until He had given us all He had.

It would have been surprising grace if He had allowed us to eat the crumbs of His bounty beneath the table of His mercy, but He will do nothing by halves. He makes us sit with Him and share the feast.

Had He given us some small pension from His royal coffers, we would have had reason to love Him eternally; but He wanted His bride to be as rich as himself, and He will not have a glory or grace in which she will not share.

He has not been content with less than making us joint heirs with himself, so that we might have equal possessions. He has emptied all of His estate into the coffers of the Church and has all things in common with His redeemed ones.

—CHARLES H. SPURGEON, "June 30—Morning," in *Morning and Evening* (Geanies House, Fearn, Scotland: Christian Focus, 1994), 382.

> **Romans 8:16–17:** The Spirit himself bears witness with our spirit that we are children of God, and if children, then heirs—heirs of God and fellow heirs with Christ, provided we suffer with him in order that we may also be glorified with him.

Here we learn what a great glory and ineffable eternal treasure the advent of God's Son has brought to those who accept Him, believe in Him, and regard Him as the Son sent from God to save the world. We believe He is the means and agency for the bestowal of both the power and the prerogative of the children of God upon all who believe in His name.

If we believe that He is the eternal Word of the Father through whom all things were made (John 1:3); if we believe that He is the Light and the Life of man (John 1:4) and the Lamb of God who bore the sins of the world (John 1:29) and takes away the sin of the world and casts them into the depths of the sea (Micah 7:19); if we call upon Him in every need and thank Him for His inexpressible grace and benefits—then we shall have the singular privilege, liberty, and right to be the dear children of a gracious Father in heaven, to be heirs of His eternal and heavenly blessings, to be, as Paul declares in Romans 8:17, heirs of God and co-heirs with Christ, and to have salvation and life eternal.

Did He grant this power and privilege to all, who, as we know, are all deserving of wrath (Ephesians 2:3)? The evangelist replies: "No, not to all; but to all without limit and to the exclusion of none who believe in His name; this means, to all who accept His Word by faith, who remain steadfast, and call upon Him."

We poor mortals, condemned and miserable sinners through our first birth from Adam, are singled out for such great honor and nobility that the eternal and almighty God is our Father, and we are His children.

—MARTIN LUTHER, *Luther's Works: Sermons on the Gospel of St. John: Chapters 1–4*, vol. 22, ed. Jaroslav Jan Pelikan, Hilton C. Oswald, and Helmut T. Lehmann (St. Louis, MO: Concordia Publishing House, 1999).

John 15:15: No longer do I call you servants, for the servant does not know what his master is doing; but I have called you friends, for all that I have heard from my Father I have made known to you.

There is no person in the world that stands in so endearing a relationship to Christians as Christ; He is our friend, our nearest friend.

—JONATHAN EDWARDS, *Sermons and Discourses 1720–1723*, The Works of Jonathan Edwards, vol. 10, ed. Wilson H. Kimnach (New Haven, CT: Yale University Press, 1992), 158.

All the kinds and degrees of friendship meet in Christ.

As His friendship is sweet, so it is constant in all conditions. If other friends fail, as friends may fail, yet this friend will never fail us. If we are not ashamed of Him, He will never be ashamed of us. How comfortable would our life be if we could draw out the comfort that this title of *friend* affords! It is a comfortable, fruitful, eternal friendship.

In friendship there is a mutual consent, a union of judgment and affections. There is a mutual sympathy in the good and ill one of another.

There is liberty, which is the life of friendship; there is a free interaction between friends, a free sharing of secrets. So here Christ opens His secrets to us, and we to Him.

In friendship, there is mutual solace and comfort in one another. Christ delights himself in His love for the Church, and His Church delights herself in her love for Christ.

In friendship there is a mutual honor and respect one of another. As He is our friend, He is also our king.

—RICHARD SIBBES, "A Discovery of the Near and Dear Love, Union, and Communion Between Christ and the Church," in *The Complete Works of Richard Sibbes*, vol. 2, ed. Alexander Balloch Grosart (reprint, Edinburgh: Banner of Truth, 1983), 36–37.

Isaiah 42:1–4:
Behold my servant, whom I uphold,
    my chosen, in whom my soul delights;
I have put my Spirit upon him;
    he will bring forth justice to the nations.
He will not cry aloud or lift up his voice,
    or make it heard in the street;
a bruised reed he will not break,
    and a faintly burning wick he will not quench;
    he will faithfully bring forth justice.
He will not grow faint or be discouraged
    till he has established justice in the earth;
    and the coastlands wait for his law.

Consider that all expressions of love issue from the nature of Christ, which is constant. God knows that as we are prone to sin, when the conscience is thoroughly awakened, we are prone to despair of sin.

Therefore, He wants us to know that He places himself in the covenant of grace to triumph in Christ over the greatest evils and enemies we fear. His thoughts are not our thoughts; He is God and not man. There are heights, depths, and breadths of mercy in Him above all the depths of our sin and misery. We should never be in such a miserable condition that there is reason to despair, considering that our sins are the sins of every man, and His mercy is the mercy of an infinite God.

Though it is true that a broken-hearted sinner ought to embrace mercy, there is no evidence that the heart does so easily, especially when it is miserable. When the Holy Spirit sprinkles the conscience with the blood of Christ and sheds His love into the heart, the conscience may cry louder than it does over the guilt of sin.

For only God's Spirit can raise the conscience with comfort above guilt because He only is greater than the conscience. Men may speak of comfort, but only the Spirit of Christ can bring true comfort.

—RICHARD SIBBES, "To the General Reader," *The Bruised Reed and the Smoking Flax*, in *The Works of Richard Sibbes*, vol. 1, ed. Alexander Balloch Grosart (reprint, Edinburgh: Banner of Truth, 2001), 89.

He cries—knowing far better than any other how much reason there is to cry: "My God, my God, why have you forsaken me?" *God for us* means simply that God has not abandoned the world and humanity in the lostness of our situation, but that He chose to bear this sin as His own, that He took it upon himself, and that He cries with us in our need.

—KARL BARTH, *Church Dogmatics*, vol. 4, pt.1, ed. G. W. Bromiley and T. F. Torrance, trans. T. H. L. Parker (London: T&T Clark, 2004), 215.

To know human sin in the form of human pride, we look to the person and sacrifice of Jesus Christ, and we think of the depth of His humiliation, of the Son of God who cried out on the cross, feeling forsaken by His Father. And although He was the Son of God, He died as a man, was dead, buried, and lay in the borrowed tomb—seeming like a contradiction to His mission, but having accomplished it in the most wonderful unity, the eternal and living and Almighty God displayed in the person of this Man, the free grace of God the Father, His unmerited justification, His underserved mercy, the gift of His creative power to save humankind.

—KARL BARTH, *Church Dogmatics*, vol. 4, pt. 1, ed. G. W. Bromiley and T. F. Torrance, trans. T. H. L. Parker (London: T&T Clark, 2004), 458.

2 Corinthians 1:3–4: Blessed be the God and Father of our Lord Jesus Christ, the Father of mercies and God of all comfort, who comforts us in all our affliction, so that we may be able to comfort those who are in any affliction, with the comfort with which we ourselves are comforted by God.

He is rich unto all; He is infinite, overflowing in goodness. He is good to a fault, to the pouring forth of riches, provision to an abundance.

—THOMAS GOODWIN, *The Works of Thomas Goodwin*, vol. 2 (Grand Rapids, MI: Reformation Heritage, 2006), 182.

He is the spring of all mercy. It is in His nature. It is His natural disposition. When He shows mercy, it is with His whole heart.

—THOMAS GOODWIN, *The Works of Thomas Goodwin*, vol. 2 (Grand Rapids, MI: Reformation Heritage, 2006), 179.

Where there is but mention made by way of supposition, or by way of question, whether God will part with, or cast off, any of His people, you will find that He throws it away with the highest indignation; His love is so great. He speaks with the highest detestation that there should be any such thought in God. He is so possessed with love for His people that He will hear nothing to the contrary. Yea, His love is so strong that if there is any accusation—if at any time the devil accuses, God is moved to bless. His love is so fixed that He takes occasion to bless even more.

—THOMAS GOODWIN, *The Works of Thomas Goodwin*, vol. 2 (Grand Rapids, MI: Reformation Heritage, 2006), 176.

Isaiah 55:6–11:
"Seek the LORD while he may be found;
    call upon him while he is near;
let the wicked forsake his way,
    and the unrighteous man his thoughts;
let him return to the LORD, that he may have compassion on him,
    and to our God, for he will abundantly pardon.
For my thoughts are not your thoughts,
    neither are your ways my ways, declares the LORD.
For as the heavens are higher than the earth,
    so are my ways higher than your ways
    and my thoughts than your thoughts.
For as the rain and the snow come down from heaven
    and do not return there but water the earth,
making it bring forth and sprout,
    giving seed to the sower and bread to the eater,
so shall my word be that goes out from my mouth;
    it shall not return to me empty,
but it shall accomplish that which I purpose,
    and shall succeed in the thing for which I sent it."

The Jesus of the New Testament has at least one advantage over the Jesus of modern reconstruction: He is real. He is not a manufactured figure suitable as a point of support for ethical maxims, but a genuine Person whom we can love. Humankind has loved Him through all the centuries. And despite all the efforts to remove Him from the pages of history, there are multitudes who love Him still.

> —J. GRESHAM MACHEN, *Christianity and Liberalism* (1923; reprint, Grand Rapids, MI: Wm. B. Eerdmans Publishing, 2001), 116.

John 14:6: Jesus said to him, "I am the way, and the truth, and the life. No one comes to the Father except through me."

There is ever one and the same unchangeable God, one only Savior Jesus Christ, the Son of God, not by adoption but by nature, God eternal and blessed forever. By Christ alone is access to the Father; even Abraham came to God by no other way than by Him who was promised. One way, one truth, one life, one Mediator between God and man, Christ Jesus. Through Him alone is access to God.

> —H. ZWINGLI, "Part Third," in *Selected Works*, trans. Lawrence A. McLouth, Henry Preble, and George W. Gilmore (Philadelphia: University of Pennsylvania, 1901), 233–234.

I. All who say that the Gospel is invalid without the confirmation of the Church err and slander God.

II. The sum and substance of the Gospel is that our Lord Jesus Christ, the true Son of God, has made known to us the will of His heavenly Father, and has with His innocence released us from death and reconciled us to God.

III. Hence Christ is the only way to salvation for all who ever were, are, and shall be.

IV. Who seeks or points out another door errs; he is a murderer of souls and a thief.

V. Hence all who consider other teachings equal to or higher than the Gospel err and do not know what the Gospel is.

VI. For Jesus Christ is the guide and leader, promised by God to all human beings, which promise was fulfilled.

VII. He is our eternal salvation and Head of all believers, who are His body, but which in itself is dead and can do nothing without Him.

> —HULDREICH ZWINGLI, "The First Zurich Disputation: The Sixty-Seven Articles of Zwingli," in *Selected Works*, trans. Lawrence A. McLouth, Henry Preble, and George W. Gilmore (Philadelphia: University of Pennsylvania, 1901), 111.

> **Ephesians 2:4–7:** But God, being rich in mercy, because of the great love
> with which he loved us, even when we were dead in our trespasses, made
> us alive together with Christ—by grace you have been saved—and raised
> us up with him and seated us with him in the heavenly places in Christ
> Jesus, so that in the coming ages he might show the immeasurable riches
> of his grace in kindness toward us in Christ Jesus.

He died for us. He gave himself for us. He rose for us. He ascended for us.
He sits at the right hand of God for us. He indeed has glory, but together
with us. Therefore, when we think of the glory of Christ, think of us in
Him.

When we celebrate His birth, think He was born for you and me; when
we remember His death, think He died for us and we die with Him; when
He was buried, think we were buried with Him. And in His resurrection
and state of exaltation, we see Him rise, sit at the right hand of God, and
know He is there to prepare a place for us.

Whatever He has, whatever He did, He considered us a part of it: it is
said in Romans 14:9, "For to this end Christ died and lived again, that he
might be Lord both of the dead and of the living."

I ask you, consider who benefits in this lordship. Is it not a profitable
lordship for us? Is it not for our good that He is our Lord in life and in
death?

—RICHARD SIBBES, "Christ's Exaltation," in *The Works of Richard Sibbes*, vol. 5,
ed. Alexander Balloch Grosart (Edinburgh; London; Dublin: James Nichol; James Nisbet and Co.; W. Robertson, 1863), 353.

Galatians 1:3–5: Grace to you and peace from God our Father and the Lord Jesus Christ, who gave himself for our sins to deliver us from the present evil age, according to the will of our God and Father, to whom be the glory forever and ever. Amen.

God became man, and it was the Lord himself who saved us.

> —IRENAEUS, *Against Heresies*, in *Ante-Nicene Fathers*, vol. 1, ed. Alexander Roberts, James Donaldson, and A. Cleveland Coxe, trans. Alexander Roberts and William Rambaut (Buffalo, NY: Christian Literature Publishing Co., 1885), 451 (*Against Heresies*, 3.21.1).

In all this the Word is the Lord, the subject of the incarnation. He becomes a creature in all His sovereign freedom as Creator; and without ceasing to be that Creator Word, He becomes flesh, without any diminishment of His freedom or of His eternal nature. But as the very Word of God, and remaining God's Word in all the fullness of His grace and truth, He comes personally to man, light into darkness, declaring and manifesting God in the flesh in a fullness from which we can all receive.

Jesus Christ is not merely man participating in God but is himself essential Deity. God did not merely descend on Jesus Christ as on one of the prophets; rather, in Jesus Christ God came to dwell among us as himself Man.

> —T. F. TORRANCE, *The Hermeneutics of John Calvin* (Edinburgh: Scottish Academic, 1988), 149–150.

DAY
311

Philippians 2:8: And being found in human form, he humbled himself by becoming obedient to the point of death, even death on a cross.

We must not deceive ourselves. The incarnation, the taking on the form of a servant, means not only God becoming a man—and how this is possible to God without an alteration of His being is not self-evident—but it means His giving himself up to the contradiction of man against Him, His placing himself under the judgment under which man has fallen in this contradiction, under the curse of death that rests upon Him. The meaning of the incarnation is plainly revealed in the question of Jesus on the cross: "My God, my God, why have you forsaken me?' (Mark 15:34). The more seriously we take this, the stronger becomes the temptation to approximate to the view of a contradiction and conflict in God himself. Have we not to accept this view if we are to do justice to what God did for man and what He took upon himself when He was in Christ, if we are to bring out the mystery of His mercy in all its depths and greatness?

—KARL BARTH, *Church Dogmatics*, vol. 4, ed. G. W. Bromiley and T. F. Torrance, trans. T. H. L. Parker (London: T&T Clark, 2004), 185.

1 Corinthians 15:50–58: I tell you this, brothers: flesh and blood cannot inherit the kingdom of God, nor does the perishable inherit the imperishable. Behold! I tell you a mystery. We shall not all sleep, but we shall all be changed, in a moment, in the twinkling of an eye, at the last trumpet. For the trumpet will sound, and the dead will be raised imperishable, and we shall be changed. For this perishable body must put on the imperishable, and this mortal body must put on immortality. When the perishable puts on the imperishable, and the mortal puts on immortality, then shall come to pass the saying that is written:
"Death is swallowed up in victory."
"O death, where is your victory?
O death, where is your sting?"
The sting of death is sin, and the power of sin is the law.
But thanks be to God, who gives us the victory through our Lord Jesus Christ. Therefore, my beloved brothers, be steadfast, immovable, always abounding in the work of the Lord, knowing that in the Lord your labor is not in vain.

Through the union of the immortal Son of God with our human nature, we His people were clothed with incorruption in the promise of the resurrection. For the solidarity of humanity is such that by virtue of the Word's indwelling in a single human body, the corruption that goes with death has lost its power. When some great king enters a large city and dwells in one of its houses, because of his dwelling in that single house, the whole city is honored, and enemies cease to molest it. Even so is it with the King of All; He has come into our country and dwelt in one body amidst the many, and in consequence the designs of the enemy against humanity have been foiled and the corruption of death, which formerly held us in its power, has simply ceased to be. Our human race would have utterly perished had not the Lord and Savior of all, the Son of God, come among us to conquer death.

—ATHANASIUS, *On the Incarnation of the Word*, A Select Library of the Nicene and Post-Nicene Fathers of the Christian Church, 2nd ser., vol. 4, ed. and trans. Philip Schaff and Henry Wace (Buffalo, NY: Christian Literature Publishing Co., 1892), 269 (*On the Incarnation*, 2.9).

Psalm 145:1–3, 8–9, 14–21:
I will extol you, my God and King,
    and bless your name forever and ever.
Every day I will bless you
    and praise your name forever and ever.
Great is the LORD, and greatly to be praised,
    and his greatness is unsearchable. . . .
The LORD is gracious and merciful,
    slow to anger and abounding in steadfast love.
The LORD is good to all,
    and his mercy is over all that he has made. . . .
The LORD upholds all who are falling
    and raises up all who are bowed down.
The eyes of all look to you,
    and you give them their food in due season.
You open your hand;
    you satisfy the desire of every living thing.
The LORD is righteous in all his ways
    and kind in all his works.
The LORD is near to all who call on him,
    to all who call on him in truth.
He fulfills the desire of those who fear him;
    he also hears their cry and saves them.
The LORD preserves all who love him,
    but all the wicked he will destroy.
My mouth will speak the praise of the LORD,
    and let all flesh bless his holy name forever and ever.

God has no pleasure in the destruction or calamity of people. He would rather they turn and continue in peace. He is well-pleased if they forsake their evil ways, that He may not have reason to execute His wrath upon them. He is a God who delights in mercy; judgment is His unfamiliar work.

—JONATHAN EDWARDS, "Impending Judgments Averted Only by Reformation," in *Sermons and Discourses, 1723–1729*, The Works of Jonathan Edwards, vol. 14, ed. Kenneth P. Minkema (New Haven, CT: Yale University Press, 1997), 221.

> **Hebrews 2:9:** But we see him who for a little while was made lower than the angels, namely Jesus, crowned with glory and honor because of the suffering of death, so that by the grace of God he might taste death for everyone.

We know we have an Advocate with the Father, Jesus Christ the righteous, or, as the epistle to the Hebrews puts it, a great High Priest (Hebrews 4:14–16), who has entered within the veil and ever lives to make intercession for us. So, let us realize that in our weakness we have the protecting arm of the King of kings and Lord of lords around us, and He will not let us slip, but will lose none whom the Father has given Him, but will raise them up at the last day.

Having been tempted like we are, though without sin, He is able to empathize with us in our infirmities. Having suffered as we do, He knows how to support us in our trials.

And having opened a way through His own blood, leading to life, He knows how to conduct our faltering steps that we may walk in it. Christ our Savior is on the throne. The hands that were pierced with the nails of the cross wield the scepter. How can our salvation fail?

—B. B. WARFIELD, "The Glorified Christ," in *The Savior of the World* (Carlisle, PA: Banner of Truth, 1916/1991), 185–186.

> **Hebrews 12:1-2:** Therefore, since we are surrounded by so great a cloud of witnesses, let us also lay aside every weight, and sin which clings so closely, and let us run with endurance the race that is set before us, looking to Jesus, the founder and perfecter of our faith, who for the joy that was set before him endured the cross, despising the shame, and is seated at the right hand of the throne of God.

Remember, therefore, it is not your hold on Christ that saves you—it is Christ himself.

It is not your joy in Christ that saves you—it is Christ.

It is not even faith in Christ, though that is the instrument—it is Christ's blood and sinless sacrifice.

Therefore, do not look so much to your hand with which you are grasping Christ, but to Christ himself.

Do not look to your hope, but to Jesus, the source of your hope.

Do not look to your faith, but to Jesus, the author and finisher of your faith.

We shall never find happiness by looking at our prayers, our good works, or our feelings.

It is what Jesus is, not what we are, that gives rest to the soul.

If we would at once overcome Satan and have peace with God, it must be by "looking to Jesus."

Keep your eye simply on Him.

Let His death, His suffering, His merits, His glory, His intercession be fresh upon your mind.

When you awake in the morning look to Him.

When you lie down at night look to Him.

—CHARLES H. SPURGEON, "June 28—Morning," in *Morning and Evening* (Geanies House, Fearn, Scotland: Christian Focus, 1994), 378.

> **Revelation 22:12–16:** "Behold, I am coming soon, bringing my recompense with me, to repay each one for what he has done. I am the Alpha and the Omega, the first and the last, the beginning and the end." Blessed are those who wash their robes, so that they may have the right to the tree of life and that they may enter the city by the gates. Outside are the dogs and sorcerers and the sexually immoral and murderers and idolaters, and everyone who loves and practices falsehood. "I, Jesus, have sent my angel to testify to you about these things for the churches. I am the root and the descendant of David, the bright morning star."

The only Son from heaven, foretold by ancient seers;
By God the Father given, in human form appears.
No sphere His light confining, no star so brightly shining
As He, our Morningstar.

Oh, time of God appointed, Oh, bright and holy morn!
He comes, the king anointed, the Christ, the virgin-born,
Grim death to vanquish for us, to open heaven before us
And bring us life again.

Awaken, Lord, our spirit to know and love you more,
In faith to stand unshaken, in spirit to adore,
That we, through this world moving, each glimpse of heaven proving,
May reap its fullness there.

O Father, here before you, with God the Holy Ghost,
And Jesus, we adore you, O pride of angel hosts:
Before you, mortals lowly cry, "Holy, holy, holy,
O blessed Trinity!"

—ELISABETH CRUCIGER, "The Only Son from Heaven," in *Lutheran Book of Worship* (1978), no. 86, trans. Arthur Tozer Russell.

Galatians 2:19–20: For through the law I died to the law, so that I might live to God. I have been crucified with Christ. It is no longer I who live, but Christ who lives in me. And the life I now live in the flesh I live by faith in the Son of God, who loved me and gave himself for me.

More like Jesus would I be
Let my Savior dwell with me.
Fill my soul with peace and love,
Make me gentle as the dove.
More like Jesus while I go,
Pilgrim in this world below.
Poor in spirit would I be,
Let my Savior dwell in me

If He hears the raven's cry,
If His ever-watchful eye
Marks the sparrows when they fall,
Surely, He will hear my call.
He will teach me how to live,
All my sinful thoughts forgive.
Pure in heart I still would be.
Let my Savior dwell in me.

More like Jesus when I pray,
More like Jesus day by day.
May I rest me by His side,
Where the tranquil waters glide.
Born of Him, through grace renewed,
By His love, my will subdued.
Rich in faith I still would be.
Let my Savior dwell in me.

—FANNY CROSBY, *Bells at Evening and Other Verses*
(New York: The Biglow & Main Co., 1905), 154.

Philippians 1:21–23: For to me to live is Christ, and to die is gain. If I am to live in the flesh, that means fruitful labor for me. Yet which I shall choose I cannot tell. I am hard pressed between the two. My desire is to depart and be with Christ, for that is far better.

Question: Why does Paul not say, I desire to be in heaven?

Answer: Because heaven is nothing without Christ. It is better to be anywhere with Christ than to be in heaven without Him. All delicacies without Christ are like a funeral banquet. Where the master of the feast is gone, there is nothing but sadness. What is anything without Christ? He is the joy of heaven.

—RICHARD SIBBES, "Christ Is Best," in *The Complete Works of Richard Sibbes*, vol. 1, ed. Alexander Balloch Grosart (Carlisle, PA: Banner of Truth, 1638/2001), 339.

Just to be with Christ is heaven. That simple thing, just to be with Christ, is all the heaven a believer wants.

The angels may be there or not, as they will, and the golden crowns and harps may be present or absent, but if I am to be where Jesus is, I will find angels in His eyes, and crowns in every lock of His hair. To me the golden streets will be my fellowship with Him, and the harpings of the harpers shall be the sound of His voice.

Only to be near Him, to be with Him—this is all we want. The apostle does not say, "to be in heaven, which is far better." No, "to be with Christ, which is far better," and he adds no description. He leaves the thoughts just as they are, in all their majestic simplicity. "To be with Christ, which is far better."

But what is it to be with Christ, beloved? In some sense we are with Christ now, for He comes to us. We are no strangers to Him. Even while we are in this body, we have communion with Jesus.

And yet it must be true that a higher fellowship is yet to come, for the apostle says that while we are present in the body we are absent from the Lord.

—CHARLES H. SPURGEON, "Forever with the Lord," in *The Metropolitan Tabernacle Pulpit Sermons*, vol. 19 (London: Passmore & Alabaster, 1873), 570–572.

> **Hebrews 12:3–4:** Consider him who endured from sinners such hostility against himself, so that you may not grow weary or fainthearted. In your struggle against sin you have not yet resisted to the point of shedding your blood.

There are no human traits lacking in the picture that is drawn of Him: He was open to temptation; He was conscious of dependence upon God; He was a man of prayer; He knew a will within Him that might conceivably be opposed to the will of God. He exercised faith; He learned obedience by the things that He suffered. It was not merely the mind of a man that was in Him, but the heart of a man as well, and the spirit of a man. In a word, He was all that a man—a man without error and sin—is, and must be understood to have grown, as it is proper for a man to grow, not only during His youth, but continuously through His life, not alone in knowledge, but in wisdom, and not alone in wisdom, but in reverence and charity—in moral strength and in the beauty of holiness.

—B. B. WARFIELD, "The Faith of Jesus and Faith in Jesus," in *Selected Shorter Writings of Benjamin B. Warfield*, vol. 1, ed. John E. Meeter (Phillipsburg: P&R Publishing, 2001), 161–162.

Believe then that this Only Begotten Son of God for our sins came down from heaven to earth and took upon himself human nature of like passions with us and was begotten of the Holy Virgin and of the Holy Spirit, and was made Man, not in seeming and mere show, but in truth; nor yet by passing through the Virgin as through a channel; but was of her made truly flesh, and did truly eat as we do, and truly drink as we do. For if the Incarnation was a phantom, salvation is a phantom also. The Christ was of two natures, Man in what was seen, but God in what was not seen; as Man truly eating like us, for He had the like feeling of the flesh with us; but as God feeding the five thousand from five loaves; as Man truly dying, but as God raising him that had been dead four days; truly sleeping in the ship as Man, and walking upon the waters as God.

—CYRIL OF JERUSALEM, "The Catechetical Lectures of S. Cyril, Archbishop of Jerusalem," in *S. Cyril of Jerusalem, S. Gregory Nazianzen*, A Select Library of the Nicene and Post-Nicene Fathers of the Christian Church, 2nd ser., vol. 7, ed. Philip Schaff and Henry Wace, trans. Edwin Hamilton Gifford (Buffalo, NY: Christian Literature Co., 1894), 133.

Luke 1:46–47: And Mary said, "My soul magnifies the Lord, and my spirit rejoices in God my Savior."

John 4:42: They said to the woman, "It is no longer because of what you said that we believe, for we have heard for ourselves, and we know that this is indeed the Savior of the world."

1 John 4:14: And we have seen and testify that the Father has sent his Son to be the Savior of the world.

Near the end, William Jay visited his friend Newton, who was then barely able to speak.

But Newton said: "My memory is nearly gone; but I remember two things: that I am a great sinner, and that Christ is a great Savior."

—JOHN NEWTON, *Wise Counsel: John Newton's Letters to John Ryland Jr.*, ed. Grant Gordon (Carlisle, PA: Banner of Truth, 2009), 401.

> **Luke 2:25–32:** Now there was a man in Jerusalem, whose name was Simeon, and this man was righteous and devout, waiting for the consolation of Israel, and the Holy Spirit was upon him. And it had been revealed to him by the Holy Spirit that he would not see death before he had seen the Lord's Christ. And he came in the Spirit into the temple, and when the parents brought in the child Jesus, to do for him according to the custom of the Law, he took him up in his arms and blessed God and said, "Lord, now you are letting your servant depart in peace, according to your word; for my eyes have seen your salvation that you have prepared in the presence of all peoples, a light for revelation to the Gentiles, and for glory to your people Israel."

Through them Christ was prophesied and made known and brought to birth. For He was prefigured in Joseph, while He was born of Levi and Judah after the flesh as king and priest. It was through Simeon in the temple that He was made known and through Zebulun He was believed on among the nations. And it was through Benjamin, through Paul, that He was glorified by having been proclaimed to the entire world.

—IRENAEUS, Fragment 17, in *Ancient Christian Doctrine: We Believe in the Crucified and Risen Lord* (Downers Grove, IL: IVP Academic, 2009), 5.

The aged Simeon met the Savior and received Him in his arms as an infant, the Creator of the world, and proclaimed Him to be Lord and God. But later, younger men would meet the Savior as Simeon did, and instead of holding Him in their arms they tossed palm branches under His feet and blessed the Lord God seated on a colt, as on the cherubim: "Hosanna, to the son of David." David in prophecy hid the spirit in the letter; children, opening their treasures, brought forth riches on their tongues.

—METHODIUS, Oration on Psalm 5, in *Ancient Christian Doctrine: We Believe in the Crucified and Risen Lord* (Downers Grove, IL: IVP Academic, 2009), 9.

Psalm 45:10–15:
Hear, O daughter, and consider, and incline your ear:
forget your people and your father's house,
and the king will desire your beauty.
Since he is your lord, bow to him.
The people of Tyre will seek your favor with gifts,
the richest of the people.
All glorious is the princess in her chamber, with robes interwoven with
gold.
In many-colored robes she is led to the king,
with her virgin companions following behind her.
With joy and gladness they are led along
as they enter the palace of the king.

Christ rejoices over His saints as the bridegroom over the bride. But there are some seasons when He especially rejoices.

The time when this mutual rejoicing of Christ and His saints will be perfected is the time of the saints' glorification with Christ in heaven. For that is the proper time of the saints' entering in with the bridegroom into the marriage. The saint's conversion is rather like the betrothing of the intended bride to her bridegroom before they come together.

But the time of the saint's glorification is the time when it shall be fulfilled: "With joy and gladness they are led along as they enter the palace of the king." That is the time when those whom Christ loved and gave himself for, He might sanctify and cleanse, as with the washing of water by the Word. They shall be presented to Him in glory, not having spot or wrinkle. It is the time wherein the Church shall be brought to the full enjoyment of her bridegroom, having all tears wiped away from her eyes.

She shall then be brought to the joys of an eternal wedding feast, and to dwell eternally with her bridegroom.

—JONATHAN EDWARDS, "The Church's Marriage to Her Sons, and to Her God,"
in *Sermons and Discourses, 1743–1758*, The Works of Jonathan Edwards, vol. 25, ed.
Wilson H. Kimnach and Harry S. Stout (New Haven, CT: Yale University Press, 2006),
181–182.

Psalm 103:11–14:
For as high as the heavens are above the earth,
    so great is his steadfast love toward those who fear him;
as far as the east is from the west,
    so far does he remove our transgressions from us.
As a father shows compassion to his children,
    so the Lord shows compassion to those who fear him.
For he knows our frame;
    he remembers that we are dust.

God sees no sin in any one of His people when He looks upon them "in Christ." In themselves, He sees sin and abomination, but if they are "in Christ," He sees nothing but purity and righteousness.

To the Christian, is it not one of the most delightful privileges to know that altogether apart from anything they have ever done, or can do, God looks upon them as righteous, and despite all the sins they have ever committed, they are accepted in Him as though they were in Christ, while He was punished for them as though He were the sinner?

When I stand in Christ—by faith—the Father's everlastingly beloved one, the Father's accepted one, He whom the Father delights to honor, I am in the most joyous spot that a creature of God can occupy.

Oh, Christian, get yourself up, get up into the high mountain, and stand where your Savior stands, for that is your place. Do not lie there on the dunghill of fallen humanity; that is not your place now. Christ has stood on your behalf. The Father made Him to be sin for us.

—CHARLES H. SPURGEON, "Christ—Our Substitute," in *The New Park Street Pulpit Sermons*, vol. 6 (London: Passmore & Alabaster, 1860), 195.

Matthew 5:14–16: "You are the light of the world. A city set on a hill cannot be hidden. Nor do people light a lamp and put it under a basket, but on a stand, and it gives light to all in the house. In the same way, let your light shine before others, so that they may see your good works and give glory to your Father who is in heaven."

He is called Christ, not having been anointed by men's hands, but eternally anointed by the Father to be High Priest on behalf of men. He is called Jesus because He is our Savior, according to the Hebrew language. He is called Son, not by adoption, but as naturally begotten. Jesus in the Greek tongue means the Healer, a physician of souls and bodies, curer of spirits. Kings among men have their royal style that others may not share, but Jesus Christ, being the Son of God, gave us the dignity of being called Christians. You are called a Christian: be a true witness of the name; let not our Lord Jesus Christ, the Son of God, be blasphemed through your life and testimony: but rather, "let your light shine before others, so that they may see your good works and give glory to your Father who is in heaven."

—CYRIL OF JERUSALEM, "The Catechetical Lectures of S. Cyril, Archbishop of Jerusalem," in *S. Cyril of Jerusalem, S. Gregory Nazianzen*, A Select Library of the Nicene and Post-Nicene Fathers of the Christian Church, 2nd ser., vol. 7, ed. Philip Schaff and Henry Wace, trans. Edwin Hamilton Gifford (Buffalo, NY: Christian Literature Co., 1894), 203, 210, 212, 216.

> **Romans 5:7–8:** For one will scarcely die for a righteous person—though perhaps for a good person one would dare even to die—but God shows his love for us in that while we were still sinners, Christ died for us.

It is common for equals to love, and for superiors to be beloved; but for the King of princes, the Son of God, Jesus Christ to love man: this is amazing, and so much more for the fact that man, the object of His love, is so low, so mean, so vile, so undeserving, as by the Scriptures he is everywhere described to be.

He is called God, the King of Glory. But the persons He calls beloved are also called transgressors, sinners, enemies, fleas, worms, shadows, vapors, vile, filthy, sinful, unclean; and are we not to be affected by the fact that He sets His eye upon us? But how much more when He will set His *heart* upon us?

Love in Him is essential to His being. God is love; Christ is God; therefore, Christ is love, *love naturally*. He may as well cease to be, as cease to love. . . .

Love from Christ requires no obvious beauty in the object to be beloved. His love can act in and of itself, without all such kinds of dependencies. The Lord Jesus sets His heart to love us.

Love in Christ does not decay, nor can it be tempted to do so by anything that happens, or that shall happen hereafter, in the object of His love.

—JOHN BUNYAN, *The Saints' Knowledge of the Love of Christ*, in *The Works of John Bunyan*, vol. 2, ed. G. Offor, reprint, (Edinburgh: Banner of Truth, 1991), 16–17.

> **John 14:27–28:** "Peace I leave with you; my peace I give to you. Not as the world gives do I give to you. Let not your hearts be troubled, neither let them be afraid. You heard me say to you, 'I am going away, and I will come to you.' If you loved me, you would have rejoiced, because I am going to the Father, for the Father is greater than I."

Many statements in Scripture imply or even assert that the Father is greater than the Son. Unfortunately, some readers have erred, through lack of careful examination, to consider the whole tenor of the Scriptures, and in so doing have transferred those things said of Jesus Christ as man to His substance before the incarnation. They say, for instance, that the Son is less than the Father, because the Lord himself said, "The Father is greater than I." In the same sense, they say the Son is less than himself because it is written, "He emptied himself." But He did not take the form of a servant and so lose the form of God, in which He was equal to the Father. The Scripture says both the one and the other, that the Son is equal to the Father, and that the Father is greater than the Son. For there is no confusion when the former is understood as speaking of the form of God, and the latter speaking of the form of a servant. This rule for clearing the question through all of Scripture is set forth in one chapter of an epistle of the apostle Paul, where this distinction is stated plainly enough: "Have this mind among yourselves, which is yours in Christ Jesus, who, though he was in the form of God, did not count equality with God a thing to be grasped, but emptied himself, by taking the form of a servant, being born in the likeness of men" (Philippians 2:5–7). The Son of God, then, is equal to God the Father in nature, but less in "fashion." For in the form of a servant He is less than the Father; but in the form of God, which He was before He took the form of a servant, He is equal to the Father. In the form of God, He is the Word, "by whom all things are made," but in the form of a servant, He was "born of a woman, born under the law, to redeem those who were under the law" (Galatians 4:4–5).

—AUGUSTINE OF HIPPO, "On the Trinity," in *St. Augustin: On the Holy Trinity, Doctrinal Treatises, Moral Treatises*, A Select Library of the Nicene and Post-Nicene Fathers of the Christian Church, ser. 1, vol. 3, ed. Philip Schaff, trans. Arthur West Haddan (Buffalo, NY: Christian Literature Co., 1887), 24.

> **Hebrews 13:5:** "I will never leave you nor forsake you."

Christ loved you before the world came into being, long before the day star flung his rays across the darkness, before the wings of angels soared. Before creation had struggled from the womb of nothingness, God, even our God, had set His heart upon all His children.

Since that time, has He once turned aside, once changed? No, you who have tasted of His love and know His grace will bear me witness that He has been a certain friend in uncertain circumstances.

You have often left Him; has He ever left you? You have had many trials and troubles; has He ever deserted you? Has He ever turned away His heart, or closed His spirit of compassion for you? No, children of God, it is our privilege to bear witness to His faithfulness.

—CHARLES H. SPURGEON, "A Faithful Friend," in *Sermons of C. H. Spurgeon* (New York, Sheldon, Blakeman, 1857), 13–14.

As God did not at first choose you because you were faithful, He will not now forsake you because you have doubts.

—JOHN FLAVEL, *Keeping the Heart: How to Maintain Your Love for God* (Fearn, Scotland: Christian Focus, 2012), 43.

DAY
328

Matthew 1:1–2, 17: The book of the genealogy of Jesus Christ, the son of David, the son of Abraham. Abraham was the father of Isaac, and Isaac the father of Jacob, and Jacob the father of Judah and his brothers. . . . So all the generations from Abraham to David were fourteen generations, and from David to the deportation to Babylon fourteen generations, and from the deportation to Babylon to the Christ fourteen generations.

If you hear the Gospel saying, "The book of the genealogy of Jesus Christ, the son of David, the son of Abraham," understand it to mean "according to the flesh"; for He is the Son of David at the end of the ages, but the Son of God before all ages, without beginning or end. The one He received, not having it before; the other, He has eternally, in that He is begotten of the Father. David is His father according to the flesh; God is His Father, after a divine manner, according to His Godhead. As the Son of David, He is subject to time, and His descent is traced; but according to His Godhead, He is subject neither to time nor place, nor descent. God is Spirit; He who is Spirit has spiritually begotten, being immaterial, an inscrutable and incomprehensible generation. The Son himself says of the Father, "The LORD said to me, 'You are my Son; today I have begotten you'" (Psalm 2:7). "Today" here is not recent, but eternal, "today" without time, before all ages.

—CYRIL OF JERUSALEM, "The Catechetical Lectures of S. Cyril, Archbishop of Jerusalem," in *A Library of Fathers of the Holy Catholic Church, Anterior to the Division of the East and West*, vol. 2, trans. Members of the English Church (Oxford: John Henry Parker, 1839), 112.

Deuteronomy 5:24: "Behold, the Lᴏʀᴅ our God has shown us his glory and greatness, and we have heard his voice out of the midst of the fire. This day we have seen God speak with man, and man still live."

The nature of this glory of Christ that they shall see will be such as will draw and encourage them, for they will not only see infinite majesty and greatness, but infinite grace, condescension, gentleness, and sweetness, equal to His majesty. The sight of Christ's kingly majesty will not be a dread to them but rather will serve to heighten their pleasure and joy. The souls of departed saints with Christ in heaven shall have Christ as it were joined to them, manifesting infinite riches of love toward them, which have been there from eternity. They shall eat and drink with abundance, swim in the ocean of love, and eternally bask in the infinitely bright and glorious beams of His divine love.

—JONATHAN EDWARDS, "True Saints, When Absent from the Body, Are Present with the Lord," in *Sermons and Discourses, 1743–1758*, The Works of Jonathan Edwards, vol. 25, ed. Wilson H. Kimnach and Harry S. Stout (New Haven, CT: Yale University Press, 2006), 233.

> **John 11:33:** When Jesus saw her weeping, and the Jews who had come with her also weeping, he was deeply moved in his spirit and greatly troubled.

It would be impossible for a moral being to stand in the presence of perceived wrong indifferent and unmoved. Precisely what we mean by a moral being is a being perceptive of the difference between right and wrong and reacting appropriately to it. The emotions of indignation and anger belong therefore to the very self-expression of a moral being and cannot be lacking to him in the presence of wrong.

Jesus approached the grave of Lazarus, in a state, not of uncontrollable grief, but of irrepressible anger. The emotion that tore His breast and clamored for utterance was rage.

Inextinguishable fury seizes upon Him. It is death that is the object of His wrath, and behind death, he who has the power of death, and whom He has come into the world to destroy. Tears of sympathy may fill His eyes, but this is incidental. His soul is held by rage. The raising of Lazarus thus becomes, not an isolated marvel, but a decisive instance and open symbol of Jesus' conquest of death and hell.

What John does for us is to uncover the heart of Jesus, as He wins for us our salvation. Not in cold unconcern, but in flaming wrath against the foe, Jesus smites in our behalf. He has not only saved us from the evils that oppress us; He has felt for and with us in our oppression, and under the impulse of these feelings has wrought our redemption.

—B. B. WARFIELD, *Person and Work of Christ* (Oxford: Benediction Classics, 2015), 107, 115, and 117.

Jesus' anger is not merely the disreputable side of His pity; it is the righteous reaction of His moral sense in the presence of evil. But Jesus burned with anger against the wrongs He met with in His journey through human life as truly as He melted with pity at the sight of the world's misery, and it was out of these two emotions that His actual mercy proceeded.

— B. B. WARFIELD, "On the Emotional Life of Our Lord," in *Biblical and Theological Studies* (New York: Charles Scribner's Sons, 1912), 12.

2 Timothy 2:11–13:
The saying is trustworthy, for:
> If we have died with him, we will also live with him;
> if we endure, we will also reign with him;
> if we deny him, he also will deny us;
> if we are faithless, he remains faithful—
for he cannot deny himself.

We needed an incarnate God, a God put to death, that we might live. We were put to death together with Him that we might be cleansed; we rose again with Him; we are also glorified with Him.

> —ST. GREGORY THE THEOLOGIAN, "The Second Oration on Holy Pascha," in *Nicene and Post-Nicene Fathers*, 2nd ser., vol. 7 (Grand Rapids, MI: Wm. B. Eerdmans Publishing, 1974), 433.

Christ came and was baptized that He might sanctify baptism: He came to work wonders, to walk upon the waters of the sea. Before His coming in the flesh, the sea saw Him and fled, and the Jordan was driven back. The Lord took upon himself a body that the sea might behold Him, and that the Jordan might receive Him. Since through Eve, a virgin, came death, from a virgin He came to life in the flesh; as through the serpent one was deceived, so through Gabriel might come the good news of great joy. Men, having forsaken God, made images in the form of men and worshiped them; God became man that they might see the light and worship the living God.

> —CYRIL OF JERUSALEM, "The Catechetical Lectures of S. Cyril, Archbishop of Jerusalem." in *A Library of Fathers of the Holy Catholic Church, Anterior to the Division of the East and West*, vol. 2, trans. Members of the English Church (Oxford: John Henry Parker, 1839), 130.

> **Luke 15:4–7:** "What man of you, having a hundred sheep, if he has lost one of them, does not leave the ninety-nine in the open country, and go after the one that is lost, until he finds it? And when he has found it, he lays it on his shoulders, rejoicing. And when he comes home, he calls together his friends and his neighbors, saying to them, 'Rejoice with me, for I have found my sheep that was lost.' Just so, I tell you, there will be more joy in heaven over one sinner who repents than over ninety-nine righteous persons who need no repentance."

Remember, you have given Jesus great joy in His saving you. He was forever with the Father, eternally happy, infinitely glorious, as God over all.

Yet out of boundless love, He came, took upon himself our nature, and suffered in our stead to bring us back to holiness and to God.

"He lays it on his shoulders, rejoicing." That day the shepherd knew but one joy. He had found his sheep, and the very pressure of it upon his shoulders made his heart light, for he knew by that sign that the object of his care was safe beyond all question.

Now he goes home with it, and his joy was so great that it filled his soul to overflowing. The parable speaks nothing of his joy in getting home again, nor a word concerning the joy of being greeted by his friends and neighbors.

No, the joy of having found his sheep eclipsed all other gladness of heart and dimmed the light of home and friendship. He turns to friends and neighbors and begs them to help him bear the weight of his happiness.

He cries, "Rejoice with me, for I have found my sheep that was lost." When one sinner repents, all heaven must celebrate.

—CHARLES H. SPURGEON, "The Parable of the Lost Sheep," in *The Metropolitan Tabernacle Pulpit Sermons*, vol. 30 (London: Passmore & Alabaster, 1884), 526.

Isaiah 54:8, 10:
"In overflowing anger for a moment
    I hid my face from you,
but with everlasting love I will have compassion on you,"
    says the Lord, your Redeemer. . . .
"For the mountains may depart
    and the hills be removed,
but my steadfast love shall not depart from you,
    and my covenant of peace shall not be removed,"
    says the Lord, who has compassion on you.

The Son of God, having clothed himself with our flesh, of His own accord clothed himself also with human emotions, so that He did not differ at all from His brethren, sin excepted.

—JOHN CALVIN, *Commentary on the Gospel according to John*, vol. 1, trans. William Pringle (Grand Rapids, MI: Baker, 2003), 440.

The emotion that we should naturally expect to find most frequently attributed to Jesus, whose whole life was a mission of mercy, and whose ministry was so marked by benevolent deeds that it was summed up in the memory of His followers as "He went about doing good" (Acts 10:38), is no doubt compassion. In fact, this is the emotion that is most frequently attributed to Him.

His heart responded with a profound feeling of pity for them. His compassion fulfilled itself in the outward act; but what is emphasized by the term employed to express our Lord's response is the profound internal movement of His emotional nature.

—B. B. WARFIELD, *Person and Work of Christ* (Oxford: Benediction Classics, 2015), 96–98.

> **John 16:4–7, 13–15:** "I did not say these things to you from the beginning, because I was with you. But now I am going to him who sent me, and none of you asks me, 'Where are you going?' But because I have said these things to you, sorrow has filled your heart. Nevertheless, I tell you the truth: it is to your advantage that I go away, for if I do not go away, the Helper will not come to you. But if I go, I will send him to you. . . . When the Spirit of truth comes, he will guide you into all the truth, for he will not speak on his own authority, but whatever he hears he will speak, and he will declare to you the things that are to come. He will glorify me, for he will take what is mine and declare it to you. All that the Father has is mine; therefore I said that he will take what is mine and declare it to you."

Do not think that because He is absent in the flesh, He is therefore absent in the Spirit. The Holy Spirit is here present with us, listening to us, guiding and helping us, knowing our thoughts and desires.

—CYRIL OF JERUSALEM, "The Catechetical Lectures of S. Cyril, Archbishop of Jerusalem," in *S. Cyril of Jerusalem, S. Gregory Nazianzen*, A Select Library of the Nicene and Post-Nicene Fathers of the Christian Church, 2nd ser., vol. 7, ed. Philip Schaff and Henry Wace, trans. Edwin Hamilton Gifford (Buffalo, NY: Christian Literature Co., 1894), 293.

Had He remained upon the earth in visible form, He could not have been as effective, for everyone could not have been with Him and heard Him. Therefore, He devised a plan to make it possible for Him to be in touch with all people, to preach to all, to be heard by all, and to be present with all. Therefore, beware lest you imagine that He has gone, and now is far away from us. The very opposite is true: while He was on earth, He was far away from us; now He is very close.

—MARTIN LUTHER, *The Complete Sermons of Martin Luther*, vol. 2, ed. Eugene F. King and John Nicholas Lenker (Grand Rapids, MI: Baker Books, 2000), 190.

1 Corinthians 13:4–8: Love is patient and kind; love does not envy or boast; it is not arrogant or rude. It does not insist on its own way; it is not irritable or resentful; it does not rejoice at wrongdoing, but rejoices with the truth. Love bears all things, believes all things, hopes all things, endures all things. Love never ends.

There is no love so great and so wonderful as the love of Christ. He delights in mercy; He is ready to console those who are suffering or are in sorrowful circumstances. He delights in the happiness of His children. The love and grace that Christ has manifested to us exceeds all that is otherwise in this world. Though parents may be full of kindness toward their children, it cannot exceed the kindness of Jesus Christ.

—JONATHAN EDWARDS, "Children Ought to Love the Lord Jesus Christ Above All," in *Sermons and Discourses 1739–1742*, The Works of Jonathan Edwards, vol. 22, ed. Harry S. Stout and Nathan O. Hatch (New Haven, CT: Yale University Press, 2003), 171.

Everything that is lovely in God is in Jesus Christ, and everything that is or can be lovely in any man is in Him, for He is man as well as God, the holiest, meekest, most humble, and in every way the most excellent man that ever lived.

—JONATHAN EDWARDS, "Children Ought to Love the Lord Jesus Christ Above All," in *Sermons and Discourses 1739–1742*, The Works of Jonathan Edwards, vol. 22, ed. Harry S. Stout and Nathan O. Hatch (New Haven, CT: Yale University Press, 2003), 172.

Seeing only His greatness, the enmity and opposition of one's heart may remain in its full strength, and the will remain inflexible; whereas, one glimpse of the moral and spiritual glory of God, the supreme kindness of Jesus Christ, piercing the heart, overcomes this opposition and inclines the soul to Christ, as it were by an omnipotent power.

—JONATHAN EDWARDS, "True Grace, Distinguished from the Experience of Devils," in *Sermons and Discourses, 1743–1758*, The Works of Jonathan Edwards, vol. 25, ed. Wilson H. Kimnach and Harry S. Stout (New Haven, CT: Yale University Press, 2006), 635.

1 John 4:9–10: In this the love of God was made manifest among us, that God sent his only Son into the world, so that we might live through him. In this is love, not that we have loved God but that he loved us and sent his Son to be the propitiation for our sins.

John 3:16: For God so loved the world, that he gave his only Son, that whoever believes in him should not perish but have eternal life.

Our transgressions called forth the loving-kindness of the Word, that the Lord should both make haste to help us and to appear among men. For we were the object of His becoming incarnate, and for our salvation He lovingly appeared, even being born in a human body.

> —ATHANASIUS, *On the Incarnation*, trans. Archibald Robertson (London: D. Nutt, 1891), 7.

They that find Christ discover that though He is so glorious and excellent a person, He is ready to receive such poor, worthless, hateful creatures as they are, which surprised them.

They did not imagine that Christ was such a person, a person of such grace. They heard He was a holy Savior and hated sin, and they did not imagine He would be so ready to receive such vile, wicked creatures as they. They thought He surely would never be willing to accept such provoking sinners, such guilty wretches, those that had such abominable hearts.

They unexpectedly find Him with open arms to embrace them, ready forever to forgive all their sins as though they had never been. They find that He runs to meet them, and makes them most welcome, and admits them not only to be His servants but His friends. He lifts them out of the dust and sets them on His throne; He makes them the children of God; He speaks peace to them; He cheers and refreshes their hearts; He admits them unto strict union with himself, and gives the most joyful entertainment, and binds himself to them to be their friend forever.

They never imagined to find Christ a person of such love and grace. It is beyond all imagination or conception.

> —JONATHAN EDWARDS, "Seeking After Christ," in *Sermons and Discourses 1739–1742*, The Works of Jonathan Edwards, vol. 22, ed. Harry S. Stout and Nathan O. Hatch (New Haven, CT: Yale University Press, 2003), 290.

1 Corinthians 2:2: For I decided to know nothing among you except Jesus Christ and him crucified.

Was not God crucified? Did He not truly die after a real crucifixion? Did He not truly rise again, after a real death? If not, then Paul's determination was mistaken, "to know nothing among you except Jesus Christ and him crucified"; mistaken too his insistence on His burial, his emphasis on His resurrection. Then our faith also is mistaken, and our hope in Christ a mere illusion. Spare us the one and only hope of the whole world, for you are destroying the indispensable glory of the faith if you deny His death and resurrection. All that is unworthy of God is for my benefit. I am saved if I am not ashamed of my Lord. For He says, "Whoever denies me before men, I also will deny before my Father who is in heaven" (Matthew 10:33). Nowhere else do I find grounds for shame that may prove me to be nobly shameless and happily foolish: "Let us run with endurance the race that is set before us, looking to Jesus, the founder and perfecter of our faith, who for the joy that was set before him endured the cross, *despising the shame*, and is seated at the right hand of the throne of God" (Hebrews 12:1–2). The Son of God was born shameful, therefore there is no shame. The Son of God died: absurd, and therefore utterly credible. He was buried and rose again: impossible, and therefore a fact.

—TERTULLIAN, *The Flesh of Christ*, 4–5 (Bettenson 1956), 125.

Oh, how should the consideration of this stir up the soul against it, and work the soul to fly from it, and to use all holy means whereby sin may be subdued and destroyed!

It was good counsel one gave: "Never let go out of your minds the thoughts of a crucified Christ."

Let these be meat and drink unto you; let them be your sweetness and consolation; your reading and meditation; your life, death, and resurrection.

—THOMAS BROOKS, *The Works of Thomas Brooks*, vol. 1, ed. Alexander Balloch Grosart (Carlisle, PA: Banner of Truth, 1666/2001), 17–18.

> **1 John 2:1–2:** My little children, I am writing these things to you so that you may not sin. But if anyone does sin, we have an advocate with the Father, Jesus Christ the righteous. He is the propitiation for our sins, and not for ours only but also for the sins of the whole world.

Christ as Priest goes before, and Christ, as an Advocate comes after. Christ, as Priest, continually intercedes; Christ, as Advocate, in case of great transgression, pleads. Christ, as Priest has need to act always, but Christ, as Advocate, sometimes only. Christ, as Priest, acts in times of peace; but Christ, as Advocate, in times of turmoil and sharp contention. Christ, as Advocate, may be called upon as a reserve, someone to stand up and plead for His own when they are clothed in some filthy sin, which they have fallen into.

—JOHN BUNYAN, *The Work of Jesus Christ as an Advocate*, in *The Works of John Bunyan*, vol. 1, ed. George Offor (Edinburgh: Banner of Truth, 1991), 169.

Christ gave for us the price of blood, but that is not all; Christ as a Captain has conquered death and the grave for us, but that is not all; Christ as a Priest intercedes for us in heaven, but that is not all. Sin is still in us, and with us, and mixes itself with whatever we do, whether what we do be religious or civil. For not only our prayers and our preaching, but our homes, our shops, our trades, and our beds, are all polluted with sin.

Nor does the devil, our constant adversary, restrain from telling our bad deeds to our Father, urging that we might forever be disinherited.

What would we do if we did not have an Advocate, no one to plead for us, no one that could prevail and that would faithfully execute that office for us? We would surely die in our sins. But since we are rescued by Him, let us lay our hand upon our mouth and be silent.

—JOHN BUNYAN, *The Work of Jesus Christ as an Advocate*, in *The Works of John Bunyan*, vol. 1. ed. George Offor (Edinburgh: Banner of Truth, 1991), 197.

> **Luke 23:34:** And Jesus said, "Father, forgive them, for they know not what they do."

Even now He prays for us, and through us. He prays through us as our High Priest and for us as our Head. We pray to Him as our God. Even while on the cross, He was praying. He could see and foresee. He knew who His enemies were, but also who would become His friends. He was interceding for them all. While they raged, He prayed. They were shouting to Pilate, "Crucify Him!" but He was crying out, "Father, forgive them!" While hanging in agony from the cruel nails, He did not lose His gentleness. He was asking for pardon for His executioners. They were gathered around Him, mocking and scorning as one man, like so many raving lunatics against the Great Physician. His heart was to forgive them, to heal them. He was suspended there, and yet dispensing goodness. Though He had the power to do so, He would not come down from the cross, because He was shedding His blood for their redemption. After His resurrection, He cured some who were present as He hung on the cross. That is why Christ came; not to destroy those whom He had found, but to seek and to save those who were lost, so that by loving His enemies, He might make them believers and friends.

—AUGUSTINE OF HIPPO, "Sermon 382—Sermon on the Birthday of St. Stephen, the First Martyr," in *The Works of St. Augustine*, vol. 3, ed. Edmond Hill (Hyde Park, NY: New City Press, 1990), 376.

He regarded not that He was being put to death by them, but only that He was dying for them. It was a great sin that was forgiven them, it was a great sacrifice that was made for them, so that no man should despair of the forgiveness of his sins when they who crucified Christ could also obtain pardon.

—AUGUSTINE OF HIPPO, "Lectures on the Gospel according to St. John," in *St. Augustin: Homilies on the Gospel of John, Homilies on the First Epistle of John Soliloquies*, A Select Library of the Nicene and Post-Nicene Fathers of the Christian Church, 1st ser., vol. 7, ed. Philip Schaff, trans. John Gibb and James Innes (Buffalo: NY: Christian Literature Co., 1888), 191.

> **Isaiah 53:7:**
> He was oppressed, and he was afflicted,
>   yet he opened not his mouth;
> like a lamb that is led to the slaughter,
>   and like a sheep that before its shearers is silent,
>   so he opened not his mouth.

Christ gave evidence that He was that mild and gentle lamb, led out to be sacrificed, as Isaiah the prophet had foretold. For not only does He abstain from revenge but pleads with God the Father for the salvation of those by whom He is most cruelly tormented (Luke 23:34). It would have been a great thing not to think of rendering evil for evil (1 Peter 3:9), as Peter did, when He exhorts us to patience by the example of Christ. But this is a far higher and more excellent virtue, to pray that God would forgive His enemies.

—JOHN CALVIN, *Commentary on a Harmony of the Evangelists, Matthew, Mark, and Luke*, vol. 3, in Calvin's Commentaries, vol. 17 (Grand Rapids, MI: Baker, 2003), 300.

Did you notice when it was that Jesus pleaded for their forgiveness? It was while they were crucifying Him! They had not just driven in the nails, they had lifted the cross and rammed it into its socket, dislocating all His bones, as He said, "I am poured out like water, and all my bones are out of joint" (Psalm 22:14). Dear friends, it was then that instead of a cry or a groan, the Son of God said, "Father, forgive them, for they know not what they do" (Luke 23:34). They did not ask for forgiveness for themselves; Jesus asked for forgiveness for them. Their hands were stained with His blood; and it was then that He prayed for them. Let us think of the great love wherewith He loved us, even while we were yet sinners. Even then He prayed for us. "While we were still weak, at the right time Christ died for the ungodly" (Romans 5:6). Bless His name tonight. He prayed for you when you did not pray for yourself. He prayed for you when you were crucifying Him.

—CHARLES H. SPURGEON, "Christ's Plea for Ignorant Sinners," https://www.spurgeon.org/resource-library/sermons/christs-plea-for-ignorant-sinners/#flipbook/.

> **Hebrews 2:14–18:** Since therefore the children share in flesh and blood, he himself likewise partook of the same things, that through death he might destroy the one who has the power of death, that is, the devil, and deliver all those who through fear of death were subject to lifelong slavery. For surely it is not angels that he helps, but he helps the offspring of Abraham. Therefore he had to be made like his brothers in every respect, so that he might become a merciful and faithful high priest in the service of God, to make propitiation for the sins of the people. For because he himself has suffered when tempted, he is able to help those who are being tempted.

The very fact that God became man in order to save us declares in no uncertain terms that the humanity of Christ is absolutely essential to our salvation.

> —T. F. TORRANCE, *Incarnation: The Person and Life of Christ*, ed. Robert T. Walker (Downers Grove, IL: IVP, 2008), 184.

It is essential to realize that Jesus Christ, the Son of God, is also man, of one and the same being and nature as we are. If He is not really man, then the great bridge that God has thrown across the gulf between himself and us has no foundation on our side of that gulf. Jesus Christ, to be Mediator in the proper sense, must be wholly and fully man as well as God. Hence the Creed stresses the stark reality and actuality of His humanity: it was for our sakes that God became man, for us and for our salvation, so that it is from a soteriological perspective that we must seek to understand the human agency and life of Jesus Christ. He came to take our place, in all our human, earthly life and activity, in order that we may have His place as God's beloved children, in all our human and earthly life and activity, sharing with Jesus in the communion of God's own life and love as Father, Son, and Holy Spirit.

> —T. F. TORRANCE, *The Trinitarian Faith* (New York: Bloomsbury, 2016), 8.

Romans 8:26: Likewise the Spirit helps us in our weakness. For we do not know what to pray for as we ought, but the Spirit himself intercedes for us with groanings too deep for words.

Christ turns the Father's eyes to His own righteousness to avert His gaze from our sins. He so reconciles the Father's heart to us that through His intercession He prepares a way and access for us to the Father's throne.

—JOHN CALVIN, *Institutes of Christian Religion*, vol. 1, ed. John T. McNeill, trans. Ford L. Battles (Louisville, KY: Westminster John Knox Press, 1960), 524–525 (*Institutes*, 2.16.16).

It is a consoling thought that Christ is praying for us, even when we are negligent in our own prayer life.

—LOUIS BERKHOF, *Systematic Theology* (Edinburgh: Banner of Truth, 1958), 400.

What a comfort it is, as we daily approach the throne, that God might minister boldness to us in all our pursuits for His kingdom, that we may go to God in the name of the One whom He loves, in whom His soul delights, that we have a friend in court, as it were, a friend in heaven for us, who is at the right hand of God, interposing himself there for us, making us acceptable, sweetening our prayers and makings them acceptable. Be sure therefore in all your endeavors and approaches to God the Father to take along your elder Brother. God looks upon us, loving us in Him. He delights in us, as we are members of His family.

—RICHARD SIBBES, "A Description of Christ," in *The Works of Richard Sibbes*, vol. 1, ed. Alexander Balloch Grosart (Edinburgh: Banner of Truth, 1983), 13.

> **Hebrews 12:22–24:** But you have come to Mount Zion and to the city of the living God, the heavenly Jerusalem, and to innumerable angels in festal gathering, and to the assembly of the firstborn who are enrolled in heaven, and to God, the judge of all, and to the spirits of the righteous made perfect, and to Jesus, the mediator of a new covenant, and to the sprinkled blood that speaks a better word than the blood of Abel.

Christ, in dying for the sins of humanity, died for those who were His crucifiers and murderers. As He died for those who actually and immediately put Him to death, as He called for mercy for them while He was suffering, so His voice in that prayer was as the voice of His blood, which spoke a better word than the blood of Abel. For Abel's blood cried for vengeance on him who shed it, but Christ's blood cries for the forgiveness of those who shed it, saying, "Father, forgive them, for they know not what they do" (Luke 23:34). His dying for those at His crucifixion, and interceding for their forgiveness, represented His dying for all the elect Jews and Gentiles, while forgiving their enmity against Him.

—JONATHAN EDWARDS, "Miscellany 762," in *The "Miscellanies," 501–832*, The Works of Jonathan Edwards, vol. 18, ed. Ava Chamberlain (New Haven, CT: Yale University Press, 2000), 408.

We could ask of Christ himself why He did not withhold this kindness from those who crucified Him, reviled Him, and blasphemed Him, but rather prayed for them: "Father, forgive them, for they know not what they do," although they were shameless villains who deserved the wrath of God and punishment. If He had been angry with them who were His enemies and practiced all manner of idolatry and ungodliness, He would have had to stay in heaven and not die for us, but say rather: I will forgive, indeed, but I will not forget.

—MARTIN LUTHER, *Luther's Commentary on the Sermon on the Mount*, trans. Charles A. Hay (Philadelphia: Lutheran Publication Society, 1892), 136.

Ephesians 1:3, 7–8, 11–12; 3:20–21: Blessed be the God and Father of our Lord Jesus Christ, who has blessed us in Christ with every spiritual blessing in the heavenly places. . . . In him we have redemption through his blood, the forgiveness of our trespasses, according to the riches of his grace, which he lavished upon us, in all wisdom and insight. . . . In him we have obtained an inheritance, having been predestined according to the purpose of him who works all things according to the counsel of his will, so that we who were the first to hope in Christ might be to the praise of his glory. . . . Now to him who is able to do far more abundantly than all that we ask or think, according to the power at work within us, to him be glory in the church and in Christ Jesus throughout all generations, forever and ever. Amen.

The promises of Scripture may very roughly be reduced to five heads. It is promised first of all, that we shall be with Christ; secondly, that we shall be like Him; thirdly, with an enormous wealth of imagery, we shall have "glory"; fourthly, that we shall, in some sense, be fed or feasted or entertained; and, finally, that we shall have some sort of official position in the universe—ruling cities, judging angels, even being pillars in God's temple.

—C. S. LEWIS, "The Weight of Glory," in *The Weight of Glory: and Other Addresses* (New York: HarperCollins, 1949/2001), 34.

My Master has such riches that you cannot count them. You cannot guess what they are, much less convey their fullness in words. They are unsearchable! You may look, search, weigh, but Christ is greater than you think Him to be even when your thoughts are at their greatest.

My Master is more able to pardon you than you to sin, more able to forgive than you to transgress. My Master is more ready to supply your needs than you are to ask, even ten thousand times more prepared to save than you are to be saved. Never tolerate small thoughts of our Lord Jesus. Your highest estimates will dishonor Him.

—CHARLES H. SPURGEON, "The Unsearchable Riches of Christ," in *Spurgeon's Sermons*, vol. 9 (Grand Rapids, MI: Baker, 1996), 259–260.

> **Luke 23:32–39:** Two others, who were criminals, were led away to be put to death with him. And when they came to the place that is called The Skull, there they crucified him, and the criminals, one on his right and one on his left. And Jesus said, "Father, forgive them, for they know not what they do." And they cast lots to divide his garments. And the people stood by, watching, but the rulers scoffed at him, saying, "He saved others; let him save himself, if he is the Christ of God, his Chosen One!" The soldiers also mocked him, coming up and offering him sour wine and saying, "If you are the King of the Jews, save yourself!" There was also an inscription over him, "This is the King of the Jews." One of the criminals who were hanged railed at him, saying, "Are you not the Christ? Save yourself and us!"

There is no prayer against them in the words that Jesus utters. It was written of old, by the prophet Isaiah, "He bore the sin of many, and makes intercession for the transgressors" (53:12), and here it is fulfilled. He pleads for his murderers, "Father, forgive them." He does not utter a single word of upbraiding. He does not say, "Why are you doing this? Why do you pierce the hands that fed you? Why do you nail the feet that followed you in mercy? Why do you mock the Man who loved to bless you?" No, not a word of accusation, much less anything like a curse. "Father, forgive them." Notice He does not say, "I forgive you," but you may read that between the lines. It is even more powerful because He does not say those exact words. But He laid aside His majesty and is nailed to a cross; He takes the humble position of someone making a request rather than the higher place of One who had the power to forgive. How often, when men say, "I forgive you," there is a kind of selfishness about it. At any rate, self is asserted in the very act of forgiving. But Jesus takes the place of a pleader, pleading on behalf of those who were murdering Him. Blessed be His name!

—CHARLES H. SPURGEON, "Christ's Plea for Ignorant Sinners," https://www.spurgeon.org/resource-library/sermons/christs-plea-for-ignorant-sinners/#flipbook/.

> **Matthew 27:45–46:** Now from the sixth hour there was darkness over all the land until the ninth hour. And about the ninth hour Jesus cried out with a loud voice, saying, "Eli, Eli, lema sabachthani?" that is, "My God, my God, why have you forsaken me?"

All that He suffered was by the special order of God. There was a very visible hand of God allowing men and devils loose upon Him and separating Him from His own disciples. "Yet it was the will of the LORD to crush him" (Isaiah 53:10). God dealt with Him as if He had been angry with Him, as though He had been the object of His dreadful wrath. This made the sufferings of Christ all the more terrible to Him, because they were from the hand of His Father, whom He infinitely loved, and whose infinite love He had experienced eternally.

It was an effect of God's wrath that He forsook Christ. This is what caused Christ to cry out from the cross, "My God, my God, why have you forsaken me?" This was infinitely terrible to Him: Christ's knowledge of the glory of the Father, and His love for the Father, and the sense and experience He had had of the worth of the Father's love to Him, made the withholding of His Father's love as terrible to Him as the sense and knowledge of His hatred for the damned, who have no knowledge of God's excellence, no love for Him, nor any experience of the infinite sweetness of His love.

—JONATHAN EDWARDS, "Miscellany 1005," in *The "Miscellanies," 833–1152*, The Works of Jonathan Edwards, vol. 20, ed. Amy Plantinga Pauw (New Haven, CT: Yale University Press, 2002), 333–334.

> **1 Corinthians 1:23–24:** But we preach Christ crucified, a stumbling block to Jews and folly to Gentiles, but to those who are called, both Jews and Greeks, Christ the power of God and the wisdom of God.

The best preaching is "We preach Christ crucified."

The best living is "We are crucified with Christ."

The best man is a crucified man.

The best lifestyle is a crucified lifestyle; may we embrace it!

The more we live beholding our Lord's unutterable griefs and understanding how He has fully put away our sin, the more holiness we will demonstrate.

The more we dwell where the cries of Calvary can be heard, where we can view heaven, and earth, and hell, all moved by His wondrous passion—the more devoted our lives will be to Him.

Nothing puts real life into humankind like a dying Savior.

Get closer to Christ and carry His presence with you from day to day, and you will do His bidding.

Come, let us crucify sin, for Christ was crucified.

Come, let us bury all our pride, for Christ was buried.

Come, let us rise to newness of life, for Christ has risen.

Let us be united with our crucified Lord in His one great object to draw the lost to himself.

Let us live and die with Him, displaying His perfect love and sacrifice.

—CHARLES H. SPURGEON, "To Lovers of Jesus: An Example," in *The Metropolitan Tabernacle Pulpit Sermons*, vol. 31 (London: Passmore & Alabaster, 1885), 202.

Romans 5:6–8: For while we were still weak, at the right time Christ died for the ungodly. For one will scarcely die for a righteous person—though perhaps for a good person one would dare even to die— but God shows his love for us in that while we were still sinners, Christ died for us.

God has come through Jesus Christ to be one with humankind, to act from within humanity, and as man to yield to the Father the obedience of a true and faithful Son, and so to lay hold of God for us from the side of humanity. It is within that union of the Son with the Father that the sinner is drawn in and given a share. In other words, the union of God and man in Christ is enacted as the reconciling event, and through it men and women are given to share by adoption in the grace of Jesus Christ.

Christ's salvation is such that it expresses the ultimate reality of guilt and exposes it in terms of the wrath of God, but at the same time manifests the infinite love of God and enacts the union of God and man in a communion that nothing can undo. In forgiveness, Jesus Christ offers himself on behalf of and in the place of the sinner, and the gulf of man and God is spanned, but in casting a bridge over the abyss, the depth and breadth of it are made still more evident. That is why Golgotha casts such a dark shadow over the world. That is why the cross unmasks the inhumanity of man, at once exposing sin and guilt and dealing with them at their worst—in humankind's ultimate attack upon God in Jesus Christ—in God's display of love upon the inhumanity of humankind—and out of the heart of that come two words that reveal the infinite guilt of humanity and the infinite love of God: "My God, my God, why have you forsaken me?" and "Father, forgive them, for they know not what they do."

—T. F. TORRANCE, *Incarnation: The Person and Life of Christ* (Downers Grove, IL: IVP Academic, 2008), 194, 256.

> **Luke 23:43:** And he said to him, "Truly, I say to you, today you will be with me in paradise."

Until now, one thief was equal in all things to his companion. He was a robber on the roads and a danger to the safety of the people. Deserving the cross, he suddenly becomes a confessor of Christ: "Jesus, remember me when you come into your kingdom." Then came the gift in which faith itself received a response. Jesus said to him, "Truly, I say to you, today you will be with me in paradise." This promise surpasses the human condition, because it did not come so much from the wood of a cross as from a throne of power. From that height, He gives a reward to faith. There He abolishes the debt of human transgression, because the "form of God" did not separate itself from the "form of a servant." Even in the midst of this punishment, both the inviolable divinity and the suffering human nature preserved its own character and its own oneness.

This cross of Christ holds the mystery of its true and prophesied altar. There, through the saving victim, a sacrifice of human nature is celebrated. There the blood of a spotless lamb dissolved the pact of that ancient transgression. There the whole perversity of the devil's mastery was abolished, while humility triumphed as conqueror over boasting pride. The effect of faith was so swift that one of the two thieves crucified with Christ, who believed in the Son of God, entered paradise justified. Who could explain the mystery of such a great gift?

Who could describe the power of such a marvelous transformation? In a moment of time, the guilt of a longstanding wickedness was abolished. In the middle of the harsh torments of a struggling soul, fastened to the gallows, the guilty one passes over to Christ, and the grace of Christ gives him a crown, the same who incurred punishment for his wickedness.

—LEO THE GREAT, "Sermon 55," in *Sermons*, vol. 93 of *The Fathers of the Church: A New Translation (Patristic Series)*, trans. Jane Patricia Freeland (Washington, D.C.: Catholic University of America Press, 1996), 239.

Psalm 119:120: My flesh trembles for fear of you, and I am afraid of your judgments.

John 6:37: All that the Father gives me will come to me, and whoever comes to me I will never cast out.

They who would come to Jesus Christ are often afraid that He will not receive them. This observation is implied in the text. But look at the largeness and openness of the promise: "Whoever comes to me I will never cast out." Had there not been a proneness in us to fear being cast out, Christ would not have needed to allay our fears, as He does in the second text.

For this word, "Whoever comes to me I will never cast out," cuts to the throat of all objections, and was spoken by the Lord Jesus to that very end, to help the faith that is mixed with unbelief. It is, as it were, the sum of all promises; no objection can be made based upon the unworthiness you find in yourself:

But I am a great sinner, you say. "Whoever comes to me I will never cast out," says Christ.

But I am an old sinner, you say. "Whoever comes to me I will never cast out," says Christ.

But I am a hard-hearted sinner, you say. "Whoever comes to me I will never cast out," says Christ.

But I am a backsliding sinner, you say. "Whoever comes to me I will never cast out," says Christ.

But I have served Satan all my days, you say. "Whoever comes to me I will never cast out," says Christ.

But I have sinned against the light, you say. "Whoever comes to me I will never cast out," says Christ.

But I have sinned against mercy, you say. "Whoever comes to me I will never cast out," says Christ.

But I have no good thing to bring with me, you say. "Whoever comes to me I will never cast out," says Christ.

This promise was provided to answer all objections, and it does answer them.

—JOHN BUNYAN, *Come, and Welcome to Jesus Christ*, in *The Work of John Bunyan*, vol. 1, ed. George Offor (Edinburgh: Banner of Truth, 1991), 279–280.

> **Philippians 2:5–8:** Have this mind among yourselves, which is yours in Christ Jesus, who, though he was in the form of God, did not count equality with God a thing to be grasped, but emptied himself, by taking the form of a servant, being born in the likeness of men. And being found in human form, he humbled himself by becoming obedient to the point of death, even death on a cross.

> **Luke 23:39–43:** One of the criminals who were hanged railed at him, saying, "Are you not the Christ? Save yourself and us!" But the other rebuked him, saying, "Do you not fear God, since you are under the same sentence of condemnation? And we indeed justly, for we are receiving the due reward of our deeds; but this man has done nothing wrong." And he said, "Jesus, remember me when you come into your kingdom." And he said to him, "Truly, I say to you, today you will be with me in paradise."

I marvel at this: that the thief on the cross could have so much faith. Peter denied Him on the ground; that fellow confessed Him on a cross. He had not seen the miracles of Christ; Christ had not said to him, "I will make you fishers of men." He not only believed but spoke openly of his own sin and was concerned for the salvation of his neighbor. Nobody, when he first enters his reign, takes a thief for a companion. Christ did just that, and did not contaminate paradise, but rather made it honored that it had such a Lord, who could purify thieves and prostitutes instantly so that they were suitable for the kingdom of heaven.

—PETER VERMIGLI, *On the Death of Christ, from Philippians*, in *Life, Letters, and Sermons*, vol. 5 of *The Peter Martyr Library*, ed. And trans. John Patrick Donnelly (Kirksville, MO: Thomas Jefferson University Press, 1999), 244–245.

Matthew 27:46: And about the ninth hour Jesus cried out with a loud voice, saying, "Eli, Eli, lema sabachthani?" that is, "My God, my God, why have you forsaken me?"

He was forsaken, bearing the sins of many, shouldering so great a work even to the death of the cross, a work that would seem shameful to most people. For it was the height of His abandonment when they crucified Him and placed above His head the disdainful inscription "This is Jesus, king of the Jews." And when they crucified Him together with thieves, and when those who passed by blasphemed Him and wagged their heads. The chief priests and scribes said, "He saved others but cannot save himself." At that time even one of the thieves reviled Him on the cross. It is easy to understand His cry "Why have you forsaken me?" when you compare the glory Christ had in the presence of the Father with the contempt He sustained on the cross. His throne was like the sun in the presence of God and like the moon established forever; He was His faithful witness in heaven. Afterward, it was written that "He was despised and rejected by men, a man of sorrows and acquainted with grief; and as one from whom men hide their faces he was despised, and we esteemed him not" (Isaiah 53:3).

—ORIGEN, "Commentary on Matthew," in *Matthew 14–28*, vol. 1b, in *Ancient Christian Commentary on Scripture*, ed. Manlio Simonetti (Downers Grove, IL: IVP, 2002), 294.

In the presence of this mental anguish the physical tortures of the crucifixion retire into the background, and we may well believe that our Lord, though He died on the cross, yet died not of the cross, but, as we commonly say, of a broken heart.

—B. B. WARFIELD, *The Person and Work of Christ* (Oxford: Benediction Classics, 2015), 133.

Hebrews 5:1–5: For every high priest chosen from among men is appointed to act on behalf of men in relation to God, to offer gifts and sacrifices for sin. He can deal gently with the ignorant and wayward, since he himself is beset with weakness. Because of this he is obligated to offer sacrifice for his own sins just as he does for those of the people. And no one takes this honor for himself, but only when called by God, just as Aaron was. So also Christ did not exalt himself to be made a high priest, but was appointed by him who said to him, "You are my Son, today I have begotten you."

The gentle dealing by the high priest as applied to Jesus Christ is a matter of the highest encouragement and consolation to believers. Were there not an absolute sufficiency of this disposition in Him, in all occurrences, He would surely turn us all away in displeasure.

The high priest can deal gently with the ignorant and the wayward. He can no more turn away poor sinners for their ignorance and wanderings than a father could turn away a newborn child for its crying. So ought it to be with a high priest, and so it is with Jesus Christ. He is able, with all meekness and gentleness, patience and moderation, to bear with the infirmities, sins, and provocations of His people, even as a mother or father bears with the weakness of a poor infant.

Christ does not, in His dealings with us, more fully display any aspect of His nature than He does His compassion, long-suffering, and forbearance.

—JOHN OWEN, *An Exposition of the Epistle to the Hebrews*, in *The Works of John Owen*, vol. 21, ed. W. H. Goold (Edinburgh: Banner of Truth, 1968), 454–456, 462.

Matthew 27:46: And about the ninth hour Jesus cried out with a loud voice, saying, "Eli, Eli, lema sabachthani?" that is, "My God, my God, why have you forsaken me?"

As a man, therefore, He doubts; as a man He is surprised. Neither His power nor His Godhead is taken by surprise, but His soul. He is taken aback by the consequence of having taken human infirmities upon himself. Since then He took upon himself a soul, He also took on the emotions of a soul, for God could not have been distressed, nor could He have died in respect to His being God. He cried, "My God, my God, why have you forsaken me?" As a man, therefore, He spoke, bearing with Him our terrors, for when we are in danger, we think ourselves abandoned by God. As a man, therefore, He was distressed, as a man He wept, as a man He was crucified.

—ST. AMBROSE, "Some of the Principal Works of St. Ambrose," in *A Select Library of Nicene and Post-Nicene Fathers of the Christian Church*, trans. H. De Romestin, E. De Romestin and H.T.F. Duckworth (Oxford: James Parker & Co., 1896), 230.

In order that Christ might be a suitable sacrifice for us, it was necessary that He should be placed as a guilty person at the judgment seat of God. Nothing is more dreadful than to feel that God is our Judge. When this temptation was presented to Christ, having God opposed to Him, already devoted to destruction, He was seized with terror, which would have been equal to a hundred times all the men in the world; but by the amazing power of the Spirit, He achieved the victory. Nor was it by hypocrisy, or by assuming a character, that He complained of being forsaken by the Father. Some allege that He employed this language in compliance with the opinion of the people, but this is an absurd mode of evading the difficulty; for the inward sadness of His soul was so powerful that it forced Him to break out into a cry. Nor did the redemption that He accomplished consist solely in what was exhibited to the eye, but having undertaken to be our payment for sin, He resolved to undergo in our place the judgment of God.

—JOHN CALVIN, *Commentary on a Harmony of the Evangelists, Matthew, Mark, and Luke*, vol. 3, in Calvin's Commentaries, vol. 17 (Grand Rapids, MI: Baker, 2003), 319.

Hebrews 4:14–16: Since then we have a great high priest who has passed through the heavens, Jesus, the Son of God, let us hold fast our confession. For we do not have a high priest who is unable to sympathize with our weaknesses, but one who in every respect has been tempted as we are, yet without sin. Let us then with confidence draw near to the throne of grace, that we may receive mercy and find grace to help in time of need.

Christ is inclined from His own heart and affections to give us help and relief and He is inwardly moved during our sufferings and trials with a sense of identity with them.

—JOHN OWEN, *An Exposition of the Epistle to the Hebrews*, in *The Works of John Owen*, vol. 21, ed. W. H. Goold (Edinburgh: Banner of Truth, 1968), 422.

I have chosen this text, as that which more than any other speaks the heart of Christ most, and sets the working of it toward sinners; and does so in a way that, as it were, takes our hands and lays them upon Christ's breast, and lets us feel how His heart beats and His affections yearn toward us, even now that He is in glory—the very scope of these words being to encourage believers against all that may discourage them, from the consideration of Christ's heart toward them now, in heaven.

The text allows us to understand how closely and sensibly affected the heart of Christ is toward sinners in all their miseries and infirmities.

—THOMAS GOODWIN, *The Heart of Christ* (Edinburgh: Banner of Truth, 2011), 48–50.

Hosea 11:1–4, 8–9:
When Israel was a child, I loved him,
    and out of Egypt I called my son.
The more they were called,
    the more they went away;
they kept sacrificing to the Baals
    and burning offerings to idols.
Yet it was I who taught Ephraim to walk;
    I took them up by their arms,
    but they did not know that I healed them.
I led them with cords of kindness,
    with the bands of love,
and I became to them as one who eases the yoke on their jaws,
    and I bent down to them and fed them. . . .
How can I give you up, O Ephraim?
    How can I hand you over, O Israel?
How can I make you like Admah?
    How can I treat you like Zeboiim?
My heart recoils within me;
    my compassion grows warm and tender.
I will not execute my burning anger;
    I will not again destroy Ephraim;
for I am God and not a man,
    the Holy One in your midst,
    and I will not come in wrath.

There is comfort in your infirmities in that your sins move Him to pity. For He suffers with us under our sins, as well as other miseries. Christ takes part with you, and is far from being provoked against you. His anger is against your sin to destroy it. His pity is increased toward you, even as the heart of a father is to a child who has a disease, or a member of his own body that has leprosy. He does not hate his own flesh, but the disease.

The greater the misery, the more the pity when a person is beloved. Of all miseries, sin is the greatest; and when you look at it as such, Christ looks upon it as such as well. He loves you and hates the sin. Therefore, fear not.

—THOMAS GOODWIN, *The Heart of Christ* (Edinburgh: Banner of Truth, 2011), 155–156.

Isaiah 53:7–10:
He was oppressed, and he was afflicted,
    yet he opened not his mouth;
like a lamb that is led to the slaughter,
    and like a sheep that before its shearers is silent,
    so he opened not his mouth.
By oppression and judgment he was taken away;
    and as for his generation, who considered
that he was cut off out of the land of the living,
    stricken for the transgression of my people?
And they made his grave with the wicked
    and with a rich man in his death,
although he had done no violence,
    and there was no deceit in his mouth.
Yet it was the will of the LORD to crush him;
    he has put him to grief;
when his soul makes an offering for guilt,
    he shall see his offspring; he shall prolong his days;
the will of the LORD shall prosper in his hand.

What is the outcome of this suffering? What was the reason for it? Our Savior could answer His own question. If for a moment His manhood was perplexed, yet His mind soon came to a clear understanding; for He said, "It is finished." He referred to the work that He had just performed.

Why, then, did God forsake His Son? I cannot conceive of any other answer than this: He stood in our place. There was no other reason why the Father should forsake Him: He was perfect, His life was without spot. God never acts without reason; and since there were no reasons in the character and person of the Lord Jesus why His Father should forsake Him, we must look elsewhere. I do not know how others answer the question. I can only answer it in this way. He bore the sinner's sin, and He had to be treated, therefore, as though He were a sinner. With His full consent He suffered as though He had committed the transgressions that were laid on Him.

—CHARLES H. SPURGEON, "Lama Sabachthani?" https://www.spurgeon.org/resource-library/sermons/lama-sabachthani/#flipbook/.

Psalm 18:35: You have given me the shield of your salvation, and your right hand supported me, and your gentleness made me great.

Isaiah 53:7: He was oppressed, and he was afflicted, yet he opened not his mouth; like a lamb that is led to the slaughter, and like a sheep that before its shearers is silent, so he opened not his mouth.

Romans 2:4: Or do you presume on the riches of his kindness and forbearance and patience, not knowing that God's kindness is meant to lead you to repentance?

No impression was left by His manifest life more deeply imprinted upon the consciousness of His followers than that of the noble humility of His bearing.

—B. B. WARFIELD, *The Person and Work of Christ* (Oxford: Benediction Classics, 2015), 140.

People are apt to have contrary concepts of Christ, but the Word tells us of His disposition, preventing hard thoughts of Him: "God's kindness is meant to lead you to repentance." We are apt to think that He, being holy, is therefore of a severe and stern disposition, particularly against sinners, and not able to tolerate them. But, in fact, He is of a meek disposition, gentle in nature and temper.

—THOMAS GOODWIN, *The Heart of Christ* (Edinburgh: Banner of Truth, 2011), 63.

> **Hebrews 13:10–16:** We have an altar from which those who serve the tent have no right to eat. For the bodies of those animals whose blood is brought into the holy places by the high priest as a sacrifice for sin are burned outside the camp. So Jesus also suffered outside the gate in order to sanctify the people through his own blood. Therefore let us go to him outside the camp and bear the reproach he endured. For here we have no lasting city, but we seek the city that is to come. Through him then let us continually offer up a sacrifice of praise to God, that is, the fruit of lips that acknowledge his name. Do not neglect to do good and to share what you have, for such sacrifices are pleasing to God.

According to His divine nature, Jesus Christ is the eternal Son who came from the bosom of the eternal Father, and who took our flesh upon Him in order to offer himself as a sacrifice for the glory of God and for our salvation. By taking our place He accomplished our reconciliation to God. But as such and in the accomplishment of this reconciliation He was rejected by men. Like the scapegoat, He suffered the sin of many to be laid upon Him (and it is the faith of His followers that their sin can and should be laid upon Him), in order that He may bear it away, out from the camp into the greatest shame, out into the darkness, that it may no longer and never again be a burden to them. For this, in our flesh, according to His human nature, as the Son of David, He was the rejected One. He was delivered up by His own people to the heathen, descending into hell, where He could only cry, "My God, my God, why have you forsaken me?" There is, indeed, no man who partakes of the shame and abandonment of the One who was abandoned by men according to the will of God. For how could any man partake of both at the same time? But in Him, who was very God and very Man, in perfect unity, the glory and the shame and abandonment were one reality.

—KARL BARTH, *Church Dogmatics*, vol. 2, ed. G. W. Bromiley and T. F. Torrance, trans. T. H. L. Parker (London: T&T Clark, 2004), 365.

Ephesians 1:3–6: Blessed be the God and Father of our Lord Jesus Christ, who has blessed us in Christ with every spiritual blessing in the heavenly places, even as he chose us in him before the foundation of the world, that we should be holy and blameless before him. In love he predestined us for adoption to himself as sons through Jesus Christ, according to the purpose of his will, to the praise of his glorious grace, with which he has blessed us in the Beloved.

Jesus loved His own people from before time began. This is a most blessed fact. He has loved them eternally. There never was a time when He did not love them.

His love is timeless. Before the heavens and the earth were made, before the stars were touched with His light, Jesus had received His people from His Father, and written their names on His heart.

"Having loved his own who were in the world, he loved them to the end" (John 13:1). Jesus, before the world, set the crown of His distinctive love upon those whom He foreordained unto His glory.

This love is infinite. Jesus does not love His own with a taste of His love, nor regard them with some token of affection, but He says, "As the Father has loved me, so have I loved you" (John 15:9). The Father's love to the Son is inconceivably great, since they are one in essence.

The Father cannot but love the Son infinitely, neither does the Son love His people less than with all His heart. It is an affection that no angelic mind could measure.

—CHARLES H. SPURGEON, "The Faithfulness of Jesus," in *The Metropolitan Tabernacle Pulpit Sermons*, vol. 14 (London: Passmore & Alabaster, 1868), 270–271.

Psalm 139:2–3:
You know when I sit down and when I rise up;
  you discern my thoughts from afar.
You search out my path and my lying down
  and are acquainted with all my ways.

Mark 2:16–17: And the scribes of the Pharisees, when they saw that he was eating with sinners and tax collectors, said to his disciples, "Why does he eat with tax collectors and sinners?" And when Jesus heard it, he said to them, "Those who are well have no need of a physician, but those who are sick. I came not to call the righteous, but sinners."

The glory and happiness of Christ are enlarged and increased as His children come to enjoy the benefits of His death and resurrection, and they know their sins are forgiven and they are sanctified by the Holy Spirit. They are comforted, knowing the fruit of His labor has resulted in a changed life, and He is glorified by it. He is pleased and rejoices with us in this transformation. His heart rejoices in satisfying the needs and desires of His children here below, to refresh them every moment by His Word and His presence.

Jesus surprises us in exercising acts of grace, and from His continual doing good unto and for His faithful ones, from His filling them with all mercy, grace, comfort, and joy, himself becoming yet more full, by filling them.

—THOMAS GOODWIN, *The Heart of Christ* (Edinburgh: Banner of Truth, 2011), 111–112.

> **Luke 23:34:** And Jesus said, "Father, forgive them, for they know not what they do."

Jesus Christ, the incarnate Son of God, hangs upon a tree. He is murdered—by His own brethren. "He came to his own, and his own people did not receive him" (John 1:11).

He bleeds, He dies, and then a cry is heard in heaven. The astonished angels arise and say, "What is this? What is this cry that we hear?"

And the mighty God answers yet again, "It is the cry of blood. It is the cry of the blood of My Only Begotten and beloved Son!" And God the Father, rising from His throne, looks down from heaven and listens to the cry.

What is the cry? It is not revenge. It is not vengeance. But the voice cries, "Mercy! Mercy! Mercy!" Did you not hear it? He said, "Father, forgive them, for they know not what they do." And then, "It is finished."

Herein, the blood of Christ speaks better things than that of Abel, for Abel's blood cried, "Revenge!" and the sword of God started from its scabbard. But Christ's blood cried, "Mercy!" and sent the sword back to its place to sleep forever.

—CHARLES H. SPURGEON, "The Voice of the Blood of Christ," https://www.spur
geon.org/resource-library/sermons/the-voice-of-the-blood-of-christ/#flipbook/.

> **Ephesians 2:8–9:** For by grace you have been saved through faith. And this is not your own doing; it is the gift of God, not a result of works, so that no one may boast.

Christ's own joy, comfort, and glory are increased and deepened by His showing grace and mercy, in pardoning, relieving, and comforting His people here on earth, in the face of their many sins, diseases, and miseries.

—THOMAS GOODWIN, *The Heart of Christ* (Edinburgh: Banner of Truth, 2011), 107.

We cannot please Christ more than by accepting His welcome, by joyfully taking part in His rich provisions of grace and mercy. It is an honor to His bounty, acknowledgment of His undeserved blessing.

—RICHARD SIBBES, *A Discovery of the Near and Dear Love, Union, and Communion Between Christ and the Church*, in *The Works of Richard Sibbes*, vol. 2, ed. Alexander Balloch Grosart (reprint, Edinburgh: Banner of Truth, 1983), 34.

Psalm 22:1–5:

My God, my God, why have you forsaken me?
  Why are you so far from saving me, from the words of my groaning?
O my God, I cry by day, but you do not answer,
  and by night, but I find no rest.
Yet you are holy,
  enthroned on the praises of Israel.
In you our fathers trusted;
  they trusted, and you delivered them.
To you they cried and were rescued;
  in you they trusted and were not put to shame.

Jesus' cry, coming from the Psalms, is a prayer. Even if Jesus dies under a "Why?" of incomprehension of God's ways, He still makes the agony into a prayer. The cry should be understood *biblically* in its relation to Jesus' mission. The unique characteristic of His death on the cross should be interpreted in relation to the Law, to the conflict of the Law with itself, which Jesus occasioned, and to which He at the same time exposed himself. A victim of this conflict, He died as a criminal, "cursed" by God, according to the Law (Galatians 3:13), abandoned by God. In any case, contrary to Luke, who interprets this moment as that of the just One abandoning himself *to* God, Mark and Matthew seem to present it as an abandonment of the just One *by* God. But the psalmist's cry, taken up by the dying Jesus, expresses abandonment by God only because the relationship with God is its condition. In fact, specialists in Christology emphasize the paradox to which this cry gives expression: an experience of abandonment by God yet endured by *faith*—the dark night of faith. Some might say, "God let Jesus die; God abandoned Him to His enemies; God did not deliver Him, and His enemies were right to deride Him." Jesus was, in the state of death, by nature separated from the living God. At the same time, Jesus proclaimed His faith, that in spite of all appearances, God "leads the dance."

—LOUIS-MARIE CHAUVET, *A Sacramental Reinterpretation of Christian Existence*,
  trans. Patrick Madigan and Madeleine Beaumont (Collegeville, MN: Liturgical Press,
  1995), 494–498.

Hebrews 7:23-25: The former priests were many in number, because they were prevented by death from continuing in office, but he holds his priesthood permanently, because he continues forever. Consequently, he is able to save to the uttermost those who draw near to God through him, since he always lives to make intercession for them.

God justifies us not by giving us laws to obey, or by becoming our example, or even by our following Him in any sense, but by His blood shed for us. He justifies us by bestowing His grace upon us, not by expecting something from us.

—JOHN BUNYAN, *The Works of John Bunyan*, vol.1, ed. George Offor (Edinburgh: Banner of Truth, 1991), 221.

As you must know Him, and how people are freely justified by Him, so you must know of His readiness to receive and to do for those who come unto God by Him. Suppose His merits were completely reputable, but if it could be proven that there was some hesitancy in Him to bestow them upon those coming to Him, there would surely be fewer who would venture to seek Him. But we do know that nothing pleases Him more than to give what He has away, to bestow what is needed upon those who ask.

—JOHN BUNYAN, "Christ A Complete Savior," in *Doctrinal Discourses* (London: Thomas Ward and Co.), 55.

ABOUT THE AUTHOR

Justin S. Holcomb is an Episcopal priest and teaches theology at Reformed Theological Seminary and Gordon-Conwell Theological Seminary. He has written, coauthored, or edited over twenty books on theology, historical theology, biblical studies, and abuse.